M

Antique
Fairs
and Auctions
of Britain

Also in the Travel Key Guide Series

Manston's Travel Key Europe

Manston's Antique Fairs and Auctions of France

Manston's Antique Fairs and Auctions of Britain

Including
where to find markets,
fairs, and auctions,
and much more

by
Peter B. Manston

A Travel Key Guide
Published by B.T. Batsford Ltd.
London

Published in the United Kingdom by
B.T. Batsford Ltd.
4 Fitzhardinge Street
London W1H OAH
Telephone 01-486 8484

Published in a different edition in the United States by
Travel Keys
P.O. Box 160691
Sacramento, California 95816 U.S.A.
Telephone (916) 452-5200

Designed by Peter B. Manston
Edited by Robert C. Bynum in the United States
    and by Alison Bolus in the United Kingdom
Illustrated by Claudia R. Graham
Type Galleys by Lithographics, Sacramento,
    California U.S.A.
Printed and bound by Interpress Budapest
Manufactured in Hungary
First Printing January 1989

ISBN 0734-6234-5

Contents

Acknowledgements

Many people helped provide information and support while this book was being written. Most of them provided help, but it isn't possible to thank them all. A few I'd like to thank specially include: Robert C. Bynum, who provided thoughtful editorial comments and strong moral support, Alison Bolus, who with great patience helped adapt this book for its British edition, Paula R. Mazuski for excellent help in clarifying the objective of this book, Joyce Williams, and Agnes A. Manston (my mother). In addition, thanks to many members of the British antiques trade.

Disclaimer of Responsibility

Markets move as the result of urban renewal, sometimes close during bad weather, or rescheduled around holidays. Dates can change because the hall, square, or other location has already been reserved for another conflicting use, or because there are not enough sellers reserving a place. Bus lines are sometimes renumbered, car parks turn into buildings, parking garages raise their rates, and occasionally new underground stations are built.

This book is as complete and accurate as possible. Facts have been checked and rechecked. Therefore, though the information is deemed to be accurate as of press date, it may not exactly mirror your experience. Neither the author nor the publisher can be responsible if you are inconvenienced by information contained herein.

The persons, companies, institutions, and organizations named in the book are believed to be reputable and engaged in the work they purport to be in. Any questions should be directed to them rather than the author or publisher. Inclusion or exclusion of a firm or organization is no reflection on the suitability of its service or product.

When you find differences, will you let us know? Fill out the "Will You Help?" form at the end of the book (or in a letter). What you find and suggest can make the next edition even more complete and more useful to those who follow your path.

Portobello Road - London

Introduction

Britain is a treasure-trove of antiques, collectables, and bric-a-brac. Even better, the British antiques trade is well organized, so that markets and fairs are frequent and large.

Britain has a centuries-old tradition of markets, and cities and other locations have vied to have the best. As early as AD 1100, royal charters authorized markets either once a year or more frequently. The market cross in many a town became the focal point of the town, and gave legal status to buying and selling in the market precinct.

While few of the antiques fairs and markets date back to the Middle Ages, a large number have been in existence for many years. At some, the right to sell is granted to all willing to pay a few pounds for a small spot on the ground; at others, one must wait for years until a permanent place is available; and at the most prestigious, one must be invited to display, and all merchandise is carefully checked for authenticity.

You can find almost anything: British specialties such as porcelain, pottery, silver, linen, furniture, glass, old industrial tools, and all types of other items too numerous to mention. There are also relics and artefacts brought from around the world.

As the result of empire and trade, some of the finest antiques and other items came from parts of the world that weren't directly under British rule: therefore, Britain is one of the best places in the world to find antique Persian carpets, French furniture, and Oriental wares of all types.

Today, hundreds of markets offer all types of items, from carefully checked items that could grace a museum, elegant country estate, or castle, as well as your home, to just plain junk.

There are also hundreds of auctions a year. Some auctions in London may offer only paintings, others may restrict themselves to silver, wine, books, or militaria. Many in the country sell whatever people bring in. Often, country auctions are where true finds may be made. Many occur on a regular schedule: weekly, or once or twice a month. Occasionally, an entire estate is auctioned, but finding these is a matter of luck and timing, since they are most often announced only in local newspapers and posters glued to walls.

This book will give information vital for the antique dealer and collector; most isn't convenietly available elsewhere. It includes:

- when and where to find antique fairs, markets, boot sales, and auctions
- types of markets and what you can expect to find at each
- names, addresses, and specialties of auction houses, as well as the regular schedule of auctions
- and much, much more.

This pocket-sized book provides all this information. At the back, you'll find a complete index, and detailed maps to help you find what you need fast.

This book is dedicated to you, the ever-hopeful collector of exciting experiences and warm memories, as well as the collector of antiques, junk, and hidden treasures.

Can You
Still Make Finds?

All of us have heard about long-lost masterpieces found in a junk shop or bought for a few pounds at a flea market. We would all like to make a "great find"—a long lost painting, an old Wedgwood service, or a piece of original Chippendale or Adam furniture, or a teapot by famed silversmiths Paul de Lamerie, Paul Storr, or Hester Bateman.

These items do exist, and can occasionally be found, usually accompanied by great publicity and newspaper headlines. Finds of this type are rare.

But minor finds can more readily be made—the antique 18th-century spoon for only a few pounds; or a massive Queen Anne sterling chocolate pot for a few hundred to several thousand; finely detailed Victorian clothing; or a minor 17th- or 18th-century artist's painting.

The more you know about a given period or class of objects, the likelier you are to recognize and make a true find. This merely reinforces the fact that specialized knowledge has potentially great value.

Remember, you're searching for the proverbial needle in a haystack; there are thousands of British dealers and collectors in competition for the same things you are.

Many British dealers only know about specialties of their own locality or country, so it is worthwhile to trying to take a broader view, surveying the products of the entire world. Often, your best finds will be products or artworks far from their home, and, therefore, whose true value is unappreciated or unknown locally.

Charnock Richard

Why Search for Antiques in Britain?

Britain is probably the best antique warehouse in the world. There are more antiques available here than in any other single country, with the possible exception of France.

Britain has many attributes that make it an excellent source of antiques: large quantities of goods, the willingness to export antiques and art, and past wealth coupled with economically difficult times.

Britain has huge quantities of goods at attractive prices. British craftsmanship has been renowned since the Middle Ages, particularly in silver and gold, porcelain, and furniture.

British sterling silver is particularly well noted for its craftsmanship, sense of good design, and its generally good state of preservation. Every antiques market and flea market will have lots of sterling, ranging from racks of sugar tongs and spoons to 18th-century teapots, coffee and chocolate pots, and serving pieces.

Britain has long been noted for furniture, from Welsh cabinets and pine work to carefully made furniture of exotic woods. The British taste in furniture tends to be for simplicity of line and exquisite taste. The Victorian age produced an unparalleled amount of furniture, possibly not quite so beautifully designed and made as in earlier times, but far more available and reasonable in cost. (Unfortunately, much modern British furniture has lost this quality.)

Britain has long been known for pottery or porcelain—who hasn't heard of Wedgwood, Royal Doulton, and a number of other famous porcelain works? Their products often span the centuries. Pottery works have been producing everything from common brown-glazed teapots to Toby mugs, and everything in between.

Now, the products of the early 20th century are becoming widely available in British markets. British Art Deco is distinctive and noteworthy, slightly understated when compared to the designs of the same period in Germany, France, and the United States.

In addition to British-made goods, many foreign items have trickled into Britain over the centuries, making Britain a prime source of Persian carpets, Oriental art, religious art from Eastern Europe, and enough other specialities that it would take an entire page to list them all.

British vendors are willing and able to sell most antiques, and the government doesn't interfere in the export of most of them. Several factors contribute to this:

- Trade and commerce have traditionally been the main source of British wealth.
- The late 20th century has been a difficult time for Britain's economy, with the result that many treasures of the past are surfacing for sale at attractive prices. This phenomenon is particularly marked in the economically devastated areas mainly in Britain's north, such as Lancashire and parts of Scotland. This factor is helped by the relative fall in the value of the British pound sterling during this century when compared with both American and Canadian dollars. (At the turn of the century, the British pound was worth about $5; today it is worth about $1.60/1.90 U.S. and about $2.00/2.40 Canadian.)
- The British sense of fair dealing has made the legal export of most antiques and collectables possible and the rules governing ex-

port of antiques and works of art clear and understandable.

The British antiques trade is large and well organized. Thousands of dealers have immense stocks of antiques. Many take their choicest items to markets, shows, and fairs. It would take a number of people to canvass all of the markets, fairs, sales, and auctions where antiques and collectables are sold.

Export arrangements are also easier to make in Britain than almost everywhere else. Many collection and packing companies provide nationwide or regional pickup, and can pack at any given standard of packing, from just jamming huge containers full of miscellaneous lots of furniture, to careful item-by-item museum- quality coddling.

Britain, for a number of reasons, is probably the best country for hunting antiques in the world today.

Bermondsey Street ~ London

Learning to See What You're Looking At

Without preparation, you can find antiques, collectables, and assorted items by the thousands. You're limited only by your money, your patience, and your transportation. But discoveries of real artistic quality items will be made only from good luck, maybe aided by intuition. But for the real finds, you must know what you're looking at.

You'll be well repaid later by the effort spent now, when you are knowledgeable enough to tell a good piece from a poor or fake one later at a boisterous flea market, auction, or antique show. You'll be faced with hundreds and thousands of items, but only a few are of interest to you, and even fewer are very good value for the serious collector.

At well-known dealers and some dealers' marts, you will often be able to obtain certificates of authenticity and provenance papers, more or less guaranteeing that you're really buying a genuine antique. Naturally such guarantees and paperwork have their (high) price.

At flea markets and junk shops, however, the motto is "let the buyer beware". The market in fakes sold to the unwary is large, and buyers' cupidity and ignorance are prime sales tools for these sellers. In Britain this is somewhat less of a problem than in countries such as Spain, Portugal, and Italy.

The time to start learning about antiques and collectables is right now. Read everything you can—style guides, price guides, antique-trade and fine arts magazines, museum catalogues, and applied arts and fine arts history. Catalogues from Christie's, Phillips, and Sotheby's auctions are treasure-troves of knowledge, with illustrations of sale items, descriptions of the creator, the item, and characteristics of the style, and estimated sales prices. These catalogues are sometimes available at libraries or museums, and, of course, are sold through the respective auction houses.

Study the text and illustrations carefully—what you remember will make it much easier to sort through the thousands of worthless pieces for the few excellent items at the market, show, or fair.

Your local library is an excellent place to begin your search. Search through "Books In Print" to supplement your search of library shelves. Small and medium-sized libraries can often obtain books through the "interlibrary loan" system. For details and to make a request, see the reference librarian.

Many college and university libraries have more extensive and specialized collections, particularly in the area of art and antiques. Usually the public is admitted to "open-stack" libraries and can use the books in the library at no charge. Often you can become a "friend of the library" at modest cost to obtain borrowing privileges.

Museums are another place to learn. In major museums you will be able to see actual examples of authentic works. Study the lines, the artistic qualities, and materials carefully. When you have a bit of knowledge but want more, seek out the curators in the museum.

Sometimes museums also have excellent art libraries, but rarely can their library materials be checked out.

Antique dealers in your area represent a valuable source of knowledge, though for obvious reasons, dealers won't usually share their sources of supply.

When buying, you're likely to find more interesting and beautiful items if you know what you're buying.

Let your sense of beauty and value for money guide you: learn to trust your instincts, based on a firm foundation of knowledge.

The Barras - Glasgow

London, 1800

British Sterling Silver

The work in silver is one of the greatest of all British art forms. For centuries, British royalty and gentry have carefully nurtured, encouraged, patronized, and carefully regulated silversmiths and goldsmiths. Several periods are unequalled in artistry and quality, but perhaps the greatest age of British silver was from the Restoration (1660) to the Regency (1820). The design and execution of silver was particularly distinguished from about 1690 to 1730.

Origin of Hallmarks

All solid British silver (but not silverplate) has been hallmarked since early in the Middle Ages. The first hallmark was introduced in 1180, and assay of precious metals was required under Henry III in 1238. The reason for hallmarking was to guarantee the purity of precious metals, both silver and gold. By requiring every piece to be assayed (tested for purity), the mark of the maker and the guild furnished proof that the metal was up to standard. As time went on, additional marks were added to record such diverse facts as the city, year of manufacture, payment of tax, and other items.

Regulation of the trade was under the protection of the government, delegated to the

Worshipful Company of Goldsmiths and Silversmiths.

Standards for Silver

There are two legal standards for British silver: Sterling (925/1000 fine) and Britannia (958/1000 fine). Sterling is shown by a lion, and Britannia by a seated figure. Foreign silver must be marked as an import with an inverted "U" in a circle before it can be sold.

Hallmarks

Silver hallmarks have changed over time, so that it is relatively simple to date British silver. The first mark was a leopard's head, introduced in 1180 by the guild of goldsmiths.

Beginning in 1336, the crowned leopard's head was joined by the maker's mark (always two letters), and the date letter.

Beginning in 1393, a city mark was introduced: each assay office had (and still has) its own mark. These are shown overleaf.

Beginning in 1545, the sterling standard was shown by a lion in a shield. Beginning in 1697, a higher silver standard (Britannia) was introduced to prevent the melting of coins for silver work.

Since 1719, British silversmiths have been able to use either the sterling or Britannia standard.

The lion mark is found on all sterling (.925) work, the Britannia on all Britannia (.958) work.

 Sterling   *Britannia*

Marks on British Silver

Modern British silver will have four marks. Each of the following must be included: the initials of the maker, the town of manufacture, the date-letter, and the lion guarantee of sterling or seated Britannia figure for Britannia standard silver. If it also has a monarch's head (1758—1890) you can be sure that the tax on silver items was paid before its initial sale.

Date letters are particularly helpful when dating silver, since they change every year. At the end of a series of letters, the style of the letters and surrounding shields are changed. Therefore, every nineteen years the letter has changed (most date-letter alphabets do not include J, W, X, Y, or Z).

Beginning in 1975, all year marks and the lettering style were standardized. In that year, date-letters began with "A"; the cycle is expected to repeat every 25 years (the letter J is not used).

Sample Marks

Here are some samples of the marks used on British sterling:

 Chester　　　　 *Sheffield*

 Exeter　　　　 *York*

 Newcastle　　　　 *London*

 Birmingham

 Scotland　　 *Glasgow*　　 *Edinburgh*

The city stamp will be one of those shown.

Note: British silver marks have changed to some degree as the result of the Hallmarking Act 1973. There are now only four assay offices: London (using the leopard's head), Birmingham (using the anchor), Sheffield (now using a rose instead of the traditional crown), and Edinburgh (using the castle). Date letters are now to be standard between assay offices, and each year's letter must coincide with the calendar year (January 1 through December 31).

A full explanation of British hallmarks can be found in a small book often sold at British markets for about £1.50.

Why is It Called Sterling, and What Was a Pound Sterling?

Coins in the Middle Ages were given value by their precious metal content. A sterling was a medieval silver coin, which for many centuries was distinguished by a star (stoer in Middle English). The silver was of a consistent standard of purity: 10 troy ounces 11 pennyweights of pure metal in the troy pound (12 ounces). One pound by weight in sterlings equalled a "pound sterling".

London, 1687

From the early 1800s until 1966, one pound's (£1) worth of copper pennies (240 pence) weighed exactly 16 ounces. Copper coins were measured at banks by weight rather then value.

The name for the main unit of British money remains today, though no coin or combination of coins worth £1 weighs anything close to a pound.

Silver Plate

Silver plate can be distinguished from solid silver, because it has very different marks. Some may be merely for decoration, but in Britain, non-silver must be marked as plated ware. This can be shown by the initials EPNS (Electro-Plated Nickel Silver), the words "Silverplate" or "Silver Plated," or if on a base of copper, "Sheffield Plate".

Gold

Pure gold is 24 karats. In Britain, to be legally sold as gold, it must contain at least 9 karats (375/1000 fine). Usually, modern cheap gold chains and earrings are 9 or 10 karat. However, good quality gold in Britain is often 18 carat (750/1000 fine).

All gold must state its gold content in carats, and be assayed and hallmarked.

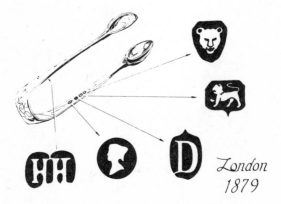

London
1879

Ardingly

When to Go for the Best Finds

The British antiques trade is a year-round activity, except for the week between Christmas and New Year's Day. While there are seasonal highs and lows to various components of the trade, some events take place all through the year. The weekly antiques markets are always going. Auctions take place on a regular basis. And antiques fairs at hotels and conference halls are also continual.

In winter, there are few tourists and the business is more for the locals. The quantity of merchandise is almost as large, but it is almost all under cover and indoors. The weekly antiques markets—many outside—are open in unpleasant weather: the dealers don't let a bit of dampness, cold, and rain interfere with the pursuit of profit and finds. However, only a few of the major, one-day sales are held before March.

In spring, outdoor sales become more frequent: the first of the large, one- or two-day sales are held. These large fairs often have 1000 vendors, some under cover in exhibition halls and some offering their wares from trucks and vans outside. Some of the major auctions of the season take place and the weekly antiques markets continue.

Summer is the high point of the outdoor market season, with seemingly the whole country involved in the buying and selling of collectables, antiques, and just plain junk. Every town and apparently every village has its market. There are also plenty of auctions in most parts of the country. Every weekend, at hundreds of "boot sales", private parties unload all types of treasures and rubbish from their cars' boots.

Autumn is probably the most active season in the antiques trade, with major fairs and exhibitions held between September and Christmas. Many highly publicised auctions of famous paintings also take place, as well as the last of the one- or two-day antiques fairs. And the open-air antiques markets continue.

Any time of year will offer opportunities to pursue and acquire antiques and collectables. And at any time of the year, there are more events than you could ever thoroughly cover.

Time of Day

Most open-air markets begin early in the morning, some as early as 3 or 4 a.m. The best finds are made as the vendors unpack. When an interesting load arrives, potential buyers cluster around to inspect. Many sales are made before the goods are all unloaded. Markets usually run until noon or early afternoon.

Most antiques fairs start later in the morning, most often 9.30 or 10 a.m., and end at 5 p.m.

Night Sales: A Special Caution

You can lose the right to any purchase made during the night at an open market, if it can be proven that the goods were stolen. In 1973, an Appeal Court ruled that all purchases made at open markets during the night could be challenged. If goods could be proven to be stolen, they can be returned to the rightful owner without recourse. Purchases made during daylight hours are yours without this restriction, as long as you don't know that goods were stolen.

This ruling doesn't seem to affect the early morning markets, probably because few stolen goods are offered at the markets.

Market Cross – Stratford

Origins of the British Markets

Britain has had recognized markets since the Roman occupation, from AD 100 to c. AD 400. In Roman Britain, London was the trading center and largest town. There were at least two markets, one of which has left its name in "Cheapside" and other streets and squares with the word Cheap in them. (*Ceap,* spoken "cheap," was the old Saxon word for market.)

The lords of the land (who could be the Crown, a monastery, or a local lord of the manor) often were granted the right to hold specific types of markets at various times and places. Generally, competing markets within a certain distance (often a league, or six and two-thirds miles) were forbidden, as was buying and selling the prescribed items outside of the market precincts. The lords were also given the right to levy various fees and taxes in order to pay for services, and, more frequently, provide the market lords with revenue.

Some of the great London markets, such as the Sunday Petticoat Lane market (hardly the place for finding antiques!), the Billingsgate fish market, the old Covent Garden vegetable market, and the Smithfield meat and cattle market developed as the result of grant of market rights.

Most antiques markets have developed much more recently, especially since the Second World War. Many of the larger and more elite markets and fairs have grown in stature along with the British realization that there is quite a lot of money to be made in antiques.

Some fairs have charitable origins: many parish churches and beneficial organizations sponsor sales to raise money. Other fairs are run strictly to provide a location for efficient buying and selling of antiques and collectables. Naturally many of these fairs are run strictly for the profit of the participants and especially the organizers. Britain has many markets surviving centuries that are not antiques or collectables fairs. Many street markets can trace their origins back for centuries, and the original royal charter granting the right to hold a fair may be on file in some dusty records office. Some street markets in the provinces are still property of the lord of the market.

With the passage of time, however, cities and other local authorities have leased or bought the rights to hold fairs and markets from private owners.

Market Crosses

Many traditional markets were marked by a market cross, erected under the authority of the owner of the fair, and blessed by the church. This allowed the owners to bring all sales under the obligations of fair dealing and (especially before the 19th century) regulated prices.

Some of the largest and best preserved market crosses (such as Malmesbury, Wiltshire) are large enough to shelter small offices and other amenities under them, even if they no longer have a large market to serve.

Some market crosses are relatively recent, such as the one in Stratford-on-Avon, which dates from the late Victorian era, and still marks the site of a boisterous street market (no antiques) once a week.

All market crosses are out in the open; only in modern times have some gained walls to turn the interior into buildings.

Boot Sale
Ascot

Types of Markets

Britain is almost overwhelmed with fairs, markets, and auctions at which antiques are sold. In addition, there are hundreds of special-interest fairs. Most of them take place in England, with only a thin scattering in Wales, Scotland, and Northern Ireland.

Many weekly markets are organized by city or regional governmental entities, such as local councils or city governments.

In addition, a number of regular markets are organized by market companies and promoted in the antiques trade press. While most of the important markets (and some of the less important ones) are listed here, you may want to check the "Antique Dealer and Collector's Guide" monthly magazine, or the weekly "Antiques Trade Gazette".

Antiques Fairs

Regularly occurring shows are often called "antiques fairs", or "antique fairs". Often, they are held indoors at a hotel or convention hall. They consist of anywhere from twenty to two or three hundred dealers who bring all kind of things to try to sell. While most of these dealers have regular shops, some strictly travel the fair circuit. The merchandise is carefully studied by experts hired by the organizer before being offered for sale. Generally, true finds will be rare at this type of show. Some of them require sellers to be members of either of the two largest British antique dealers' associations, the British Antique Dealers Association (BADA), and the London and Provincial Antique Dealers Association (LAPADA).

Antiques Shows

Antiques shows are similar to antiques fairs, but it is often even harder for dealers to obtain the right to sell there. There is no restriction on who may come to look and to buy. Generally, admissions are more costly than at other events (as much as £5), but the price of admission often includes a wonderful, fully illustrated glossy catalogue. At the best of these shows, most of the items are of museum quality; all will carry a guarantee, and sometimes complete papers of provenance (the history of the item). Items for sale must be in perfect condition. Some shows limit those offering goods to members of the two British antiques associations, BADA, and LAPADA.

Dealers are invited to display at these shows; some dealers wait decades before they're invited to display. These shows form the high point of the British antiques circuit, and generally take place in the spring and, especially, during the autumn months.

Collectors' Fairs

Specialized fairs catering to limited types of items are often called collectors' fairs. They are often smaller than antiques fairs; some may be limited to Toby mugs or antique swords, or Belgian postage stamps, or almost any other type of collectable. Often, they are announced in the hard-to-find specialist newsletters and magazines rather than (or in addition to) the general antiques trade newspapers.

Britain is certainly a nation of collectors! These specialists are knowledgeable, and often are fountains of information for the interested amateur.

These fairs are held as much for enlightenment of the collectors as well as the purchase and sale of items. As a result, they are generally more relaxed and informal than the larger antiques events.

Boot Sales

Boot sales are thus called "boot sales" because sellers can sell whatever they can fit into the car's boot. Many are small, local affairs; others are still local but may have hundreds of sellers and thousands of potential buyers. While a few of the larger, most regular ones are listed here, often many can be found only by small, tacked-up signs along the road with an arrow pointing in the right direction.

Most sellers are private parties rather than regular dealers. Most prohibit dealers from selling, though these are some of the most fertile grounds for bargain hunters. Many dealers regularly canvass the boot sales, since this is one place where the sellers may not know what they have.

Boot sales are usually a summer, fair-weather event: they're extremely scarce from November to April. Some are held rain or shine, but others are only held if it isn't raining. Saturday and Sunday are the usual days for boot sales.

Admission charges are usually low—anywhere from 10p to 50p—and parking will often be available either for free or for a modest fee.

Jumble Sales

Often these sales are sponsored by churches or civic or charitable groups. The quality of items is usually low—old clothes, broken small appliances, and other leftovers of the industrial age. But also, many discoveries and finds can be made here for bargain prices. Jumble sales take place on an irregular basis; they are often advertised in local newspapers, and local tourist offices may list them on the calendar of the week's events.

Exhibitions

Exhibitions are usually displays of antiques, where the items are not for sale (though the dealers or exhibitors sometimes will talk discreetly about selling). Many are specialist meetings, held to show what is currently of interest in the antiques trade.

Sometimes, an antiques show or fair is called an exhibition to imply exclusivity and large size. In this case, sales are openly promoted.

Antiques Markets

Indoor antiques markets are regular collections of full-time dealers, usually open during regular business hours. While some are located in the vicinity of markets (such as the Bermondsey Antiques Market in London, adjacent to the Bermondsey Market), others are free-standing.

Often from twenty to one hundred dealers share quarters in these buildings. They are efficient ways for visitors to see large quantities of antiques and collectables quickly. Sometimes, finds may be made. However, only a few of these full-time collections of dealers are listed, when either they are very large, or when there just isn't much else in the neighbourhood.

Craft Fairs

Craft fairs are usually the fruit of one of the most endearing of British characteristics: the love of the amateur endeavour. Many of the fairs are for new work only, and only the people who created the work can offer the goods for sale. As a result, few antiques will be found at a craft fair. There are lots of interesting people, as well as products ranging from the best of British crafts to some items that, because of low quality and poor conception, make you wonder whether anyone would buy them.

Flea Markets

British flea markets are mainly for the sale of lower-quality, new and cheap goods: pots and pans, clothes, motor oil and car parts, hardware, tools, and plumbing fixtures. For example, the St. Martin's Market in Birmingham (Tuesday, Thursday, and Saturday) is a huge hall and adjacent outdoor lot, with hundreds of vendors of cheap, often poorly made clothes, new pots and pans, a few fruit and vegetable vendors, and a man selling toothpaste, aspirins, and similar items with the help of an amazing, home-built computer system hooked to an old television. (However, every six weeks, usually on a Wednesday, this site is the location of one of the best antiques and collectors markets in Britain.)

Street Markets

Street markets come in all types, but most are general collections of fruit and vegetable vendors, fish mongers, sellers of new and used clothes, demonstrations and sales of kitchen gadgets guaranteed to cut corkscrews of potatoes and mile-long curls from carrots, and shred mountains of cabbage for cole slaw.

Though they are interesting and great events in themselves, few of them offer antiques or collectables of any type.

Terms That Define a Fair or Market

Every trade has a shorthand that quickly communicates to potential visitors the type and special conditions that the fair offers. Here are several you're likely to find:

"Dateline"

Usually you'll see this term in conjunction with a year, frequently 1880 or 1930. It signifies that nothing newer can be offered for sale at this event. Generally, only the higher quality and

carefully   monitored   events   have   formal
datelines.

"No New or Reproduction"

This term means that only items of a certain age
(dependent on the organizer) can be sold.
Reproductions are widespread in Britain and are
not always very clearly marked. New items in
the style of old are also easy to find. Fair organizers often state the minimum age in their
contracts with sellers, and advertise it in an-
nouncements of forthcoming fairs and markets.
However, this doesn't mean that experts have
screened every item.

"Vetted"

When this term appears, it means that experts
have inspected every item offered to ensure that
it meets stated requirements for items to be sold
at the fair, and that the goods are authentic and
of good quality. Generally this term (and procedure) is only used at the very top quality fairs.

"BADA"

BADA, the British Antique Dealers Association,
is the most prestigious organization of antiques
dealers. It is elitist in character, with membership limited to the upper crust of dealers.
Dealers must be nominated, and if admitted,
must subscribe to a strict code of ethics. Member
dealers usually have the portrait logo prominent-
ly affixed in their shops or displays, and sometimes put it on their cards and letterheads as
well.

This organization can be contacted at its
headquarters:

British Antique Dealers Association
20 Rutland Gate
London SW7
Telephone 01-589 4128

"LAPADA"

LAPADA, the London and Provincial Antique Dealers Association, is the other major organization of antique dealers. It is newer, and was frankly formed as an alternative to BADA. While membership requires several years in business and adherence to a strict code of ethics, its character is not as elite as BADA. Member dealers often display the organization's logo, a Chippendale chandelier.

This organization can be contacted at its headquarters:

London and Provincial Antique
   Dealers Association
3 Cheval Place
London SW7 1EW
Telephone 01-584 7911

(Note: some dealers are members of both organizations.)

"PBFA"

PBFA, the Provincial Booksellers Fairs Association, an organization of antiquarian book sellers, have formed an association to promote their interests and organize book fairs. This organization sponsors a regular London fair every month, and issues a free calendar of other antiquarian book fairs all over Britain. Members of this organization can be identified by the logo of a cat sitting on a book. For a calendar schedule and list of members, contact:

Provincial Booksellers Fairs Association
P.O. Box 66
Cambridge, Cambridgeshire CB1 3PD
Telephone (0223) 240921.

Sugar tongs – Bath

Special Favours for the "Antiques Trade"

The antiques trade is highly organized. As in so many other fields, special favours and terms are given to those individuals who are in the same line of work. These favours can range from preferential pricing to early and/or free admission to fairs and markets.

How to Identify Favours to the "Trade"

Many times, notices of fairs and markets will include one or two code words to let you know that special courtesies are extended to others in the antiques trade. In advertisements, look for words such as "Trade Free", "Trade _____ Only", "Open 11.0; 9.30 by Invitation or (Trade) Card Only", or similar half-hidden wording, often placed in fine print in a corner.

Special Favours to Dealers

Many but not all antiques fairs, markets, and other events discriminate in favor of members of the antiques trades. Several different types of discrimination are practised, though with forethought and planning, they can be minimized.

Early Admission

Most antiques fairs and shows held one to four times a year allow (and encourage) dealers and others clearly in the antiques trades to have an advance look at the goods to be sold, and to "skim the cream" from the goods offered before the public is allowed to enter.

Individual organizers set the rules as they choose. Early admission for some fairs is only an hour or two before the public is admitted. At others, it may be a whole day.

During the "trade" periods, you're expected to know what you're looking at, or at least not betray your ignorance. On the other hand, prices are more favourable.

A few organizers (such as Penman Fairs) utterly refuse to allow dealers to have first pick during the trade preview.

A few other organizers let members of the antiques trade in early, but charge a higher admission to the early birds.

Free Admission

Many fairs (but not many boot sales) allow members of the antiques trade in for free, while the general public has to pay admission fees, running anywhere from 10p to £5. At some of the very famous and exclusive sales, usually those with beautifully printed colour catalogues, members of the antiques trade pay just as much as anyone else.

How to Prove You're in the "Trade"

The best proof that you're in the antiques trade is printed. A business card announcing the name of an antiques shop with address, telephone number, and your name, fills the bill.

Membership of an antiques trade organization (as shown by a membership card) is also usually considered proof.

A number of knowledgeable collectors have secured "trade" privileges by merely having business cards printed before they leave home.

British dealers may have to provide their VAT number and, rarely, show a (pocket-sized) VAT Special Scheme Stockbook.

Discounts to Members of the "Trade"

Almost without exception, you can obtain a discount if you can demonstrate you're in the "trade". Often, merely asking, "What is the best price to the trade?" will obtain a reduction of 10 to 15%. Occasionally, you may have to produce some proof; as above, your business or membership card will be the best proof. Don't be bashful about asking for the "trade price", since it offers a way of saving money.

Naturally, the more you know about the subject, and the more you can talk knowledgeably about the items and the trade, the more credible your request for trade treatment becomes.

Auction House
Hamilton ~

Auctions

Probably a larger proportion of antiques and collectables passes through the auction houses in Britain than most other countries. And at auction, occasionally great finds can be made and prices can be quite reasonable. The vast majority of items offered for auction are sold for less than £200.

Auctions vary greatly in formality and how they are conducted. Some country auctions are rowdy, informal gatherings mainly consisting of local dealers and used-goods merchants where it seems that everyone knows each other, with auctioneers joking with the bidders. At these auctions, to bid you need only raise or wildly wave your hand, shout out, or almost anything else to have your bid noted.

Other auctions, primarily those dealing with very expensive fine arts often held in London, are formal, tension-laden affairs, with bidders risking huge sums to buy well-known, unique items. Suits and ties and dresses are expected. The atmosphere is formal. Buyers must pre-register to obtain admittance or to bid.

And there are all types of auctions in between.

If You Wiggle Your Ears Will You Spend All Your Money?

One of the fears that many people have at auctions is that they'll spend an outrageous amount of money for something that they don't want by wiggling their ear, looking at their watch, or scratching their nose. However, these discreet signs are usually used only by prior arrangement at auctions where the privacy of the buyer is important.

When this hasn't been arranged, this type of bid has been known to occur. They are extremely rare and, if you shake your head, are not binding. (When a bid has not been truly made, the auctioneer will restart the bidding on the spot at a lower price.)

In addition to the auctioneer watching for bids, there are usually one or more assistants also watching.

They are skilled at gaining bidders' eyes, and rarely misinterpret.

Often, auctioneers will determine early in the sale who is likely to bid on certain types of items, and direct most of their attention to those potential bidders.

Auction Schedules

Auctions basically are held when the auctioneer knows (or hopes) that there will be enough goods to draw lively bidding.

In London and other large cities, a number of auction houses hold regular auctions, with greater or lesser specialization.

Other auction houses hold auctions only infrequently on a schedule or irregularly when there are enough goods to sell. Finding the dates and times can be difficult; while local newspapers and antiques trade newspapers will invariably carry auction notices, the best source of information is the auction house itself. Most will be glad to answer when you write or telephone and request information.

Most auction houses will, upon request, provide a calendar of all auctions for three months to a year at a time.

Inspection (Viewing) Before the Sale

Every auction (except the extremely rare mail-order auction) provides inspection periods before the auction. While the exact times may vary, generally inspections can be made on the day before the sale, sometimes two days before the sale, and on sale day before the auction begins.

If a catalogue has been issued, and you don't want to buy one, several will be available for reference during the inspection period. If you don't see them around, ask at the information desk for a catalogue.

Catalogues

Most auction houses issue a catalogue, often several weeks before the sale. The catalogue can range from crude, mimeographed sheets with conditions of sale on one side and one- or two-line descriptions of each lot, to lavish, full-colour catalogues with knowledgeable commentary. If the lot is very important or unique, it will usually have a longer description, and often a photograph as well.

For the auctions of Old Masters and similarly rare items, catalogues may be issued a month or two before the sale date.

For regular sales, catalogues will usually be available about one month before the sale date.

If the auction is a regular weekly sale, the catalogue may not be available until a week before the sale.

At country auctions offering miscellaneous items, there may not be a catalogue.

Most catalogues aren't free: for the exquisite catalogues of the finest antiques and artwork, you may have to pay as much as £1 to £4. Exceptional sales may have catalogues costing as much as £20. In addition, you may have to pay extra if you want it posted to you.

Major auction houses have catalogue subscription services. If you want all catalogues for sale of a particular class of item, you can arrange to have catalogues sent to you. Contact the auction house's "general office" for further information.

How to Read a Catalogue

Most catalogues are easy to read. Somewhere on the first few pages, you'll find the Standard Conditions of Sale. This may be from one to five pages of legalese; however, read the conditions carefully to avoid surprises when the time comes to pay the bill.

General Conditions of Sale

Every catalogue includes the auction house's general conditions of sale. Variations are minor. They generally state that the highest bidder will purchase, that the auctioneer has the sole discretion to accept or reject bids for any reason or for no reason, and special provisions for items with a minimum reserve.

The general conditions will also cover payment policy, whether a buyer's premium is charged, and policy for removing purchased goods.

Estimated Sale Price

Many auction catalogues, particularly when the sale is relatively specialized, will provide estimated sales prices for every lot. Invariably, these figures do not include any buyer's premium or Value Added Tax. Somewhere, most catalogues will have a disclaimer about estimated sale prices such as this notice in Phillips' catalogues, "The estimated figures are our opinion of the prices we expect lots to realise".

Lots and Items

Auction houses decide how they want to sell various items: either as a single item or as a lot. Frequently items which were brought in together by one seller and have a relationship (for example, a tea set) will be sold as one lot. Sometimes, however, a set can be divided into two or more lots. For example, if the tea set has a matching coffee pot as well, the coffee pot may be sold as a separate lot.

The auction house has total discretion in the matter, and how and whether related items are divided depend on how the auctioneer believes they will bring a higher price.

Bidder Registration

Bidders in most auctions are requested (or required) to register before they make their first bid. The bidder's registration form asks for your name, address, sometimes verified by some identification such as a passport or identity card. At this type of auction, as you bid, a record of your purchases is kept, and you can pay for all of your purchases at the cashier.

At other auctions, most likely country auctions, you need not register; you just go in and bid. When the item is sold to you, you're handed the item, and you hand over the money to the roving auctioneer's assistant.

The Hammer and Hammer Price

The hammer is the auctioneer's symbol of office. The hammer, a small eight- or ten-inch long mallet, is actually used at every auction, and no item is considered sold until it is "knocked down" by three taps of the hammer.

The "hammer price" is the price you bid. However, at many auctions, this is not the total price you'll pay. Some auctions add a charge called a "buyer's premium", and Value Added Tax as well.

Buyer's Premium

When you buy an item for perhaps £100, that doesn't mean that is the price you must pay. Many auctions, particularly those run by the largest three auction companies (Christie's, Phillips, and Sotheby's) also charge a buyer's premium. This charge, actually a commission, is added to your bill. Some buyer's premiums are as high as 10%. Since this charge is determined by the auction house, different auctions often have a different percentage as a buyer's premium.

Even when there is a buyer's premium, the auction house still also collects a seller's premium (see "seller's premium" below).

Value Added Tax

Value Added Tax (VAT), a general tax on most sales and other transactions, is added to the buyer's premium, and therefore, to your bill. This tax is 15% of the buyer's premium (if it is charged), and is added to the auctioneer's commission or premium.

In addition, on some types of items, generally newer items, you may have to pay VAT on the price of the item as well. However, antiques, art, and most types of used goods are exempt from VAT.

Seller's Premium

Every auction house makes its money on commissions, also called premiums. These commissions are charged on a percentage basis, although the percentage may be on a sliding scale at some auction houses. It may range from about a maximum of 15% down to about 5%. The seller's premium or commission is included in the price that you pay for the goods.

If the lot is not sold because it doesn't meet the reserve price (see next section), the commission is still charged to the would-be seller.

Reserve Prices

Many items are consigned to auction houses with a firm reserve price: that is, the minimum price which the item or lot must bring. If the item doesn't bring the minimum it is not sold, but a commission is still charged to the person consigning the item.

The amount of the reserve (if any) is a secret between the auctioneer and the person consigning the item. It will not be revealed, even if you ask. You won't even be able to find out which items (if any) have a minimum reserve price. Some auction houses have general rules for minimum reserve amounts. This will be stated in the General Conditions of Sale. Often, if an item isn't sold at the reserve on the first try, it will reappear at the next sale with a lower reserve, or no reserve at all. Surprisingly, often it will bring not only the lower reserve price, but the final hammer price may exceed the higher reserve at the earlier auction.

Bought-In Items

Sometimes the auction house will itself purchase an item (or acquire it in other ways, such as nonpayment of storage fees), and sell it on its own behalf. In this case, the auction house treats it exactly as it would a consigned item, and may set a reserve and collect the premiums from the buyer in the normal way.

Bidding When You're Not There

Most auction houses welcome bids from bidders who aren't in attendance during the sale. These bids are called "Commissions". There is no charge for this service. If you wish to use this process, you must make arrangements before the auction begins. When you contact the auction house, ask for the "Commissions" office or department.

Bids can be made by telephone, mail, or by a bid left with the auction house after you have inspected the items to be sold.

Left Bids and Posted Bids

A left bid is a bid that you leave in person after inspecting the goods for sale. For posted bids, you must first obtain a catalogue or inspect the merchandise personally at the sale site. If you wish to make a bid, fill out a form (usually provided by the auction house) in which you state the maximum hammer price you're willing to pay for each separate item.

You must also provide your name, signature and date, address, and telephone number where you can be reached during the sale.

List the items you wish to bid on: lot number, description, and maximum price. The auction's commission bidder will bid for you, only to the maximum price (usually called the "limit") you have stated.

Note that the "limit" is the price before any buyer's premium and VAT; if you want your price to include these figures, lower the amount of your limit. Do not put the total price and state "including premium and VAT".

Telephone Bids

For telephone bids, the procedure is a bit more complicated. You must register as a bidder, and inform the auction house about how you intend to pay, and the items you wish to bid on.

Contact the Commissions office well in advance of the sale to arrange for telephone bidding.

Bidding by the House

When you're at the auction and you see employees of the auction house making bids, don't worry. In reality, they are making bids not for themselves or for the house, but rather for people who have left written bids or are relaying bids from telephone bidders.

Shills

Shills are prohibited at British auctions. Owners of items at auction are also generally prohibited from bidding on the items they're trying to sell. Failure to follow these rules will exclude the seller from future auctions.

Storage After the Auction

Generally, most antiques auctions require that all purchases be removed in a short period. Some require removal by dark, while others will let you take as long as one week. The free period depends on the auction house's policy.

After this period expires, all items are put in storage at your expense; you'll have to pay the storage and sometimes transportation charges before you can claim the purchases.

In any case, you won't be permitted to take the goods until you have a bill of sale in your possession.

If you have a removal company making collections, you may make arrangements with the auction house to hold the items until the collection truck arrives. Make sure that you work out arrangements before you leave the sale! Make sure that the collections truck driver has the original or copy of the bill of sale and your authorization to take the items.

Paying for Purchased Items

You must pay for the items you bought before you can take them. Since most auctions do not accept credit cards, payment must usually be made in pounds, either by British cheque drawn on a British bank, by sterling travellers' cheque, or by cash.

Usually, large antiques auction houses allow up to several days to make payment before action will be taken. Small country auctions may wish to collect payment on the same day as the auction. It is entirely up to the auction house to set its own policy.

Receipts and Other Documents

When you pay for your purchases, you'll be given a receipt with the lot number, probably a short description of what the lot contains, and the price, plus an additional amount for any buyer's premium and VAT.

You have the right to a receipt for every purchase.

Regulation of Auctioneers and Auctions

Legally, auctions are not considered retail sales. Unlike antique dealers, auctioneers are not bound by the "Trade Description Act", which requires accurate descriptions of items sold, and are specifically excluded from coverage under the "Unfair Contract Terms Act", which in general prohibits general disclaimers of responsibility. As a result, while auctioneers try accurately to assess the goods they offer, they are not legally liable for misdescription of merchandise and often offer no guarantee.

However, remember that many of the true experts in identification of antiques are found at the auction houses. The larger firms often have specialists in particular types of items.

Usually, if you can prove that the item was misrepresented or a fake, you can take your evidence and information to the auction house, which will often have the sale annulled, and you may be able to get your money back.

Fine Art Auctioneers Trade Association

Most auctioneers of antiques belong to the trade association. You can contact this organization if you wish:

Society of Fine Arts Auctioneers
7 Blenheim Street
London W1Y 0AS
Telephone 01-620 2933

Birmingham

Who Are the Sellers?

You always hope to find friendly, helpful vendors who don't know the value of what they're selling, and therefore sell it to you for a song. While such sellers do exist, they are only slightly more common than hens' teeth. Do not expect to find them very often.

Sellers may vary widely in knowledge of their chosen field. Most use reference books and price guides to help them keep their pricing current with the British market. The day of the untutored and ignorant seller of antiques has passed almost completely.

Most sellers at antiques fairs, shows, and regular antiques markets are full-time dealers, who may close their shops or leave an assistant to mind the main store. Depending on the nature of the market, they either take their best or worst—whatever they think will sell.

Some dealers have no fixed place of business, except their vans and trucks, and maybe a dusty barn at their home in the country or part of an old warehouse. They are "pickers"—that is, picking up the best around the country, and serving as the city dealers' source of supply. If you can find them, they can also be a cheaper source of supply for you. These traveling dealers have the time and patience to seek out house sales, country auctions, and fund-raising sales of

45

charity groups. They often cultivate a grapevine to lead to tips and sources of supply. Because they have no fixed place of business, they often thrive on large turnover and take low markups. Some vendors are junk dealers pure and simple. They clean out basements and attics, old barns, warehouses, and garages. Some even go on early morning safaris looking for salvageable items in the rubbish! Even so, they may ask the same amount that the price guides suggest and consider their time as their investment.

Part-time vendors are usually found in strength only at weekend antiques fairs where permanent stands aren't available. During the week, they are members of other trades and professions. While many do not have the choicest items, they may be more willing to negotiate and they are often more happy to share experiences. Many of their items may only be of boot-sale or jumble-sale quality.

Bermondsey Street-London

Bargaining

While prices at antique fairs and shows are often marked, they are rarely fixed—you can usually obtain reductions of 10 to 30% of the first asking price if you try. These reductions are often possible in the most elegant of fairs and exhibitions. Knowing the economics of the market helps.

As a rule of thumb, most dealers try to double the prices of everything they sell. They feel entitled to this for their time, trouble, skill, and luck.

British bargaining is unlike the "let's make a deal" attitude so common in Italy. It's much more likely to be a softly spoken, "Is that your best price?" answered by "I think I could do a little better".

The first price almost always include a "fudge factor", since most sellers (and most buyers) expect to haggle and reduce the initial price. In fact, if you fail to bargain, some vendors may be puzzled and deprived of the conversational ritual to set the final price. The conversations as well as the money constitute much of the income many part-time vendors expect and enjoy.

Here are a number of tactics to try to bring the price down:

1. The seller will always make a profit: his or her initial cost is also base price. Some sellers keep markups low to increase turnover; this will

make initial prices seem more reasonable, but there may be less price flexibility.

If the dealer just obtained the item, the price may be reduced to provide a quick profit to raise cash. The dealer may know of another more desirable object he or she may need some added money to buy. On the other hand, if the item has been a longtime dust collector, and you're the first person even casually interested, the price may be less.

2. Have enough cash to buy what you want. At antiques markets, all payments are expected to be cash. You'll be amazed at some of the sums of cash discreetly changing hands. No checques or credit cards.

3. The price is usually on an "as is—where is" basis. If there's an imperfection, use it as a way to try to reduce the price.

4. Bargain even if you know an item is an incredibly good buy. You can still always pay the initial asking price later. Failure to bargain may make the vendor believe that either you're foolish or that the item is very valuable (and the seller may decide to keep it).

5. Treat sellers as *people* first—this will solve many of your price problems. Politeness, courtesy, and consideration will almost always make a difference.

6. When you first see an item you want, set a price on it in your mind even before you pick it up to examine it. Don't pay more if you can help it. The "get it now" mentality used by auctioneers and high-pressure salespeople can lead you to spend far more than you planned. Conversely, there are sometimes a few items you must have, or you'll regret it forever.

7. If you find an item you know is unique, don't wait and plan to come back later. You probably won't, or it will be sold when you do return. You may never see a similar item again, and be reminded of it every time you see the empty space on your mantelpiece at home.

8. Don't make a beeline for the only item you want. Showing too much interest right away may lead to a higher final price. Better to pick up five or six items of lesser interest and look at them as well as the items you want.

One manœuvre that sometimes works well is to ask the price of a group of unrelated items, then ask the price of smaller groups, single items, and eventually ask the price of the item you really want.

Often, using this approach, the price of the item you want is less than its proportional share of the whole group—and a bargain besides.

9. Ask for the "best price to the trade". If you use this tactic, it helps if you know or can act knowledgeably about the field, and if you can "prove" you're a dealer by possession of a business card of an antique dealer with your name as owner or manager.

Not a Tactic

Some dealers are contrary and won't reduce the price at all. Don't insult them by being loud and rude. The fixed price may be only for a particular item, only for foreigners, or people with certain colour eyes. The firmly fixed price is uncommon in antique markets, even in the very expensive ones in London and Bath.

Bristol

Transport

Where information about access via convenient public transit is available, it's included in the description of each market, fair, or auction.

Public transport as the basis for a tour of markets, fairs, and auctions has serious drawbacks, however. Not all markets are conveniently reached using public transport. Many are in suburbs, obscure country villages, or even motorway rest areas beyond the reach of underground, train, or bus service.

Most markets start early; they're at their best early Saturday and Sunday morning (and Friday for Bermondsey in London) soon after dawn. Buses and the underground will probably be running on a night or weekend schedule—which means long waits or even no service. As the market opens, dealers and regulars pick over and buy the best of this week's harvest of antiques, while you still stand in the station waiting for a train or bus to come along. Or, you can easily spend two or three hours getting to a suburban market only 10 miles away; when you finally arrive, you may find the market has been cancelled, or is packing up.

When using public transport, you have to carry your purchases with you, send them along, or arrange for a collection service to gather them together. There's a limit to how much luggage you can carry, and porters or baggage carts are often scarce.

In London, there are often half a dozen markets to cover on a single day. Each market has its own character and unique offerings. The markets are an hour or more from each other by public tranport—but 20 minutes by car or van.

Public transport is often the fastest way to get around large cities on weekdays. During the week, a car or van in a city can be a hindrance. During the week, city driving is an exercise in fighting through the thick molasses of traffic. Cars are often best left in a parking place.

Car or Van—The Advantages

A vehicle is almost a necessity for serious collector or dealer.

Take a hint from the sellers: they don't usually arrive by public transport. They drive.

Drive Everywhere

Small towns and villages in the countryside or city suburbs often hold antiques markets, antiques fairs, and auctions. Public transport is either unavailable or very inconvenient.

If you limit yourself to major cities, you eliminate a large proportion of items for sale. You also deprive yourself of some of the most picturesque market settings, and friendly (and often lower priced) provincial sellers. You may also miss country style furniture, folk art, and new but traditional artefacts.

Your Vehicle as Depository

Carrying purchases around a market can be exhausting—especially if you have bought heavy crystal, small bronze statues, or delicate porcelain. If you have a car, you can slip back to it to unload your purchases, reducing fatigue and worry.

If several of you travel together, you can search the market independently and find the car a convenient meeting place. Each separate marketer should have a car key. (Keys are made at a locksmith, and may cost as much as £4.)

Probably Save Money

Unless your entire expedition is limited to London and its suburbs, renting a small car or a basic van (not a fully equipped camper!) can save you a substantial amount of money, even after you consider the 15% Value Added Tax and the high price of petrol.

Parking: A Potential Problem

One drawback of driving is parking. Most cities (except for the new towns and the old cities totally reconstructed after being flattened during the Second World War) were not designed for motor vehicles, or for parking. If you arrive at the market early, you'll probably get a parking place within a few blocks of the market's centre—impossible later in the day. Street parking places may be free, especially on Sunday. Watch, however, for no-parking signs. Sometimes the police will tow illegally parked cars away. Tow-away zones are usually signed: there will be two yellow lines embedded or painted on the side of the road, and a small yellow sign with black writing will be near by. To redeem a towed car may cost as much as £100. Alternatively, you may be clamped—a frustrating and expensive procedure.

You may find signs directing you to pay car parks, where for 10p to £2 you'll have a legal parking place.

Pay parking garages operate several payment systems. Some require you to take a ticket as you enter, and you pay a cashier as you leave. Others operate on a self-serve system: you find a parking place, find the coin-operated ticket machine, buy a ticket, and place it on the windshield of your car (Pay and Display). At still others, you just pay as you enter.

Parking meters are also unfortunately wide-spread. Some in London take £1 coins, while giving as little as twenty minutes of freedom from the traffic warden.

Antiques Market-Windsor

Carrying Your Finds at Market

Sellers' Packing Materials

Few sellers have adequate, secure, convenient packing materials. Most will hand you the item, possibly wrapped in an old newspaper or a flimsy shopping bag. These bags, though better than nothing or a newspaper, are lightweight, and stretch and tear if filled with heavy or sharp-pointed objects. Bring your own bag.

Selecting a Market Bag

There is a large variety of carrier bags available. Nylon bags are best: they are strong, light, fold into small places, and shield the contents from the prying eyes of potential thieves. Shoulder straps leave your hands free to inspect items. Carefully check a bag before you buy it. Look for durability and convenience, not style. A good bag has these qualities:

1. The material is strong. Rip-stop nylon is the most durable lightweight fabric. Canvas is heavier (in weight, not strength) and can rot if left in the damp for extended periods.

2. The stitching is strong and seams are secure.

3. The zippers are strong and substantial, and open and close easily.

4. All metal parts are thick and strong: solid brass is best.

If you plan on extensive purchases of small items, take an extra bag with you.

Luggage Carriers

Visitors to very large markets sometimes bring wheeled luggage carriers. They have a number of limitations that make them less useful there than at airports and train stations. Many markets have a lot of barriers to the small wheels of these devices. Markets are often held on dirt, gravel, or uneven cobblestone surfaces. Curbs may interfere with smooth rolling. Many indoor markets have stairs, which further reduce the utility of these carriers.

Flea markets and antique fairs by their very nature are very crowded, full of jostling people intent on their business. They don't expect to find luggage carriers in their way and may trip over them.

If you do use a luggage carrier, be sure it is strong and will take a lot of punishing use without breaking. And be sure that boxes or suitcases can be securely fastened to the carrier.

London

Amenities at the Antiques Market

Food at the Fair

Most markets and fairs have food and drink for sale at concession stands. Such convenience food, not noted for offering quality or good value, can range from vendors of fizzy drinks, sandwiches, and meat pies, to fish-and-chips, small pizzas, and, at the elegant hotel shows, the entire dining room of the hotel.

Snack food sold at markets is usually as safe as such food is generally. Use the same precautions you would use anywhere.

If the market is also a general market with vegetable vendors as well as a antiques and junk, you may find lower prices, better variety and more quality for your money.

Toilets

There are toilets at most markets or close by. Some can be most portable, primitive, smelly, and ill-maintained. There may not be any toilet paper—or the paper may have the texture and consistency of waxed paper. Some of the worst ones have an attendant to collect money, usually 5p, 10p, or 20p per use.

Often facilities for women are unequal to the demand—plan to wait.

In a number of markets held in open spaces or fields, toilets may be placed in portable trailers. Look for the trailers looming up above the stands. They are often but not always marked.

Birmingham

Volvo Estates—Sign of a Good Market

You *know* you're at a good market to find antiques and collectables when you see lots of Volvo estates parked close to the market. Many antique dealers and pickers use these vehicles, because Volvos are boxy and hold a larger volume of merchandise than streamlined estates. Many are fitted with roof racks, to hold the excess.

Sometimes, Volvos seem to outnumber all other cars!

While the scene illustrated above was seen at the Birmingham antiques market held every six weeks, the scene could have been seen at many, many markets.

Cities A to Y

Alcester, Warwickshire

"The Ragley Hall Antiques Fair", twice a year (near the start of March and October), Friday from 1 to 9 p.m., Saturday from 11 a.m. to 6 p.m., and Sunday from 11 a.m. to 5 p.m., at Ragley Hall, about one mile southwest of Alcester on A441. This fair, held in a historic home, offers all types of very good quality antiques, including clocks, Persian rugs, glass, porcelain, jewellery, silver, and other objets d'art. All items are vetted by outside experts. The dateline is 1885 to 1920 depending of the particular type of item (for example, furniture 1885, paintings 1920). Admission is £2.50. Free parking is available. This fair is not easily accessible by public transport. For exact dates and further information, contact Robert Bailey Antiques Fairs, 1 Roll Gardens, Gants Hill, Ilford, Essex IG2 6TN, telephone 01-550 5435.

Aldershot, Hampshire

(Please also see Farnham, Godalming, Guildford, and Hook.)

Antiques and collectors fair every eight to ten Sundays at The Princes Hall. This is a local antiques fair; most items are small items rather than furniture. For exact sale dates and further information, contact Kingston Promotions, 157 Plymouth Drive, Hill Head, Fareham, Hampshire PO14 3SN, telephone (0329) 661780.

Alnwick, Northumberland

"The Border Antiques and Interior Design Fair" held the second weekend of June, on Friday from 11 a.m. to 9 p.m., Saturday and Sunday from 10 a.m. to 6 p.m. at Alnwick Castle, an 18th- and 19th-century restoration of a 12th-century castle.

This event mixes antiques with a few modern items for interior design purposes. All types of antiques are sold, including furniture, silver, clocks, paintings and prints, and other items. All items are vetted. The general dateline is 1880. Admission is £2, accompanied children free. This is a good regional fair by an established organiser. Access by car to Alnwick Castle, just east of the town. Free parking is available at the grounds. Access by public transport is by bus from Newcastle-upon-Tyne, or by rail to Bilton and then by bus or taxi to Alnwick. For exact dates and further information, contact Mr. Robert Soper, Castle Fairs, Bowcliffe Road, Bramham, Wetherby, Yorkshire, telephone (0937) 845829.

Ampleforth, North Yorkshire

"The Dales Antiques and Interior Design Fair" the last weekend of March, on Friday from 11 a.m. to 9 p.m., Saturday and Sunday from 10 a.m. to 6 p.m. in the village of Ampleforth. This event mixes antiques with a few modern items for interior design purposes. All types of antiques are sold, including furniture, silver, porcelains, clocks, and other specialized items. All items are vetted. The general dateline is 1880. Admission is £2, accompanied children free. This is a good regional fair by an established organiser. Access by car from York, north on B1363 to Ampleforth College. The event is signposted. Free parking is available at the grounds. There is no easily used public transport to this fair. For exact dates and further information, contact Mr. Robert Soper, Castle Fairs, Bowcliffe Road, Bramham, Wetherby, Yorkshire, telephone (0937) 845829.

Ardingly, Sussex

(Please also see Haywards Heath and Horsham.)

"Antiques Trade and Collectors' Fair" five times a year on Wednesday, on varying dates (end of January, late April, mid-July, late September, beginning of November) from 7.30 a.m. to 4 p.m., except July, 2 to 8 p.m. These fairs are held at the South of England Showgrounds 5 miles north of Haywards Heath on B2028. The September fair is the oldest and largest one-day fair in the southern part of England, with more than 900 covered stands. Every sale has at least 300 stands. Antiques and collectables of all types, sizes, ages, and authenticity are in profusion. The management does not inspect or vet the items offered. Food, toilets, and currency exchange booth are available. Admission is £2 until 9 a.m., £1 after 9 a.m. Access on B2028 north of Haywards Heath. Plenty of free parking is available. Access by British Rail to Northgate or Haywards Heath station, then take courtesy buses to the show. Also, charter buses from and returning London are available for about £10, leaving Marble Arch about 6 a.m. (for information call 01-249 4050). The antiques trade is not admitted before the public or for free. Organised by Geoffrey Whitaker Antique Fairs, 25B Portland Street, P.O. Box 100, Newark, Nottinghamshire NG24 1LP, telephone (0636) 702326.

Arundel, West Sussex

(Please also see Fontwell.)

"Treasure House Antiques Market" every Saturday year round from 9 a.m. to 5 p.m. at 31 High Street. Most of it is indoors but in summer the courtyard is also used. It is accessible from High Street through a passage next to the Red Lion. All types of antiques and collectables are sold at this relatively small market, including silver, Victoriana, china, copper, brass, and miscellaneous odds and ends. There is no entry fee. Parking is free in winter and 50p—£1 in summer at the Crown Yard car park. Access by public transport on the Southdown Bus to High Street, or British Rail to Arundel and walk to High Street. For further information, contact Mrs. D. Henderson, Treasure House Antiques Market, 31b High Street and Crown Yard, Arundel, West Sussex BN18 9AG, telephone (0903) 883101.

Ascot, Berkshire

(Please also see Windsor.)

"Ascot Boot Sale" every Saturday from March to October from 8 a.m. to about 2 p.m. This is one of the largest regularly held boot sales in England and offers hundreds of vendors selling all types of used goods, including some collectables and antiques. Admission is 20p, which is donated to charity. Parking is available on the roads (free) and in adjoining fields. The sales are not held on the racecourse, but are across the street under the oak trees. Access by car from Windsor on A332 and A329. This market is not easily accessible by public transport.

Ashbourne, Derbyshire

Antiques fair every three months, usually around March 1, June 15, end of August, and first weekend of December at the Town Hall. This is a regional fair, with all types of collectable items and antiques. Admission is 25p, but is free to members of the antiques trade. Parking is available near the hall. For exact dates and further information, contact Peak Fairs, Hill Cross, Ashford, Bakewell, Derbyshire DE4 1QL, telephone (062981) 2229.

Ashburton, Devon

(Please also see Newton Abbot).

"Antiques & Collectors' Fair and Book Fair" one Saturday in May, July, September, October, and November from 9 a.m. to 4 p.m. at the Town Hall. Admission is free. This is a small local fair. Organised by Gerry Mosdell, West Country Antiques & Collectors Fairs, The Dartmoor Antiques Centre, off West Street, Ashburton, Devon TQ13 7DV, telephone (0364) 52182.

"The Dartmoor Antiques Centre", open every Wednesday from 9 a.m. to 4 p.m., is an indoor gallery off West Street of regular dealers offering all types of antiques and collectables. Organised by Gerry Mosdell, West Country Antiques & Collectors Fairs, The Dartmoor Antiques Centre, off West Street, Ashburton, Devon TQ13 7DV, telephone (0364) 52182.

Ashford, Kent

Cobb, Burrows, & Day Auctions
One auction per month is held on a Tuesday (often third or fourth but varies) at Victoria Crescent, Ashford. Each auction consists of several hundred lots, mainly of Victorian and more recent furniture, plus any odds and ends of bric-a-brac and other goods that are offered. Previews are offered the day before the sale, and the morning of the sale. Exact sale dates and further information is available from Cobb, Burrow, & Day Auctions, 39-41 Bank Street, Ashford, Kent, telephone (0233) 24321.

Hobbs Parker Antique & Fine Art Sales
Eight auction sales of antiques are held at regular intervals throughout the year, usually on Thursday. Each sale includes antique and old furniture, china, glass, jewellery, metalware, pictures, and collectors' items, usually about 900 lots. These sales are complememted by general sales of household furniture and effects held on the second Wednesday of every month. A free calendar of sales is available upon request. For further information, please contact Hobbs Parker, Romney House, Ashford Market, Elwick Road, Ashford, Kent, telephone (0233) 22222, fax (0223) 46642.

Bakewell, Derbyshire

(Please also see Buxton and Matlock.)

Antiques fair held every Monday from 10 a.m. to 5 p.m. at the Town Hall. In addition to the Monday fair, the same organisers hold fairs every second weekend (Friday, Saturday, and Sunday) from mid-April to the end of July and almost every weekend in August. The fairs are small regional and local ones, but offer various interesting small items. The region offers tourists famous stately homes, including Haddon Hall and Chatsworth. Access by car to Bakewell, which is a small town. Free parking is available near the hall. Access by bus is possible from Derby, Manchester, and Sheffield, but can be infrequent. For further information, contact Peak Fairs, Ashford, Bakewell, Derbyshire DE4 1QL, telephone (062981) 2449.

Barnstaple, Devon

"North Devon Antique Dealers' Fair" last Thursday and Friday of May and of December at Queens Hall in Barnstaple. On the first day, hours are 2 to 8 p.m.; the second day from 10 a.m to 5 p.m. This is a regional fair. Only dealers may sell here. Organised by Gerry Mosdell, West Country Antiques & Crafts Fairs, The Dartmoor Antiques Centre, off West Street, Ashburton, Devon TQ13 7DV, telephone (0364) 52182.

Barnstaple Friday Antiques & Collectors Market most Fridays, 9 a.m. to 3 p.m., The Queens Hall in Barnstaple. Admission is free. Organised by Gerry Mosdell, West Country Antiques & Crafts Fairs, The Dartmoor Antiques Centre, off West Street, Ashburton, Devon TQ13 7DV, telephone (0364) 52182.

Bath, Avon

Antiques market every Wednesday year round from 7 a.m. to 3 p.m. in the old school building on Guinea Lane and Walcott Street. About 60 to 100 dealers cram the nooks and crannies of this old building with collectables and junk as well as medium-quality antiques. There is no admission charge. For information contact (0225) 22510.

"Bath Saturday Antiques Market" every Saturday year round from 7 a.m. to 5 p.m. on Walcott Street along the wide part near Guinea Lane. This market offers all types of antiques and collectables. For further information contact (0225) 60909.

Antiques and collectors' fair second Sunday morning of every month at the Pavilion next to the Leisure Centre on North Parade Road, off A36 along the river Avon. This is a fair with all types of items, including furniture, glass, jewellery, postcards, and bric-a-brac. A car park is right next to the Pavilion. Organised by Parade Fairs, Bath, telephone (0225) 66497.

"The Bath Antiques Fair" third weekend of May at the Guildhall in High Street in the town centre. This is a vetted fair, and only antiques may be sold. Admission is charged, but is free to members of the antiques trade. Organized by Robert Bailey Antiques Fairs, 1 Roll Gardens, Gants Hill, Ilford, Essex IG2 6TN, telephone 01-550 5435.

"Bath Guildhall Antiques Fair" second weekend of August at the Guildhall in High Street. About 30 stands offer fine antiques. All items are vetted and guaranteed to be antiques. An admission charge is made. Organized by Tony Keniston, Hopton Castle, Craven Arms, Shropshire SY7 0QJ, telephone (05474) 356 and 464.

A number of indoor, year-round collections of permanent stalls (such as the Bartlett Street Antiques Centre, Great Western Antiques Centre, and Paragon Antiques) are open Monday through Saturday all along Bartlett Street. Better quality antiques and collectables abound, including large quantities of glass and furniture. Worth a browse, but few bargains are found in these markets.

Several auction houses are also found in Bath. Contact them for exact sale schedule and further information:

Aldridges of Bath
130-132 Walcot Street,
Bath, Avon
Telephone (0225) 52839

Stanley, Alder & Price
The City Auction Rooms
4 Princes Buildings, George Street
Bath, Avon

Phillips Fine Arts Auctioneers
1 Old King Street
Bath, Avon BA1 2JT
Telephone (0225) 310609 and 310709,
fax (0225) 446675

Battle, East Sussex

Antiques market every Saturday morning from
early morning until about noon. The market
takes place in open fields along the main road
near Battle Abbey. A varying number of dealers
and collectors offer all types of junk, collectables,
and antiques.

Burstow & Hewett, Auctioneers
Auctions are held two or three times per month
at the different two salesrooms in Battle. The
Abbey Auction Galleries (Lower Lake, Battle) offers antiques, clocks, watches, porcelain, silver,
and collector's items. These auctions start Wednesdays at 11 a.m. Viewing for these sales is on
the Tuesday before the sale from 9 a.m. to 8 p.m.
This saleroom also has one Wednesday evening
auction of paintings and other pictures at 6.30
p.m.; viewing is held from 9 a.m. to 1 p.m. and 2
to 6 p m. on the day of the sale. The Granary
Salerooms (Station Road, Battle) is the site of
monthly sales on a Wednesday at 10.30 a.m.
Items offered include antique and modern items,
with an emphasis on household furnishings.
Viewing is held the Tuesday before the sale from
9 a.m. to 1 p.m. and 2 to 9 p.m. A free listing of
all sales during an entire year is available upon
request. Catalogues are issued for all sales, and
cost between 20p and £1, depending on the sale.
Bids may be left or made by post or telephone.
There is no buyer's premium. For sale dates and
further information, contact Burstow & Hewett,
Abbey Auction Galleries, Lower Lake, Battle,
East Sussex TN33 0A7, telephone (04246) 2374
or (04246) 2302.

Beaconsfield, Buckinghamshire

"Beaconsfield Antique Market" second Thursday of each month from 9.30 a.m. to 4 p.m. at Burnham Hall. Information from the organiser in Beaconsfield, telephone (04946) 5338.

Antiques fair Spring Bank Holiday (last Sunday and Monday of May) from 11 a.m. to 6 p.m. at The Bell House Hotel about 2 miles west of the town centre on A40. This is a midsized regional fair. Free parking available. Organised by Midas Fairs, Beaconsfield, telephone (04946) 4170.

Beaminster, Dorset

"Antique and Bygone Fairs" held the third Saturday of every month (occasionally second or fourth Saturday) from 10 a.m. to 4 p.m. at the Beaminster Public Hall. This is a small local fair. Free parking is available. For further information, contact the organisers on (09389) 395.

Beckenham, Greater London

(Please also see London and Streatham.)

Antiques fair every Wednesday from 9.30 a.m. to 2 p.m. at The Old Council Hall on Bromley Road. Access by British Rail to Beckenham, or by Green Line bus. Organised by Ray Ratcliff, London, telephone 01-764 3602.

Bedford, Bedfordshire

Antiques and collectors fair seven Sundays per year (third of January, second of February, third of April and July, second of September, and fifth of October and first of December) from 11 a.m. to 5 p.m. at the Corn Exchange (telephone (0234) 59691), town centre. These are good regional fairs, but most items are small. There is not much large furniture. The general dateline is 1930. Admission is 50p, but members of the antiques trade are admitted free. The fairs are signposted, and parking is available. Organised by Herridges Antiques and Collectors Fairs, Chanctonbury, 8 Kimbolton Avenue, Bedford, Bedfordshire MK40 3AD, telephone (0243) 45725.

Beeston, Cheshire

Wright-Manley Auctioneers
These auctioneers hold several kinds of auctions: about six furniture and fine art sales per year, always held on the Thursday nearest to the first of every other month. Sales of miscellaneous items are held the first and third Wednesday of every month. Viewing is held every day before the sale, beginning the Saturday before the sale from 10 a.m. to 4 p.m., and Tuesday evening until 7.30 p.m. There is no buyer's premium. Catalogues are issued for sales and are available from the auctioneers. Information from and sales site is Wright-Manley Furniture & Fine Art Department, Beeston Sales Centre, near Tarporley, Cheshire, CWE6 0DR, telephone (08293) 2151.

Bexleyheath, Kent

(Please also see Crayford, Greenwich, and London.)

Antique and collectors' fair on May and August Bank Holiday (last Monday of May and August) from 10 a.m. to 5 p.m. at the Crook Log Sports Centre on Brampton Road. These are large fairs, with over 300 stands. All types of antiques and collectables are shown, but reproductions and modern items are prohibited. Access by car on A2. Free parking is available at the site. Access by train to Bexley station. Organised by Bartholomew Fayres, Executive House, The Maltings, Station Road, Sawbridgeworth, Hertfordshire CM21 9JX, telephone (0279) 725809.

Billingshurst, West Sussex

(Please also see Horsham.)

Sotheby's
Sotheby's hold fine art auctions in a Victorian mansion set in more than 40 acres of parkland. Weekly specialist sales include furniture, paintings, books, silver, jewellery, carpets, ceramics, glass, clocks, toys, guns, militaria, garden statuary, and all other types of items. Catalogues issued in advance of each sale can be purchased singly or by annual subscription and can be obtained either at Billinghurst or from Sotheby's London. The buyer's premium is 10%. Access by public transport on BritRail to Billingshurst, but the last distance may call for a taxi or long walk. Parking is available for cars on the site. Information and sales site is Sotheby's, Summers Place, London Road, Billingshurst, West Sussex RH14 9AD, telephone (040381) 3933, fax (040381) 5133, telex 87210 GAVEL.

Birmingham, West Midlands

(Please also see Bridgnorth, Kinver, Knowle, and Wombourne.)

*@FIRSTPARA = "St. Martin's Rag Market", a general market place and large covered market hall in the middle of Birmingham, is the location for a number of markets. It is easily accessible by public transport: take British Rail to New Street Station, and walk south through the Bull Ring Shopping Centre to the market, or from the Birmingham Bus Station across the street, through the Bull Ring Shopping Centre, and across Edgbaston Street. Street parking is impossible, since on most streets parking is forbidden and cars will be promptly ticketed and towed. Off-street parking is available in the Moat Lane Car Park (pay and display), and other structures on Queensway and Digbeth Street.

The "Flea Market" offers many different types of items, mostly new and cheap, such as clothes, pots and pans, tools, etc., and is of small or no interest to the antique collector. These markets take place every Tuesday, Thursday, and Saturday from 11 a.m. to 5.30 p.m. No admission charge. For further information, contact the City of Birmingham Markets Department, Manor House, 40 Moat Lane, Birmingham, West Midlands B5 5BD, telephone (021) 622 3452.

The "Monday Antique Market" takes place at the same site as the St. Martin's Market every Monday from 7 a.m. until 2 p.m. Between 150 and 200 dealers from all over central England offer collectables and antiques. For information, contact Alan Kipping, Wonder Whistle Enterprises, London, telephone 01-249 4050. There is no admission charge. For further information, contact the City of Birmingham Markets Department, Manor House, 40 Moat Lane, Birmingham, West Midlands B5 5BD, telephone (021) 622 3452.

"The Big Brum" antique market, a true antique dealer's and collector's paradise, is held every six weeks on Wednesday, from 10 a.m. to 6 p.m. inside the hall. Between 600 and 800 dealers and thousands of buyers cram the hall. All types of items are displayed, but the emphasis is on small items such as silver, porcelain, coins, and all types of collectables rather than furniture. However, the real buying and selling begin on the surrounding streets at dawn. Almost no selling takes place on the grounds to the north of the building, since the market police are vigilant. However, on the south and east, as the dealers wait to get in (there is no admission by either dealers or buyers until 10 a.m) all types of transactions are common. The greatest crush takes place within the first 15 minutes after the doors are opened. Most of the good buys are gone by noon, and by 1 p.m. some of the dealers are packing up. Information about exact dates and charter buses from London to this fair (leaving Marble Arch about 6:50 a.m.) are available from Alan Kipping, Wonder Whistle Enterprises, 1 Ritson Road, London E8, England, telephone 01-249 4050. Organised by Antique Forum, Flat 2, 98 Maida Vale, London W9, telephone 01-624 3214 (after 6 p.m. only). The Birmingham Markets Department also can inform you about dates of these fairs.

"British International Antiques Fair" the entire first week of April at the National Exhibition Centre. This is a large fair, held indoors. All types of items are shown, including furniture, jewellery, silver, and all types of miscellaneous items. Admission is charged. Information from the Exhibitions Division, National Exhibition Centre, Birmingham B40 1NT, telephone (021) 780 2518.

"Miniatura", a twice yearly specialists fair of dollhouse crafts, third Sunday in March and fourth Saturday in September from 10.30 a.m. to 5 p.m. at the Pavilion Suite, County Cricket Ground, Edgbaston Banqueting Centre, Edgbaston, southwest of the city centre on Bristol Road. This is one of the largest specialist shows for nearly all new handmade miniature craftwork: dolls, dollhouses, and miniature pottery, furniture, miscellaneous items. About 100 exhibitors show. Most but not all items are 1/12 scale. Nothing larger than 1/10 size may be shown. Merchandise is inspected by the management, but there is no date line. Admission is £2; no discounts or free admission to the antiques trade. Parking on the grounds is free. Access by public transport is on bus lines 45 and 47 from New Street British Rail station. Organised by Bob Hopwood, Miniatura, 41 Eastbourne Avenue, Hodge Hill, Birmingham, B34 6AR, telephone (021) 783 2070.

"NEC August Fair" first Thursday through Sunday of August at the National Exhibition Centre, near the Birmingham International Airport. About 270 exhibitors show antiques of all types. Datelines are: pictures and jewellery, not later than 1930; all other exhibits, not later than 1900; all items are vetted. Admission is £2.70, chidren and senior citizens £1.50. Parking is free, and catalogues are available at the fair. Organised by the Exhibitions Division, National Exhibition Centre, Birmingham B40 1NT, telephone (021) 780 2518.

"Warwickshire Antiques Fair" last Thursday, Friday, and Saturday of September at the Warwickshire County Cricket Ground at Edgbaston, southwest of the city centre. This fair has approximately 50 stands. Only antiques may be sold—no reproductions or new items. There is enough parking on the site; admission is £1. Organised by Bob Harris & Sons, 2071 Coventry Road, Sheldon, Birmingham, telephone (021) 743-2259.

The Birmingham Antique Centre is an indoor market open every Thursday from 9 a.m. to midafternoon. Thirty dealers offer all types of antiques and collectables. It is located at 141 Bromsgrove Street, Birmingham B5 6RQ, telephone (021) 622 2145. (Weller & Dufty, auctioneers, are at this location. Please see next entry.)

Weller & Dufty Ltd.

Auctions of arms, armour, and militaria are held every five weeks on Wednesday and Thursday, beginning at 9.30 a.m., at 141 Bromsgrove Street. Hundreds of lots of rifles, shotguns, ammunition, and other related items, as well as armour are offered by this specialist auction house. Catalogues are issued for all sales at least two weeks in advance, price £2 plus postage (one catalogue for each day). Catalogues can also be obtained by annual subscription. Viewing is held the day before the sale from 9 a.m. to 5 p.m. and each morning before the sale begins. Bids may be left, or made by post or telephone. Telephone bids must be confirmed in writing by letter, telegram, or telex before the sale begins. The buyer's premium is 10%. All items must be paid for and removed within one day, except that special arrangements can be made for postal, telephone, and left bids. If known to the auction house, purchasers have 28 days to pay for and remove their purchases. All firearms purchasers must be non-residents or, if British residents, must hold firearms certificates of the correct category for that item. Access by car is to central Birmingham. Street parking is difficult, but any of the Pay and Display car parks near the Bull Ring Market and New Street station are within walking distance. Access by train to New Street station and walk. For further information and exact sale dates, contact Weller & Dufty Ltd., 141

Bromsgrove Street, Birmingham, West Midlands
B5 6RQ, telephone (021) 692 1414 and 692 1415.

Bletchingley near Godstone, Surrey

Lawrences Fine Art Auctioneers
Auctions are held every six weeks from Tuesday
to Thursday, during which more than 2000 lots
are sold. The sales include antiques, specialising
in furniture, silver, pictures, and porcelain, plus
all types of collectables, bric-a-brac, and some
rather uninteresting modern items. Previews are
held the Friday and Saturday before the sale.
There is a 10% buyer's premium. There is no
readily available public transport. Access by car
on M25 to Exit 6, south to Godstone, and on A 25
to Bletchingley. The sales take place and information can be obtained from Lawrences Fine Art
Auctioneers, Norfolk House, 80 High Street,
Bletchingley, telephone (0883) 843323.

Boston Spa, West Yorkshire

Antiques fairs five Sundays per year (end of May,
beginning of July, September, mid-October, and
end of November) at the Village Hall. This is a
small regional fair, always held indoors. Admission 50p. Dateline 1930. Organised by Borough
Fairs, 83 Huntstanton Road, Old Huntstanton,
Norfolk, telephone (0485) 33732.

Botley, Hampshire

(Please also see Southampton.)

Antiques and collectors' fair every sixth Sunday
(approximately) from 11 am. to 5 p.m. at The
Botley Centre. This is a local fair. Small antiques
and collectables are available, but not much furniture. Admission is 25p, accompanied children
free. For exact dates and further information,
contact Kingston Promotions, 157 Plymouth
Drive, Fareham, Hampshire PO14 3SN,
telephone (0329) 661780.

Bournemouth, Dorset

Antiques and collectors' fair the second Saturday of every month from 10.30 a.m. to 4 p.m. from March to December at The Sacred Heart Institute Hall on Richmond Hill. This is a local fair with about 20 to 25 stands. Admission is 20p. Street parking can be difficult, but there is a parking garage at Richmond Hill and Wessex Way. Organised by Linda Forster, Forest Fairs, 28 Glenwood Road, West Moors, Dorset, telephone (0202) 875167.

"The Bournemouth Antiques Fairs", held one weekend in mid February and mid November, Friday from 1 to 9 p.m., Saturday from 11 a.m. to 6 p.m., and Sunday from 11 a.m. to 5 p.m., at the Wessex Hotel. This fair offers all types of very good quality antiques, including clocks, Persian rugs, glass, porcelain, jewellery, silver, and other objets d'art. All items are vetted by outside experts. The dateline is 1885 to 1920 depending of the particular type of item (for example, furniture 1885, paintings 1920). Admission is £2.50. Access by public transport to Bournemouth Central Station. For exact dates and further information, contact Robert Bailey Antiques Fairs, 1 Roll Gardens, Gants Hill, Ilford, Essex IG2 6TN, telephone 01-550 5435.

Antiques and collectors' fair the first Saturday of June from 10 a.m. (9 a.m. for members of the antiques trade) to 5 p.m. at the Bournemouth International Centre. Reproductions and new work are prohibited. This is a large regional fair, with more than 250 dealers, who each take up one or more tables, selling all types of antiques and collectables. Admission is 25p. Access by car to the Bournemouth International Centre along the shore; the route is AA signposted. Parking is available at the site, for which a charge is made. Organised by P S Enterprises, P.O. Box 268, Poole, Dorset BH14 8DE, telephone (0258) 840224.

Bradford-on-Avon, Wiltshire

Antiques and collectors' weekly market every
Thursday from 9 a.m. to 4 p.m. at St. Margaret's
Hall. This is a newly-established fair, and is
small and local in scope. Organised by Westfairs
Ltd., P.O. Box 43, Weston-super-Mare, Avon
BS23 2DS, telephone (0934) 33596.

Brandon, Suffolk

(Please see Lakenheath.)

Brecon (Aberhonddu), Powys, Wales

"Welsh Annual Antiques Fair" in April of each
year during Easter week, Thursday to Saturday,
at the Castle Hotel (telephone (0874) 4611). This
is a good, long-established regional fair; most
items offered are older than 1890. Only dealers
may sell. Organised by Tony Keniston, Hopton
Castle, Craven Arms, Shropshire SY7 0QJ,
telephone (05474) 356 and 464.

Bridgnorth, Shropshire

Antique fair one Sunday in January, March, May,
June, July, September, October, and November
from 10 a.m. to 5 p.m. at Bridgnorth Leisure
Centre, on the outskirts of town. This is a small
regional sale of approximately 40 vendors of
small antiques and collectables. Organised by
Waverly Fairs, Boreley Cottage, Boreley, Near
Ombersley, Worcestershire, telephone (0205)
620697.

Brighton, East Sussex

*(Please also see Lancing, Fontwell, Haywards
Heath, and Worthing.)*

"Brighton Saturday Morning Market" held every
Saturday from 7 a.m. to 1 p.m. on Upper
Gardner Street, near the Brighton railway sta-

tion. This market offers about 80 stands of antiques and collectables, including coins, silver,
porcelain, some furniture, glassware, and other
items, as well as additional stands of fruit,
vegetables, and flowers. Access by car is simple:
the market is between Gloucester Road and
North Road, between Grand Parade and Queens
Road. Parking, however, can be difficult, though
there are some car parks, for which a charge is
made. Access by train to Brighton station (main
line from Victoria station in London) then walk
200 feet along Queens Road, then left at
Gloucester Road. Access by many buses to
Brighton Station or Queens Road. Organised by
Brighton Borough Council, Town Hall, Brighton
BN1 1JA, telephone (0273) 29801. Secretary of
Traders Association is P.J. Smith, telephone
(0273) 505560.

"Brighton Sunday Market and Boot Sale" held
every Sunday from about 7 a.m. to 2 p.m. at the
Brighton station car park. This boot sale offers a
bit of everything: collectables, antiques, clothes,
and food. It is a general market as well as offering odds and ends. Organised by Bray
Enterprises, telephone (0883) 42671.

"Hove Town Hall Antiques Fair" second or third
Tuesday of every other month from May through
November at the Town Hall at Church Road and
Norton Road in Hove. About 65 indoor stalls,
1930 dateline. Admission 30p, parking in struc-
ture across the street. Nearest train station:
Brighton, about a mile east of the hall, also ac-
cess by city bus. Organised by Mostyn Fairs, 64
Brighton Road, Lancing, Sussex, telephone
(0903) 752961.

Antiques and collectors fairs every month (days
vary) from 10 a.m. to 5 p.m. at the Brighton
Centre on the sea at King's Road and West St.
Between 100 and 200 vendors (mostly but not
entirely dealers) offer all types of antiques and
collectables, dateline approximately 1930. Admission is 60p; free to the antiques trade. All of
this is indoors. Parking is difficult, but available
at the Council Car Park at the adjacent Church
Street Shopping Centre. For exact dates and fur-

ther information, contact Brenda Lay, Dyke Farm, West Chiltington Road, Pulborough, West Sussex, telephone (07982) 2447.

"The Brighton Antiques Fair" one Wednesday to following Saturday in July from 11 a.m. to 6 p.m. (Friday 11 a.m. to 9 p.m.) at the Corn Exchange on the grounds of the Royal Pavilion. This is one of the best regional fairs, with about 70 stands. All types of items are offered, including furniture, glass, porcelain, some silver, and collectables. The dateline is 1870, except for 1900 for jewellery and collectables, and 1920 for paintings. All items are vetted; new items and reproductions are prohibited. Admission is £2, which includes a brochure. Readmission is free. Access by car to the Royal Pavilion; there is parking on the street or the Church Street car park. Access by train to Brighton, and then a 15-minute walk to the Royal Pavilion. Organised by Penman Fairs, P.O. Box 114, Haywards Heath, West Sussex RH16 2YU, telephone Lindfield (04447) 2514 and 4531.

Raymond P. Inman Auctions
Auctions of antiques, used goods, and some reproductions are held at 9.30 a.m. every five weeks on Monday. Viewing is the previous Friday and Saturday from 9.30 a.m. to 4 p.m. and just before the sale. Sales are held at Raymond P. Inman Auctions, 35-40 Temple Street, Brighton, East Sussex, telephone (0273) 774777.

Graves, Son & Pilcher Fine Arts
Auctions of antiques of all types are held every month, usually on a Thursday and following Friday at Palmeira Fine Art Auction Rooms, 38 Holland Road, Hove. Catalogues are issued at least one week before the sale. Viewing is held on Tuesday and Wednesday before the sale. Bids may be left or made by post or telephone. The buyer's premium is 8%. Parking can be difficult, and is not available on the premises. Access by public transport by train to Brighton or Hove stations, then by bus. For exact sale dates and further information, contact Graves, Son & Pilcher Fine Arts, 71 Church Road, Hove, East Sussex BN3 2GL, telephone (0273) 735266.

"The Lanes", the quaint and well-touristed old area between the Royal Pavilion and the Brighton Centre, offers lots of antiques in small, often elegant shops, but does not have an antiques market at regular intervals.

Bridport, Dorset

Antiques stalls as part of the general Wednesday and Saturday market from early morning until about noon in the town centre. A few dealers of antiques, bric-a-brac, and junk are next to vendors of fruit, vegetables, and other new items.

Bristol, Avon

(Please also see Filton Portishead, Weston-super-Mare, and Yatton.)

Antique and collectable section of the regular weekday market at the Exchange Hall on Corn Street. Antiques are mixed in with all other types of merchandise, including glass, baking, art, and crafts. Over 180 stands are full most days, and many vendors are regulars.

Antique market every other Saturday, early morning to early afternoon, held at the Hope Centre. This is a regional market worth visiting if you're in the area.

"Antiques and Collectables Market" second Sunday of every month from 10 a.m. to 4.30 p.m. at the Brunel Great Train Shed at Temple Meads station. All types of antiques and collectables are offered. Admission is 50p, not charged to members of the antiques trade. A charge is made for parking. Access by train or bus to Temple Meads station (the main Bristol station). Organised by Talisman-Evergreen Fairs, P.O. Box 58, Weston-Super-Mare, Avon BS22 8ER, telephone (0934) 636648.

"West of England Antiques Fair" from early to mid May at the Bristol Exhibition Centre,

Canon's Road, Bristol. This long-established fair is organised by Anne Campbell Macinnes, 9 George Street, Bath, Avon BA1 2EH, telephone (0225) 463727.

"Antiques, Collectors' and Book Fair" on New Year's Day, last Sunday of March, August Bank Holiday Monday (last Monday of August), and third Sunday of October at the Bristol Exhibition Centre from 10 a.m. to 5 p.m. These are large regional fairs worth attending if you're in the area. Organised by West Country Antiques & Collectors Fairs, The Dartmoor Antiques Centre, off West Street, Ashburton, Devon TQ13 7DV, telephone (0364) 52182.

"Antique and Collectors' Fair" one Saturday in January, May, and August at Ashton Court Mansion, Long Ashton, across the Suspension Bridge from Bristol. Admission is 50p, children free. For further information, contact the organiser Kay Crisp, Evergreen Promotions, P.O. Box 58, Weston-Super-Mare, Avon BS22 8ER, telephone (0934) 636648.

"Antique and Collectors' Fair" several Sundays a year (usually the beginning of March, June, October, and December) from 10 a.m. (members of the antiques trade 9 a.m.) at Transport House on Victoria Street. About 100 dealers set up stalls and tables to sell all types of antiques and collectables. For further information and exact dates, contact Hallmark Antiques Fairs, Keynsham (02756) 3975.

"Antiques & Collectors' Fair" one Sunday in August, September, October, November, and December at the New Webbington Hotel, near Bristol off A38, 10.30 a.m. to 4.30 p.m. There are 80 stalls. For information contact the organiser, KS Fairs, P.O. Box 58, Weston-Super-Mare, Avon BS22 8ER, telephone (0934) 636648 or (0278) 784912.

Prudential Fine Art Auctioneers
Auctions of fine arts and antiques every two weeks on Wednesday at 11 a.m. at the Bristol Sales Rooms. The items offered are general antiques and collectables, but every two months there are specialized sales of antiques, models, books, and silver, also on Wednesday. Catalogues are issued and sold (usually £1) two to three weeks before sales. Viewing is the day before the sale from 9.30 a.m. to 6 p.m. and morning of the sale. Bids may be left or made by post or telephone. The buyer's premium is 10%. Parking is not available at the salesrooms, and street parking can be difficult. Sales are held at and more information is available from Prudential Fine Art Auctioneers, 71 Oakfield Road, Bristol, Avon BS8 2BE, telephone (0272) 734052.

Brockenhurst, Hampshire

(Please also see Bournemouth, Christchurch, and Ringwood.)

Antiques and collectors' fair second Sunday of most months (occasionally first Sunday) from 11 a.m. to 5 p.m. at the Balmer Lawn Hotel on Lyndhurst Road (hotel telephone (0590) 23116). These are local fairs; small items are sold. Admission is 25p, accompanied children are free. Organised by and further information is available from Kingston Promotions, 157 Plymouth Drive, Hill Head, Fareham, Hampshire PO14 3SN, telephone (0329) 661780.

Buckingham, Buckinghamshire

"The Stowe School Antiques Fair" five days in March at Stowe School, an 18th-century estate a mile northwest of the town on A421 and then on local lanes. This is a major regional fair, offering all types of good quality antiques, including Persian rugs, glass, porcelain, jewellery, silver, and other objets d'art. All items are vetted by outside experts. The dateline is 1885 to 1920 depending on the particular type of item (for example, furniture 1885, paintings 1920). Admission is £2.50.

Free parking is available. Access by public transport to Burton-upon-Trent, then walk or take a taxi. For exact dates and further information, contact Robert Bailey Antiques Fairs, 1 Roll Gardens, Gants Hill, Ilford, Essex IG2 6TN, telephone 01-550 5435.

Budleigh Salterton, Devon

"The Budleigh Salterton Antiques Fair" a Friday and Saturday in May, July, and October at the Masonic Hall. Hours vary by day: usually on Friday the fair is open from 2 p.m. to 8 p.m., on Saturday from 10 a.m. to 5 p.m. Organised by Gerry Mosdell, West Country Antiques & Collectors Fairs, The Dartmoor Antiques Centre, off West Street, Ashburton, Devon TQ13 7DV, telephone (0364) 52182.

Burnley, Lancashire

Antique and flea market every Wednesday from early morning until noon at the market hall. The rest of the week, this is a general market. The five days following the first Saturday in July is a large pottery fair. Access by road to the market hall. Access by rail to Burnley, then walk. For further information, call (0204) 691511.

Bury St. Edmunds, Suffolk

Antiques fair last Friday and Saturday of April at the Athenaeum. This is a middle-sized regional fair with about 40 sellers. In the area, follow the yellow AA signs to the fair. Parking is available on the grounds. Organised by Crown Antiques Fairs, 55 Barton Road, Cambridge, Cambridgeshire CB3 9LG, telephone (0223) 353016.

"East Anglia Antiques Fair" first Thursday to Saturday, March and September, from 10.30 a.m. to 8 p.m. at the Athenaeum (telephone (0284) 4785). This is a regular and long-established regional fair with about 60 vendors. Most items are older than 1890, and a money-back guarantee is offered on all items. Organised by Tony Keniston, Hopton Castle, Craven Arms, Shropshire SY7 0QJ, telephone (05474) 356 and 464..

Antiques and collectors' fair, seven Saturdays per year (first of February, first of April, third of July, third of September, second of October, and third of December) from 10 a.m. to 5 p.m. at the Corn Exchange (telephone (0284) 3937). These are regional fairs with all types of small and medium-sized antiques and collectables. Admission is 50p, free to members of the antiques trade. The fair is signposted, and parking is available. Organised by Herridges Antiques & Collectors Fairs, Chanctonbury, 8 Kimbolton Avenue, Bedford, Bedfordshire MK40 3AD, telephone (0234) 45725.

"Wakefield Ceramics Fair" in late July at The Athenaeum. This is a specialist fair with all types of ceramics, including crocker, stoneware and and porcelain. Organised by Wakefield Ceramics Fairs, 1 Fountain Road, Stood, Rochester, Kent ME2 3SJ, telephone (0634) 723461.

Buxton, Derbyshire

(Please also see Bakewell.)

"The Buxton Antiques Fair" starting the Saturday following May Bank Holiday at the Pavilion Gardens. This is a long-established, good-size regional fair. Antiques include furniture, paintings, prints, clocks, books, silver, and metalware. All antiques are vetted, and must be older than 1851. Admission is charged to all; price includes an illustrated catalogue. Organised by Roger Heath-Bullock, Cultural Exhibitions Ltd., 8 Meadrow, Godalming, Surrey GU7 3HN, telephone (04868) 22562.

This site is frequently used during the year by other organisers for antiques shows: one organiser using this site is Unicorn Fairs (several weekends per year), P.O. Box 30, Hereford, Hereford & Worcester, telephone (061)

773 7001. Information on forthcoming events is available from the Pavilion Gardens office, telephone (0298) 3114.

Caerleon near Newport, Gwent (Wales)

"Antique and Collectors' Fair" last Sunday of every month from 11 a.m. to 5 p.m. at the Priory Hotel in High Street, Caerleon, about 3 miles northwest of the Newport railway station. Several dozen dealers display indoors; reproductions must be clearly marked. Welsh specialties including furniture, brass, copper, and china are offered. Admission is 30p to the public, free to the trade. Access by car on M4 to Junction 25, then northeast to Caerleon; access by public transport on the hourly Sunday bus from Newport station is to the hotel front door. Organised by Doug Burnell-Higgs, Isca Fairs, 10 Norman Street, Caerleon nr. Newport, Gwent, NP6 1BB, Wales, telephone (0633) 421527.

Cambridge, Cambridgeshire

Cambridge book market last Wednesday of every month from 10 a.m. to 5 p.m. at Fisher Hall. Only used and antiquarian books may be sold at this fair. Organised by the Provincial Booksellers Fairs Association, P.O. Box 66, Cambridge, CB1 3PD, telephone (0223) 240921.

"The Cambridge Antiques Fair" the second weekend in October at The Corn Exchange. All items are vetted by outside experts. The dateline is 1885 to 1920 depending on the particular type of item. For exact dates and further information, contact Robert Bailey Antiques Fairs, 1 Roll Gardens, Gants Hill, Ilford, Essex IG2 6TN, telephone 01-550 5435.

Cheffins Grains & Comons Auctioneers
Weekly sales of period furniture, pictures, textiles, ceramics, silver, jewellery, domestic and rural bygones, and general household furniture and effects at the Cambridge Sale Room at Cher-

ry Hinton Road, Cambridge CB1 4BW, telephone
(0223) 358721 and 213343.

Canterbury, Kent

Antiques and crafts market every Saturday year
round from 9.30 a.m. to 5 p.m. at the Sidney
Cooper Centre on St. Peters Street in the town
centre. This indoor market is where about 40
local dealers show off small items, such as silver,
porcelain, ceramics, glass, coins, and books.
There isn't much furniture. There is no admission charge. The market is easily accessible by
rail from the British Rail Canterbury West station. Parking is difficult; the nearest is on Pound
Lane (20p per hour). Organised by the Amenities
Department, Canterbury City Council, Military
Road, Canterbury, Kent, CT1 1YW, telephone
(0227) 763763, extension 4704.

Antiques market first and third Saturday of
every month from 8 a.m. to 4.30 p.m. at the Red
Cross Hall, Lower Chantry Lane, about a block
toward Dover from the city walls and bus station.
Dealers offer porcelain, silver, jewellery, and
scales with weights. Dateline 1930; no reproductions or modern works are allowed. Admission is
free. Free parking is available in front of the
building and on some surrounding streets. For
information, contact the organiser, Mr. A.W. Gar-
ratt, The Old Court House, Upper Hardres,
Canterbury, Kent, telephone (0227) 70437.

G.A. Property Services Auctioneers
Monthly auctions of antiques, furniture, fine
arts, and clocks once a month, usually on a
Thursday. Sales with special interests, particularly books, pictures, and paintings, are held
irregularly in addition to the monthly sales.
Viewing is held the day before the sale. Sales site
and information from G.A. Property Services
Fine Art Auctions, 40 Station Road West, Canterbury, Kent CT2 8AN, telephone (0227) 763337.

Cardiff, South Glamorgan (Wales)

Antiques markets every Thursday and Saturday year round. One is in the city centre on St. Mary Street, and the other is Jacob's Market on Canal Wharf. These two are among the better markets in Wales, offering antiques and lots of collector's items. There is no admission charge.

Antiquarian book fair second Saturday of April and November from 10 a.m. to 5 p.m. at St. Davids Hall in The Hayes. Only used books and related items may be sold. Organised by the Provincial Booksellers Fairs Association, P.O. Box 66, Cambridge, Cambridgeshire CB1 3PD, telephone (0223) 240921.

Phillips Fine Art Auctioneers
Auctions are held on two Wednesdays per month at 11 a.m. at the auctioneers' office on Westgate Street. Sales are specialized, with topics such as Victoriana (a frequent classification), silver and jewellery, furniture, etc. Catalogues are issued at least one week before the sale, price between £1 and £2. Viewing is Monday from 9 a.m. to 5 p.m., Tuesday from 9 a.m. to 6.30 p.m. and from 9 a.m. on sale day. A free schedule of yearly sales is available upon request. Bidders must register at the office before bidding. Bids may be left or made by post or telephone. Access by road on M4 to A48 to Junction 29,then follow signs to City Centre. Phillips is just west of the castle. No parking is available on site, but there is a car park at the Cardiff Arms Park, off Westgate Street. Access by rail to Central station, then walk about 300 yards. Sales are held at and further information is available from Phillips in Wales, 9-10 Westgate Street, Cardiff, South Glamorgan CF1 1DA, telephone (0222) 396453.

Prudential Fine Arts Auctioneers
Auctions of fine arts and antiques on Wednesdays, every third week at 11 a.m. at the Cardiff Auction Rooms. The items offered are period furniture, art works, clocks, ceramics, glass, silver, jewellery, and carpets and rugs. Catalogues are issued (price usually £1) about two weeks before the sale. Off-street parking is available opposite

the Auction Rooms, 56 Machen Place, Cardiff
CF1 8EQ, telephone (0432) 272413.

Cark, Cumbria

"The Lake District and Interior Design Fair" the
first weekend of November (Friday are from 11
a.m. to 9 p.m., Saturday and Sunday from 10
a.m. to 6 p.m.), at Holker Hall, (telephone
(044853) 328), a stately home originally built in
the 17th century but almost totally rebuilt since.
In addition to the hall, there are about 200 acres
of grounds and several museums. This event
mixes antiques with a few modern items for interior design purposes. All types of antiques are
sold, including furniture, silver, clocks, paintings
and prints, and other items. All items are vetted.
The general dateline is 1880. Admission is £2,
accompanied children free. Access by car from
Grange-over-Sands on B5277 to Cark, and then
north on B5278 for about one mile. Free parking
is available at the grounds. Access by public
transport is by rail to Cark and then by taxi to
Holker Hall. For exact dates and further information, contact Robert Soper, Castle Fairs,
Bowcliffe Road, Bramham, Wetherby, Yorkshire,
telephone (0937) 845829.

Carmarthen, Dyfed (Wales)

John Francis Auctioneer
Auctions are held every six weeks on Tuesday at
11 a.m. "precisely" either at the Curiosity Sale
Room, King Street (antiques, catalogue issued,
price £1), or the Household Sale Auction Room,
Old Station Road. Antique auctions include
paintings, prints, some carpets, silver, some silver plate, clocks, large quantities of (mainly Victorian) furniture, porcelain, and miscellaneous
other items. Catalogues are published at least
two weeks in advance, price £1 (postpaid £1.40).
Viewing is held the day before the sale from 3 to
6 p.m. and the morning of the sale from 9 a.m.
Bids may be left, made by post, or by telephone if
confirmed in writing. Parking is available close
by in public car park. Access by train to Carmar-

then, then walk from the station. For exact sale dates and further information, contact John Francis Auctioneers, King Street, Carmarthen, Dyfed, telephone (0267) 233456.

Castle Ashby, Northamptonshire

"The Castle Ashby Antiques Fair" five days in mid-August. All items are vetted. The dateline is 1885 to 1920 depending on the particular type of item. Admission is charged for the public, but members of the antiques trade are admitted free with a business card. For dates and details, contact Robert Bailey Antiques Fairs, 1 Roll Gardens, Gants Hill, Ilford, Essex IG2 6TN, telephone 01-550 5435.

Castle Combe, Wiltshire

(Please also see Chippenham.)

Car boot sales every three weeks on Sunday from the end of April to October from 10 a.m. to 3 p.m. at Castle Combe Circuit. This large boot sale takes place inside the main entrance. All types of used goods and some antiques can be found here. This is often a good place to make true finds— the dealers come early and look. Access by car is on B4039 between Bristol and Chippenham. Admission is 25p (donated to charity). For exact dates and further information, contact Castle Combe Circuit Ltd., Chippenham, Wiltshire SN14 7EY, telephone (0249) 782417.

Castle Howard, Yorkshire

(Please also see York.)

"The Castle Howard Antiques Fair" the first Friday to following Tuesday of December at Castle Howard. This is a new regional fair, with about 60 dealers. All items are vetted, and the dateline is 1890 for many types of items, but 1930 for others. Admission is charged to the public, but is free to members of the antiques trade with a business card. Parking is available at the site. Organized by Robert Bailey Antiques Fairs, 1 Roll Gardens, Gants Hill, Ilford, Essex IG2 6TN, telephone 01- 550 5435.

Chard, Somerset

Antique and collectors' market every Thursday from 8 a.m. to 4 p.m. at the Guildhall. This is a small, regional market. No admission is charged; parking is availble nearby. Organised by Mr. Gill, Illminster, telephone (04605) 2873.

Charnock Richard, Lancashire

(Please also see Preston.)

"Park Hall Charnock Richard Antique and Collectors' Fair" every Sunday from dawn or 6 a.m. (whichever comes first) to 4 p.m. at Park Hall Leisure Centre. This is one of the largest and best antique fairs in Britain, and richly rewards the early bird. In the middle of one of the regions richest in antiques, dealers from all over Britain converge here to buy and sell. All types of antiques and other collectable items are sold, ranging from silver, porcelain, glass, and jewellery, to furniture, old machinery, flatirons, and hip baths. Outdoors, over 100 vans, estate and saloon cars operate more or less in boot sale fashion until about 9.30, though the quality is far higher than the typical boot sale. Inside, as many as 300 dealers and other sellers offer all types of antiques and collectables. (More than a few dealers buy outside, and bring their purchases inside at double the price.) There is no admission charge to the outside portion, but 75p is charged for the indoor fair. All items are supposed to be older than 1950, but this doesn't seem to be closely monitored. Access by car is easy: take the M6 to the Charnock Richard Service Area, and drive out through the open gate that says "no entry except for service" (really!), and turn right on the road at the bridge. Follow it for about half a mile, and turn into the Park Hall Leisure Centre. Follow the road all the way to the far end (about 500 yards) until you see cars parked on the gravel. There is no public transport to this fair. For further information, contact Unicorn Fairs Ltd., P.O. Box 30, Hereford, Hereford & Worcester HR2 8SW, telephone (061) 773 7001.

Chatham, Kent

Baldwin and Partners Auctions
This general sale of antiques and other odds and ends is held the first Wednesday of every month. Previews are the Saturday and Tuesday before the sale. Auction site and information is available from Baldwin & Partners, 26 Railway Street, Chatham, Kent, telephone (0634) 400121.

Cheam, Surrey

(A suburb of London.)

Parkins Auctioneers & Valuers
Auctions are held on the first Monday of each month at 10 a.m. and one Friday each month at 7 p.m. for antiques and collectables at the auction rooms. Viewing is held on Friday and Saturday for the Monday sale, and from 2 to 7 p.m. on the day of the evening sale. There is also a general furniture and effects sale held every remaining Monday at 10 a.m. For exact sale dates and further information, contact Parkins Auctioneers & Valuers, 18 Malden Road, Cheam, Surrey SM3 8SD, telephone 01-644 6633.

Chelmsford, Essex

(Please also see Ipswich.)

"Antique and Collectors' Fair" of more than 150 stalls, four times a year (about every three months but call for exact dates) from 10.30 a.m. to 5 p.m. at the Riverside Ice & Leisure Centre, Victoria Road. Organised by Bartholomew Fairs, Executive House, The Maltings, Station Road, Sawbridgeworth, Hertfordshire CM21 9JX, telephone (0279) 725809 and 725699.

Cooper Hirst, Auctioneers
Weekly auctions are held every Friday at 10 a.m.
at the Granary Saleroom, Victoria Road,
Chelmsford. These are auctions of all types of
used goods and household items. In addition,
there are special sales of antiques and collectables, usually held on Wednesdays. For further
information, contact Cooper Hirst at the Granary
Saleroom, Chelmsford, Essex CM2 6LH,
telephone (0245) 260535.

Cheltenham, Gloucestershire

Antiques fair second Sunday of each month year
round from 10 a.m. to 4.30 p.m. in the Golden
Valley Hotel 2 miles west of the town centre on
Gloucester Road (A40). This is a regional fair
with about 50 dealers selling. Parking is available on the site. Organised by Somerset & Avon
Antique Fairs, telephone (0278) 784912; the
hotel telephone is (0242) 32691.

Antiques and collectors' fair the third Sunday of
every month from 10 a.m. (members of the antiques trade 9 a.m.) to 5 p.m. in the Prestbury
Suite at the Cheltenham Racecourse. These are
local fairs, with not more than 80 vendors. Admission is 30p. Most vendors are dealers.
   In addition, the same organisers sponsor the
"Midsummer Magnet" the last Tuesday of June
at the same location, and all over the racecourse
grounds. The midsummer fair has over 500
vendors. Admission is £1, but members of the
antiques trade are admitted for free at 8 a.m.
Access from M5 Junction 10, through
Cheltenham on A435 to the racecourse. Access by
public transport is difficult. There is plenty of
free parking at this fair. Organised by Westfairs,
P.O. Box 43, Weston-super-Mare, Avon BS23
2DS, telephone (0934) 33596.

Antiques fair the second weekend of February,
last weekend of May, and in mid-September at
the Town Hall, Imperial Square. These are
regional fairs.

"Wakefield Ceramic Fairs" for three days at the end of March and beginning of April (not Easter) at the Pitville Pump Room, Cheltenham. Organised by Fred Hynds, Wakefield Ceramic Fairs, 1 Fountain Road, Rochester, Kent ME2 3SJ, telephone (0634) 723461.

Hobbs & Chambers, Auctions
Auctions are held fortnightly on Tuesdays at the Chapel Walk Saleroom, Cheltenham. Items sold include antique and general secondhand furniture, paintings, prints, silver, jewellery, and collectables. For exact schedule and further information, contact Hobbs & Chambers, Market Place, Cirencester, Gloucestershire GL7 1QQ, telephone (0285) 4736.

Chester, Cheshire

Phillips in Chester, Auctioneers
Auctions are usually held the second Friday of every month, except in March, April, July and November, when they continue for three days, Wednesday to Friday. Most sales begin at 11.30 a.m. Contact any Phillips office for the exact schedule. Catalogues are available several weeks in advance for all antiques sales, and cost between £1 for one-day sales and £5 for the three-day sales. Auctions are usually specialized; antique furniture, paintings, silver and jewellery, etc. Each specialized sale takes one day. Special sales here include fishing tackle, golfing memorabilia, and oriental rugs. In addition, sales of less spectacular household goods are held once a month on Monday. Viewing is the day before the sale from 10 a.m. to 4 p.m. and the morning of the sale. The buyer's premium is 10% of the hammer price. Bids may be left, posted, or telephoned; however, telephone bids must be made at least one hour before the beginning of the sale. Access by public transport from Chester station on bus lines 4 or 5. Access by car is on A41 about 2 miles east of the rail station. Free parking is available on the site. Sales are held at and further information is available from Phillips in Chester, New House, 150 Christleton

Road, Chester, Cheshire CH3 5TD, telephone (0244) 313936 and 313937.

Sotheby's
Sales held fortnightly at Booth Mansion, usually on Tuesday, Wednesday, and Thursday at 11 a.m. and sometimes also at 2 p.m. All sales are specialised: categories include applied arts and Doulton, fine clocks and watches, Staffordshire and European ceramics, Oriental ceramics, oak and country furniture, silver, jewellery, paintings, and collectors'items. Major sales are held quarterly for silver, jewellery, objects of vertu, miniatures, furniture, European and Oriental ceramics, paintings, Oriental rugs, and carpets. Viewing begins on the Saturday prior to the sale, and continues daily (except Sunday) until the sale begins. Catalogues and further information are available from Sotheby's, Booth Mansion, 28-30 Watergate Street, Chester, Cheshire CH1 2NA, telephone (0244) 315531, fax (0244) 46984, telex 61577 SOBART G.

Chichester, West Sussex

(Please also see Fontwell.)

Street market every day except Sunday in the town centre. A small number of antiques dealers offer odds and ends of mainly collectables and some small antiques.

"The South East Counties Antique Dealers' Fair" held three weekends a year: the second weekend of February, the third weekend of June, and the last weekend of November. Hours on Friday are from 11 a.m. to 9 p.m. and Saturday and Sunday from 10 a.m. to 6 p.m. at Goodwood House, a fine 17th- and 18th-century stately home (telephone (0243) 774107). This event mixes antiques with a few modern items for interior design purposes. All types of antiques are sold, including furniture, silver, clocks, paintings and prints, and other items. All items are vetted. The general dateline is 1880. Admission is £2, accompanied children free. These are some of the top antiques fairs in Britain. Access by car from Chichester 3 miles northeast on A27, then follow signs north to Waterbeach. Free parking is available at the grounds. Access by public transport is by rail to Chichester and then by taxi to Goodwood House. For exact dates and further information, contact Robert Soper, Castle Fairs, Bowcliffe Road, Bramham near Wetherby, Yorkshire, LS23 9JS, telephone (0937) 845829.

Stride & Son, Auctioneers
Auctions are held the last Friday of every month at the auction room at the auctioneers' offices. Auctions consist of antiques, miscellaneous items, and household furniture. Previews are held on the day before the sale. Information from and sales are held at Stride & Son, Southdown House Saleroom, St. John's Street, Chichester, West Sussex, PO19 1XQ, telephone (0243) 782626.

Prudential Fine Art Auctioneers
Auctions are held monthly on Thursdays (call for exact schedule) at the sale rooms at Baffins Hall. Sales usually consist of antique and reproduction furniture, silver, porcelain, clocks, eastern carpets and rugs, etc. Sales usually contain more than 400 lots. Previews are the day before the sale. For information and schedule, contact Prudential Fine Arts Auctioneers, Baffins Hall, Baffins Lane, Chichester, West Sussex PO19 1UA, telephone (0243) 787548.

Chingford, Greater London

"Antique and Collectors Fair" of more than 80 stalls, three Saturdays a year from 10.30 a.m. to 5 p.m. at Chingford Assembly Hall, The Green, Station Road, Chingford, London E4. Organised by Bartholomew Fairs, Executive House, The Maltings, Station Road, Sawbridgeworth, Hertfordshire CM21 9JX, telephone (0279) 725809 and 725699.

Chippenham, Wiltshire

(Please also see Castle Combe.)

Street market including antiques vendors is held as the general market on Fridays and Saturdays. Only a few vendors (usually less than 20) sell antiques, collectables, and junk.

Antiques and collectors' fair the last Sunday of every month from 10 a.m (9 a.m. to members of the antiques trade) to 5 p.m. at Neald Hall. These are regional fairs, with odds and ends of antiques and collectables. Admission is 30p, but is free to members of the antiques trade and children. Organised by Westfairs, P.O. Box 43, Weston-super-Mare, Avon BS23 2DS, telephone (0934) 33596.

Christchurch, Dorset

(Please also see Bournemouth, Brockenhurst, and Lyndhurst.)

Antique and collector's fair every Monday from 9 a.m. to 3.30 p.m. at Druitt Hall, High Street. This is a local fair of about 20 stands, and free admission. Street parking is available but can be difficult to find. Organised by Linda Forster, Forest Fairs, 28 Glenwood Road, West Moors, Dorset, telephone (0202) 875167.

Antique and collectors' fair the last Sunday of most months at the Kings Arms Hotel, Castle Street (hotel telephone (0202) 484117). This is a fair of local interest. Organised by and further information is available from Kingston Promotions, 157 Plymouth Drive, Hill Head, Fareham, Hampshire PO14 3SN, telephone (0329) 661780.

Cirencester, Gloucestershire

Antique market every Friday from 9 a.m. to 3 p.m. at the Corn Hall in the town centre. This is a small market in a provincial town in the well-touristed Cotswolds. This hall is also used on the first to fourth Saturday of every month for crafts markets from 9.30 a.m. to 4 p.m.

Antiques fairs are held every three or four weeks on Friday from 10 a.m. (9 a.m. for members of the antiques trade) to mid-afternoon at Bingham Hall, on King Street. All types of items are sold, including furniture, various antiques, and collectables. These are small, local fairs, with less than 40 sellers. Fairs are also held at this location on the second Sunday of every month. Admission is 30p, but is free to members of the antiques trade and children. Organised by Westfairs, P.O. Box 43, Weston-super-Mare, Avon BS23 9DS, telephone (0934) 33596.

Hobbs & Chambers Auctions
Auctions are held monthly at Bingham Hall, King Street. These are country auctions; all types of items, both antiques and all other types of items, are sold. Exact schedule and further information is available from Hobbs & Chambers, Market Place, Cirencester, Gloucestershire GK16 1QQ, telephone (0285) 4736.

Fraser, Glennie & Partners
Auctions are held monthly at Bingham Hall, King Street. Auctions include all types of items, both antiques and used goods. For further information, contact Fraser, Glennie & Partners, Cirencester, telephone (0285) 3938.

Cleeve, Avon

(Please also see Bristol.)

"Antique and Bric-a-Brac Fair" usually the first Sunday of every month from 10 a.m. to 4 p.m. at Cleve Village Hall, about 8 miles from Bristol on A370. The sales are held indoors, and are small (26 stalls) country sales of collectables and some antiques. Admission is 25p, but free to members of the antiques trade. Free parking is available. Organised by Evergreen Promotions, P.O. Box 58, Weston-Super-Mare, Avon BS22 8ER, telephone (0934) 636648.

Clitheroe, Lancashire

(Please also see Hurst Green and Burnley.)

Street market with a number of antique stalls every Tuesday and Saturday from early morning to just after noon on New Market Street. In addition to collectables and small antiques, several dealers offer used books and related items. Access to Clitheroe is easiest by car on A59.

McKennas Auctioneers
Auctions of antiques, fine art, and collectables are held monthly on Thursdays at the Bank Salesrooms, Harris Court. Viewing is held on Monday, Tuesday, and Wednesday prior to sale, and morning before sale. Quarterly catalogues are £1.25, including postage. Parking is available close by. For information and exact sale dates, contact McKennas, Bank Salesrooms, Harris Court, Clitheroe, Lancastershire BB7 2DP, telephone (0200) 25446 and 22695.

Cobham, Kent

"Dateline Fair" antiques fair fourth Sunday and Monday of May at Cobham Hall in Cobham, a historic house near Rochester. Organised by Fred Hynds, Wakefield Antiques Fairs, 1 Fountain Road, Rede Court, Rochester, Kent ME2 3SJ, telephone (0634) 723461.

"Wakefield Ceramic Fairs" last weekend in May at Cobham Hall, Kent. Organised by Fred Hynds, Wakefield Ceramic Fairs, 1 Fountain Road, Rochester, Kent ME2 3SJ, telephone (0634) 723461.

Cobham, Surrey

(Please also see Bletchingley, Dorking, Epsom, Guildford, and Woking.)

Antiques and collectors' fair last Saturday and Sunday of September at the Ladbroke Seven Hills Hotel, 1-1/2 miles south of the town on

A245 (hotel telephone (09325) 4471). This is a good regional fair, with all types of small antiques and collectables. The dateline is 1930. For further information, contact Kingston Promotions, 157 Plymouth Drive, Hill Head, Fareham, Hampshire PO14 3SN, telephone (0329) 661780.

Colwyn Bay, Clwyd (Wales)

Phillips Auctioneers
Auctions are held the last Thursday of most months at 10 a.m. Sales at this relatively small auction house include a wide variety of antiques and collectables, including quantities of furniture, paintings, and small quantities of silver and other metalware. Sales consist of at least 200 lots. Catalogues are issued the Sunday before the sale, price £1. Viewing is the day before the sale. The buyer's premium is 10%. Parking is 20p per day. Access by train to Colwyn Bay station, then walk. Sales are held at and further information is available from Phillips Colwyn Bay, 9 Conwy Road, Colwyn Bay, Clwyd LL29 7AF, telephone (0492) 533406.

Crayford, Kent

Albert Andrews Auctions and Sales
Auctions of all types of used goods and antiques are held every Wednesday at 10 a.m. at the auction offices. Not all items are antiques; nor are antiques separated from other items in the sale's organization. For example, consecutive lots in a recent sale included "bosun's whistle, gilded brooch, porcelain desk set, George III silver punch ladle, model boat in glazed case", etc. Catalogues are issued the day before the sale. Viewing is Tuesday from 4.30 to 8.30 p.m. and Wednesday from 9 a.m. until the sale begins. There is no buyer's premium. Telephone bids may be made. Payment must be made and all items removed by Thursday afternoon. Parking is available on the road outside the salesroom. Access by train to Crayford, then take the local bus. Sales are held at and further information is available from Albert Andrews Auctions and Sales, Farm Building, Maiden Lane, Crayford, Kent, DA1 4LX, telephone (0322) 528868.

Crowborough, East Sussex

(Please also see Tunbridge Wells.)

Black Horse Agencies—Geering & Colyer
Fine art and antiques auctions are held every two months on Wednesdays in the Ballroom at the Winston Manor Hotel on Beacon Road (telephone (0892) 652772). All types of antiques are offered in every sale, including furniture, porcelain and glass, art objects, and silver, plate, and jewellery. Catalogues are issued two weeks before the sale, price £1 plus postage. Viewing is held Tuesday from 11 a.m. to 5 p.m. and Wednesday from 9 a.m. until the sale begins. There is no buyer's premium. Payment must be made the day of the sale and all items removed by 11 a.m. on the next day. Free parking is available at the hotel or in the public car park near the hotel. Further information is available from the auctioneer's offices, Black Horse Agencies—Geering & Colyer, Highgate, Hawkhurst, Cranbrook, Kent TN18 4A, telephone (05805) 3181.

Croydon, Surrey

Antiques and collectors' fair first Saturday of every month from 8 a.m. to 4 p.m. at the Parish Hall at Reeves Corner. There are at least 50 stalls every month, with odds and ends of antiques and collectables. Information from telephone 01-657 7414.

Cullompton, Devon

"Devon & Somerset Antiques, Collectors' & Book Fair" one Sunday in May, June, October, November, and December from 10.30 a.m. to 4 p.m. at Verbeer Manor. This is a good regional fair. Admission is 50p. Parking is available. Access by car is from M5, Junction 28. There is no easy access by rail; the nearest station is Tiverton Junction station, several miles to the north. Organised by Gerry Mosdell, West Country Antiques & Collectors Fairs, The Dartmoor An- ti-

ques Centre, off West Street, Ashburton, Devon
TQ13 7DV, telephone (0364) 52182.

Dawlish, Devon

"Antiques & Fine Arts Fair" one weekend in October at the Langstone Cliff Hotel, on A379 2
miles north of Dawlish, from 2 to 8 p.m. Saturday and 10 a.m. to 5 p.m. on Sunday. Organised
by West Country Antiques & Collectors Fairs,
The Dartmoor Antiques Centre, off West Street,
Ashburton, Devon TQ13 7DV, telephone (0364)
52182.

Deal, Kent

(Please also see Dover.)

"Deal Braderie" on Easter Monday at the Deal
Town Centre, Astor Theatre, and St. George's
Hall. This large boot sale and craft sale offers
antiques, crafts, and odds and ends. Admission is
free to all. Parking is available at the Walmer
Green car park, 50p, with free bus to the centre
of events. Organised by East Kent Fairs, 201
London Road, Dover, Kent CT17 0TF, telephone
(0304) 201644.

Derby, Derbyshire

"Wakefield Ceramics Fair" one weekend in September at the Royal Crown Derby Museum. All
types of ceramics are offered. Organised by Fred
Hynds, Wakefield Ceramics Fairs, 1 Fountain
Road, Strood, Rochester, Kent ME2 3SJ,
telephone (0634) 723461.

Devizes, Wiltshire

Antique market every Tuesday from 9 a.m. to 4
p.m. in the Shambles. This small market is in a
long-established country market town, but offers
only a small to moderate selection of antiques

and collectables. The same location is used Tuesdays and Thursdays for a general street market.

"Devizes Annual Antiques Fairs" the fourth Friday and Saturday of January at the Bear Hotel in the Market Place in the town centre. Hours on Friday are 2 to 8 p.m.; on Saturday are 10 a.m. to 5 p.m. Organised by Gerry Mosdell, West Country Antiques & Collectors Fairs, The Dartmoor Antiques Centre, off West Street, Ashburton, Devon TQ13 7DV, telephone (0364) 52182.

Doncaster, South Yorkshire

Antiques and collectables section of the general market every Wednesday from early morning to noon at the Corn Market in the city market area. This is a local market for antiques and collectables.

"Giant Indoor Event" four Saturdays per year (May, July, August, and November) from 10 a.m. to 5 p.m. at the Doncaster Racecourse Grandstand. Since the dates are subject to change, please confirm them in advance. All types of antiques and collectables are offered by 150 to 200 vendors, most of whom are dealers. The dateline is 1930; no new items or reproductions may be offered. Admission is 80p for adults, 40p for persons over 65, and accompanied children are admitted free. Access by car on M1 to Junction 4, then west on A18 to the racecourse. Free parking is available at the racecourse. For exact dates and further information, contact Bowman Antiques Fairs, P.O. Box 37, Otley, West Yorkshire LS21 3AD, telephone (0943) 465782 or (0532) 843333.

Tudor Sale Rooms
Auctions every Saturday of general antiques, shipping, and modern furniture at the sale rooms, 28 High Street, Carcroft, Doncaster (telephone 0302 725029). Viewing is held on Fridays and Saturday before the sale. Organised by George H. Allen, Tudor Sale Rooms, 8

Hillcrest Skellow, Doncaster, South Yorkshire, telephone (0302) 723338 or 725029.

Dorking, Surrey

(Please also see Epsom, Guildford, and Godalming.)

Crow's Market Auction

Auctions are held every Monday year round at the auction rooms at Dorking Market off High Street, Dorking. Sales include antiques and household items. Viewing is held the morning of the sale. For information contact Crow's Market Auction, High Street, Dorking, Surrey RH4 1AQ, telephone (0306) 740382.

P.F. Windibank Auctions

Auctions are held every month to six weeks on Saturdays at the Dorking Halls. Previews are the Friday before the sale. This sale consists of antiques, paintings and books. The buyer's premium is 10%. For further information contact P.F. Windibank Auctions, 18-20 Reigate Road, Dorking, telephone (0306) 884556.

Dover, Kent

(Please also see Deal.)

Summer Sunday Boot Fairs every Sunday from June to September from 9.30 a.m. to 3 p.m. at the Plough Inn on A20. Free admission and free parking. Organised by East Kent Fairs, 201 London Road, Dover, Kent CT17 0TF, telephone (0304) 201644.

"Dover Braderie" third weekend in July (may vary from year to year) from 10 a.m. to 5 p.m. This long- established fair includes an antiques fair in Maison Dieu, craft fair in the Town Hall on Ladywell Park Street, and a boot fair throughout the town centre. Admission is free to all events. Parking can be difficult. Access by public transport to the train station, then walk.

Organised by East Kent Fairs, 201 London Road, Dover, Kent CT17 0TF, telephone (0304) 201644.

"Three-Day Dover Boot Sale" on Spring Bank Holiday weekend in conjunction with the annual Great East Kent Garden Show at Crabble Athletic Ground. Admission is 50p. Parking at the nearby recreation ground, but may be difficult. Organised by East Kent Fairs, 201 London Road, Dover, Kent CT17 0TF, telephone (0304) 201644.

"Dover Annual Boot Fair" last Monday of August at the Crabble Athletic Ground in the inland River district from 8.30 a.m. (admission £1 until 10 a.m., then 25p). This is a large holiday boot fair, with all types of items both used and antique. Antique dealers search this fair. Access by car on the London Road, parking at the nearby recreation ground, but may be difficult. Organised by East Kent Fairs, 201 London Road, Dover, Kent CT17 0TF, telephone (0304) 201644.

Driffield, East Yorkshire

Dee & Atkinson Auctions
Antique sales are held every two months at the Exchange Saleroom, Exchange Street, Driffield. Sales are on Friday and Monday beginning at 10.30 a.m., with viewing on Wednesday and Thursday prior to the sale from 10 a.m. to 7 p.m. and 10 a.m. to 4 p.m., respectively. Catalogues are £1.50 each. Monthly sales of household furniture and effects are held on Saturday mornings at 9.30 a.m.; catalogues are 30p. The saleroom has its own private car park, and Driffield is well served by public transport. Organised by Dee & Atkinson, The Exchange, Exchange Street, Driffield, East Yorkshire YO25 7LJ, telephone (0377) 43151, fax (0377) 241041.

Eastbourne, Kent

Edgar Horn Auction Room
A regional auction house of antiques and used goods. Three-day sales are held every five weeks

Tuesday, Wednesday, and Thursday. Viewing is held on the Monday before the sale. For exact sale dates and further information, contact Edgar Horn, Auctioneer, 47 Cornfield Road, Eastbourne, Kent, telephone (0323) 22801. Auctions are held at 46-50 South Street, Eastbourne.

Ely, Cambridgeshire

Ely Auction Market
Sales of general household contents and outside effects every Thursday at 11 a.m. at the Auction Market, Brays Lane. Viewing is in the morning prior to the sale. There are no catalogues. Parking is available immediately adjoining the market, and public transport, both bus and train, is close by. Information from Cheffins Grain & Comons, 25 Market Place, Ely, Cambridgeshire CB7 4NP, telephone (0353) 662266.

Epping, Essex

(Please also see Hatfield, Harlow, Hertford, London, and Ware.)

"Antique and Collectors' Fair" Saturdays five times a year (dates vary and are subject to change) at the Public Hall, St. Johns Road, Town Centre, Epping, from 10.30 a.m. to 5 p.m. This is a small market, with about 40 stalls of antiques and collectables, including silver, porcelain, coins, and other types of items. Modern items and reproductions are prohibited. Organised by Bartholomew Fayres, Executive House, The Maltings, Station Road, Sawbridgeworth, Hertfordshire CM21 9JX, telephone (0279) 725809 or 725699.

Epsom, Surrey

(Please also see Cheam, Esher, London and Redhill.)

Antique and collectors' fair the last Sunday of every month year round from 10 a.m. to 5 p.m. at

the Drift Bridge Hotel on Reigate Road, Epsom.
This is a middle-sized but regular fair in the London suburbs. Organised by Ray Ratcliff,
telephone 01-764 3602.

Esher, Surrey

(Please also see Epsom, London, and Woking.)

"Sandown Park Antique Fair" four times a year
(February, April, June, October) on a Tuesday
from 3 p.m. to 8 p.m. at Exhibition Centre at
Sandown Park Racecourse. This is a large
quarterly indoor fair; up to 550 dealers offer all
types antiques and collectables. New work or
reproductions are prohibited. Long aisles have
everything from silver and porcelain to bric-a-brac and small pieces of furniture. Access by car
to Esher on A3, then right to the racecourse,
where there is free parking. Access by train to
Esher station (main line from Waterloo to
Guildford), then by free (courtesy) bus to the
show. Access by charter bus leaving Marble Arch
at about 11 a.m. for £3; call the organiser for
details. Admission for the antiques trade begins
at 1 p.m. for £10; the public is admitted at 3 p.m.
for £3 and at 5 p.m. for £1.50. For exact dates
and further information contact Alan Kipping,
Wonder Whistle Enterprises, 1 Ritson Road, London E8 1DE, telephone 01-249 4050.

Exeter, Devon

(Please also see Cullompton and Exmouth.)

"Exeter Antique Fairs" the second Wednesday
and Thursday of March and Thursday and
Friday of November at St. George's Hall, Fore
Street, Exeter. The first day of each show is open
from 2 to 8 p.m., the second 10 a.m. to 5 p.m.
This is a regional show, and only dealers may
sell. Organised by Gerry Mosdell, West Country
Antiques & Collectors Fairs, The Dartmoor Antiques Centre, off West Street, Ashburton, Devon
TQ13 7DV, telephone (0364) 52182. This hall is

also used occasionally for other antique and collectable events.

Antiquarian book fair first Saturday of March, June, September, and December from 10 a.m. to 5 p.m. at the Arts Centre on Gandy Street. Only used and antiquarian books and related items may be sold. Organised by Provincial Booksellers Fairs Association, P.O. Box 66, Cambridge, Cambridgeshire CB1 3PD, telephone (0223) 240921.

Phillips Fine Art Auctioneers
Auctions of antiques and collectables are held most Thursdays at 11 a.m. at the auction offices. Each auction is limited to specialized areas, such as Victoriana (frequently), antique furniture, paintings, silver and jewellery, or similar categories. Catalogues are issued about 10 days before each auction and cost from £1 to £2. An annual schedule of sales is available upon request. Viewing is Tuesday from 9 a.m. until at 5 p.m. and Wednesday 9 a.m.to 7.30 p.m. The buyer's premium is 10%. Bids may be left or made by telephone or post. All purchases must be paid for and removed by the end of the second working day after the sale. Access by car from M5 exit 31, then right at the each of two roundabouts, then left at Alphin Brook Road. Free parking is available at the salesroom. Sales are held at and further information is available from Phillips in Exeter, Alphin Brook Road, Alphington, Exeter, Devon EX2 8TH, telephone (0392) 39025 and 39026, fax (0392) 410361.

Exmouth, Devon

(Please also see Budleigh Salterton and Exeter.)

"Sunday Antiques & Collectors' Bazaars" second Sunday of every month except December and every Sunday from July to the end of September from 10.30 a.m. to 5 p.m. at the Pavilion. The market in summer is larger but caters to the tourists. Organised by West Country Antiques & Collectors Fairs, The Dartmoor Antiques Centre, off West Street, Ashburton, Devon, TQ13 7DV, telephone (0364) 52182.

"Antiques & Collectors' Fairs" during a number of holidays: May Bank Holiday, first Friday, Saturday, and Sunday of May; Whitsun, usually in late May; Annual Antiques, mid September; Christmas, usually the second Sunday in December, from 10.30 a.m. to 5 p.m. at the Pavilion in the town centre. Access by train to Exmouth. Organised by Gerry Mosdell, West Country Antiques & Collectors Fairs, The Dartmoor Antiques Centre, off West Street, Ashburton, Devon TQ13 7DV, telephone (0364) 52182.

Farnham, Surrey

(Please also see Aldershot, Godalming, Guildford, and Hook.)

"The Farnham Antiques Fair" third Saturday and Sunday of May at the Church House, Farnham. Parking is available at the car park, the first right turn past the house. Organised by Gamlins Exhibition Services, telephone (045) 285 2557 or (0272) 621424.

Antiques and collectors' fair the last Sunday of February, May, August, and November at the Maltings. These are local fairs of local interest. Exact dates and further information is available from Kingston Promotions, 157 Plymouth Drive, Hill Head, Fareham, Hampshire PO14 3SN, telephone (0329) 661780.

Filton, Avon

"Antiques & Collectors Fair" one Sunday a month from 10.30 a.m. to 4.30 p.m. at the British Aerospace Leisure Centre, 589 Southmead Road. Admission is 40p, children free. Items are not vetted, but must have some age, except for coins and stamps. Leisure Centre is near the M4/M5 junction. From M5 (Junction 16) drive about 2-1/2 miles to the Anchor Pub roundabout at Filton, then turn right to the Centre. Organised by

J.A. Day, 17 Elm Close, Yatton, Avon, telephone (0934) 838187.

Folkestone, Kent

(Please also see Dover and Hythe.)

Phillips Fine Art Auctioneers
Monthly auctions of antiques, arts, and furniture are held on Wednesdays on irregular dates. Call or write for exact dates since they vary. Previews are held the day before and the morning of the sale before it begins. For further information, contact Phillips Fine Art Auctioneers & Valuers, Bayle Place, Bayle Parade, Folkestone, Kent CT20 1SQ, telephone (0303) 45555.

Fontwell, Sussex

"Drive-in Antiques Market" several Wednesdays in the summer (usually the first or second) at the Fontwell Racecourse about 4 miles east on A27 from Chichester. Outdoor, admission free, free parking, not accessible by public transport. Organised by Mostyn Fairs, 64 Brighton Road, Lancing, Sussex, telephone (0903) 752961.

Glastonbury, Somerset

(Please also see Wells.)

Monthly antiques market the last Saturday of the month from 9 a.m. to 4 p.m. at Glastonbury Town Hall. This is a small, local market. For further information, contact Mr. Holley, Stalbridge, telephone (0963) 62478.

Godalming, Surrey

(Please also see Dorking and Guildford.)

"The Charterhouse Antiques Fair" in early April (Friday from 1 to 9 p.m., Saturday from 11 a.m. to 6 p.m., and Sunday from 11 a.m. to 5 p.m.) at the Charterhouse. This is a major regional fair, offering all types of good quality antiques, including Persian rugs, glass, porcelain, jewellery, silver, and other objets d'art. All items are vetted by outside experts. The dateline is 1885 to 1920 depending on the particular type of item (for example, furniture 1885, paintings 1920). Admission is £2.50. Parking is available. Access by public transport to Godalming station, then walk or take a taxi. For exact dates and further information, contact Robert Bailey Antiques Fairs, 1 Roll Gardens, Gants Hill, Ilford, Essex IG2 6TN, telephone 01-550 5435.

Hamptons Fine Art Auctions
Auctions of household goods (which may include old furniture and collectables) are held the first and third Saturday of every month beginning at 9.30 a.m. at the Bridge Street Salesroom. Catalogues, not illustrated, are 30p. At these sales, previews are the day of the sale and there is a buyer's premium of 10%. Payment must be made and all items removed on the day of the sale; items not removed by Monday are stored at £1 per lot per day.

Auctions of true antiques are held once or twice a month at 10.30 or 11 a.m. at the auction room at 93 High Street, Godalming. Previews are held at least two days before the sale. Sales include antique furniture, carpets, and rugs; china, glass, silver, and objects d'art; pictures; and books. Usually each sale is limited to one to three types of items. Illustrated catalogues are available about two weeks before sales; cost is £2. The buyer's premium is 10%. Bids may be left, posted, or made by telephone. Payment must be made within three days of the sale, and items left longer will be stored at least £1 per day at the auctioneer's discretion. Parking is available at several Council car parks. Access is by train to Godalming, then walk. Information and exact dates are available from Hamptons Fine Art, 93 High Street, Godalming, Surrey GU7 1AL, telephone (04868) 23567, fax (0483) 426392.

Grantham, Lincolnshire

"The Harlaxton Manor Antiques Fair" two weekends a year near the end of May and beginning of October (Friday from 1 to 9 p.m., Saturday from 11 a.m. to 6 p.m., and Sunday from 11 a.m. to 5 p.m.) at Harlaxton Manor, near the village of Harlaxton. This is a major regional fair, offering all types of good quality antiques, including Persian rugs, glass, porcelain, jewellery, silver, and other objets d'art. All items are vetted by outside experts. The dateline is 1885 to 1920 depending on the particular type of item (for example, furniture 1885, paintings 1920). Harlaxton Manor is one mile west of the Grantham railway station on A607, about half a mile west of the roundabout at A1. Admission is £2.50. Parking is available. Access by public transport to Harlaxton station, then take a taxi. For exact dates and further information, contact Robert Bailey Antiques Fairs, 1 Roll Gardens, Gants Hill, Ilford, Essex IG2 6TN, telephone 01-550 5435.

William H. Brown Fine Art Auctioneers
Sales on alternate Wednesdays at 10 a.m. in Westgate Hall. Viewing is from 11.30 a.m. to 4.30 p.m. the Tuesday before the sale and until 10 a.m. on the morning of the sale. Items include general antiques and fine art, alternating with general household furniture and effects. Catalogues are £1.20 postpaid. Public car parking is nearby, and the Hall is a 10-minute walk from the railway station (main line from London, King's Cross station). For information, contact William H. Brown Fine Art Auctioneers, Westgate Hall, Westgate, Grantham, Lincolnshire NG31 6LT, telephone (0476) 68861.

Greenwich, Greater London

(Please also see Crayford and London.)

"Greenwich Antique Market" every Saturday and Sunday from early morning to mid afternoon in the old Fruit and Vegetable Market on High Street, near the Cutty Sark museum ship. This market expands to High Street across the street from St. Alpmage Church in the summer. Antiques and collectables of all types are sold. (Above the entrance to the market hall is a beautiful saying lettered in 18th-century gold leaf, "A FALSE BALANCE IS ABOMINATION TO THE LORD, BUT A JUST WEIGHT IS HIS DELIGHT".) Access by car to Greenwich Park; you must find street parking. Access by train on British Rail to Greenwich. But perhaps the most pleasant means of access is by river boat from Charing Cross Pier, along the Embankment near Charing Cross Station. It is only a short walk from the pier at Greenwich to the antiques market. Organised by Sherman & Waterman Associates, 12/13 Henrietta Street, Covent Garden, London WC2E 8LH, telephone 01-240 7405.

Guildford, Surrey

(Please also see Godalming and Farnham.)

"Surrey Antiques Fair" early October at the Civic Hall on London Road. This is a long-established regional fair. Items offered include furniture, glass, ceramics, silver, and other types of items. Only antiques may be sold; all items are vetted, with an 1840 dateline. Admission is charged to all and includes a catalogue. Organised by Roger Heath-Bullock, Cultural Exhibitions Ltd., 8 Meadrow, Godalming, Surrey GU7 3HN, telephone (04868) 22562.

Clarke-Gammon Auctioneers
Auctions are held on one Tuesday of the month (the Tuesday varies) at the Auction Rooms on Bedford Road, Guildford. Previews are the Saturday morning and all day Monday before the auction. These sales consist of fine arts, including old paintings. The buyer's premium is 10%. For exact sale dates and further information, contact Clarke-Gammon, 45 High Street, Guildford, Surrey, telephone (0483) 572266.

Halifax, West Yorkshire

Flea market and collectors' fair four or five times
a year on Sunday from 9.30 a.m. to 5 p.m. at the
Civic Theatre. At this local show, over 60 vendors
offer all types of antiques and bric-a-brac. For
exact sale dates and further information, contact
Panda Promotions, 24 Westgate, Honley, Huddersfield, West Yorkshire HD7 2AA, telephone
(0484) 666144.

Harlow, Essex

(Please also see Epping, Hertford, and Ware.)

Antiques and collectables fair the first Sunday of
every month from 10.30 a.m. to 5 p.m. at the
Moat House Hotel on Southern Way (hotel
telephone (0279) 22441). About 60 dealers and
collectors offer all types of antiques, including
porcelain, silver, and prints. Few large items
such as furniture are offered. Admission is 50p.
Organised by Bartholomew Fayres, Executive
House, The Maltings, Station Road,
Sawbridgeworth, Hertfordshire CM21 9JX,
telephone (0279) 725809 and 725699.

"Mammoth Antique & Collectors' Fair" on the
Sunday nearest to the first day of February, May,
August, November, and January from 10 a.m.
(antiques trade only) to 5 p.m. at the Harlow
Sportcentre on Hammarskjold Road (telephone
(0279) 635100). These are major regional fairs,
with over 200 vendors of all types of antiques
and collectables, including toys, linen, porcelain,
postage stamps, silver, and some furniture. Admission is £1 from 10 to 11 a.m., 70p from 11 a.m.
to 5 p.m. Accompanied children are free. Access
by car from Junction 7 on M11, and follow signs
to the fair. Free parking is available at the
Sportcentre. Access by train from London to Harlow Town station (Liverpool Street station), and
walk about half a mile to the Sportcentre. Organised by Bartholomew Fayres, Executive
House, The Maltings, Station Road,
Sawbridgeworth, Hertfordshire CM21 9JX,
telephone (0279) 725809 and 725699.

Harrogate, North Yorkshire

Flea market and collectors' fair several times a year on Sunday from 9.30 a.m. (exact dates vary) at the Conference and Exhibition Centre on Ripon Road. All types of antiques, collectables, and bric-a-brac are offered by over 100 vendors at this indoor location. Parking is available at the north end of the site. For exact sale dates and further information, contact Panda Promotions, 24 Westgate, Honley, Huddersfield, West Yorkshire HD7 2AA, telephone (0484) 666144.

"The Pavilion of Yesteryear" first Friday, Saturday, Sunday, and Monday of May (Bank Holiday), from 10 a.m. to 6 p.m. at Ripley Castle (telephone (0423) 770152), in the village of Ripley. This is an 18th-century stately home, with large grounds and a 1410 gatehouse. This event mixes antiques with a few modern items for interior design purposes. All types of antiques are sold, including furniture, silver, clocks, paintings and prints, and other items. All items are vetted. The general dateline is 1880. This is a huge fair, held at the same time and place as "The British Homes & Gardens Exhibition". Admission is £2, accompanied children free. Access by car on A61, 4 miles north of Harrogate station on A61. This is one of the larger regional fairs and worth attending. For exact dates and further information, contact Robert Soper, Castle Fairs, Bowcliffe Road, Bramham, Wetherby, West Yorkshire, telephone (0937) 845829.

"The Harrogate Granby Hotel Antiques Fair" three weekends a year, in early February, late July, and late November (Friday from 1 to 9 p.m., Saturday from 11 a.m. to 6 p.m., and Sunday from 11 a.m. to 5 p.m.) at the Granby Hotel. This is a regional fair, offering all types of good quality antiques, including Persian rugs, glass, porcelain, jewellery, silver, and other objets d'art. All items are vetted by outside experts. The dateline is 1885 to 1920 depending on the particular type of item (for example, furniture 1885, paintings 1920). Admission is £2.50. Access by public transport to Harrogate station, then walk or take a taxi. For exact dates and further information, contact Robert Bailey Antiques Fairs, 1 Roll Gardens, Gants Hill, Ilford, Essex IG2 6TN, telephone 01-550 5435.

"Northern Antiques Fair" the last week of September to beginning of October at the Royal Baths Assembly Rooms. This is a long-established quality fair. About 60 dealers have stands. All antiques are vetted; dateline 100 years old. Admission is £6 on the first day and £4 on subsequent days; admission includes an illustrated fair handbook. Parking is available at the fair, but is not free. For information, contact Robert Aagaard, Secretary, Northern Antique Dealers' Fair Limited, Manor House, High Birstwith, Harrogate, North Yorkshire HG3 2LG, telephone (0423) 770385.

"The Christmas County Antique Dealers' Fair" the first weekend of December (Friday from 11 a.m. to 9 p.m., and Saturday and Sunday from 10 a.m. to 6 p.m.) at Rudding Park House in the village of Ripley. All types of antiques are sold, including furniture, silver, clocks, paintings and prints, and other items. All items are vetted. The general dateline is 1880. Admission is £2, accompanied children free. This event mixes an antiques fair with a Christmas gift and fashion fair. This is one of the larger regional fairs and worth attending. For exact dates and further information, contact Robert Soper, Castle Fairs, Bowcliffe Road, Bramham, Wetherby, West Yorkshire, telephone (0937) 845829.

"Wakefield Ceramic Fair" three days in November (exact dates vary from year to year) at the Crown Hotel. There are from 40 to 60 stands. There is an identification service for members of the public and collectors to bring porcelain for free evaluation. Organised by Fred Hynds, Wakefield Ceramics Fairs, 1 Fountain Road, Strood, Rochester, Kent ME2 3SJ, telephone (0634) 723461.

Morphets Fine Art Auctioneers
Catalogue sales are held on second Thursdays at 4-6 Albert Street, Harrogate, in the town centre

and are devoted to period and reproduction furniture, silver, paintings, porcelain, and objets d'art. Viewing is on the Wednesday priot from 10 a.m. to 4 p.m. Catalogues are £1.75 postpaid. Sales of Victoriana and household effects are held on other Thursdays, Bank Holidays permitting. For exact dates and further information, contact Morphets of Harrogate, 406 Albert Street, Harrogate, North Yorkshire HG1 1JL, telephone (0423) 502282.

Harrow, Greater London

Antiques, crafts, and collectables market every Thursday at Centre Crafts, 308A Station Road. Organised by Centre Crafts, telephone (0923) 46559.

Antiques, crafts, and collectables market every Thursday from 10 a.m. to 4.30 p.m. at Victoria Hall, Sheepcote Lane at the junction of Station Park Road. Access by tube to Harrow-on-the-Hill, then walk. Organised by Mr. M. Morris, M & S Fairs, 38 Oakwood Avenue, Southgate, London N14, telephone 01-440 2330.

Hatfield, Hertfordshire

(Please also see Hatfield House, Hertford, and Ware.)

"Antique and Collectors' Fair" the third Sunday of every month (except second Sunday of April and December) at The Red Lion on Great North Road from 10.30 a.m. to 5 p.m. This regional fair attracts about 60 vendors of all types of antiques and collectables. Free parking is available at the hotel. Organised by Bartholomew Fayres, Executive House, The Maltings, Station Road, Sawbridgeworth, Hertfordshire CM21 9JX, telephone (0279) 725809 and 725699.

Hatfield House, Hertfordshire

(Please also see Hatfield, Hertford, and Ware.)

"Living Crafts Exhibition", a crafts fair and antique show the second weekend of May (Friday, Saturday, and Sunday) at the well known stately home, Hatfield House. It is near Hatfield, about 1-1/2 miles west of Hatfield railway station. Ample parking (for a fee) is available on the grounds. Information from Mrs. Jean Younger, Harpenden, telephone (05827) 61235.

Haywards Heath, West Sussex

(Please also see Ardingly and Lewes.)

T. Bannister & Company, Auctioneers
Auctions are held approximately every six weeks, always on Wednesdays at the salesroom on the market place. This auction specializes in antique furniture. Viewing is held the day before the sale. Most auctions consist of about 300 to 500 lots. For exact schedule and further information, contact T. Bannister & Company, Market Place, Haywards Heath, telephone (0444) 412402.

Sussex Auction Galleries
Auctions are held on Tuesdays and the following Wednesdays about every six weeks at 10 a.m. at the Galleries on Perrymount Road. Antiques of all types are offered and each sale has more than 600 lots. Previews are held the Friday before the sale from 9 a.m. to 4.30 p.m., Saturday prior from 9 a.m. to noon, and Monday prior from 9 a.m. to 4.30 p.m. For exact dates and further information, contact Sussex Auction Galleries, 59 Perrymount Road, Haywards Heath, West Sussex RH16 3DS, telephone (0444) 414935, telex 87650.

Heathfield, East Sussex

Street market every Tuesday and Saturday from early morning to early afternoon in the town centre. This general market has a number of dealers of antiques and collectables as well as used items.

E. Watson & Sons Auctions
This monthly auction of Victorian and more recent furniture is held on one Tuesday (varying) during every month. Viewing is the Monday before the auction and the morning of the sale. Catalogues are not issued. Information and exact dates are available from the auctioneer, E. Watson & Sons, Heathfield Furniture Salerooms, The Market, Heathfield, East Sussex, telephone (04352) 2132.

Hemel Hempstead, Hertfordshire

Antique market every Wednesday year round at the market place. Up to 100 dealers offer antiques and collectables of all types. Organised by Antique Forum, Flat 2, 98 Maida Lane, London W9, telephone 01-624 3214.

Henley-on-Thames, Oxfordshire

"Henley Antiques Fair" first or second weekend of May (beginning Friday for members of the antiques trade and Saturday for the public) at the Town Hall. Organised by LaChaise Antiques, telephone (0367) 20427.

Antiques and junk market, third Thursday of May from 10 a.m. to 3.30 p.m. at the Town Hall. Organised by Granny's Attic, telephone (06284) 3658.

Simmons & Sons Auctioneers
Auctions are held eight times a year, almost always on a Friday, beginning at 10.30 a.m. at the salesrooms at Watcombe Manor, Ingham Lane, off B480 just south of Watlington Village. Items for sale include glass and crystal, porcelain and pottery, rugs, costumes, prints, paintings, silver and silver plate, jewellery, furniture, household items, and other miscellaneous items. While most of them are antiques and collectables, since

most of these items are from estates, modern items may be offered as well. Catalogues are issued about two weeks before each sale, price is usually £1. Viewing is held the day before the sale from 10 a.m. to 5.30 p.m., and the day of the sale from 9 a.m. until the sale begins. Bids may be left or telephoned. There is no buyer's premium. Buyers must register and receive a bidder's number before their first bid. All items must be paid for and removed the day of the sale or next morning. For exact sale dates and further information, contact Simmons & Sons, 32 Bell Street, Henley-on-Thames, Oxfordshire RG9 2BHH, telephone (0491) 571111, fax (0491) 579833, telex 847621.

Hereford, Hereford and Worcester

Prudential Fine Art Auctioneers
Sales of fine arts and antiques one Tuesday a month (sometimes twice a month) at 11 a.m.. Viewing is from 10 a.m. to 4 p.m. the day prior to sale. For information, contact Prudential Fine Art Auctioneers, Portland Street, Hereford, Hereford and Worcester HR4 9JE, telephone (0432) 272413.

Hertford, Hertfordshire

(Please also see Epping, Harlow, Hatfield, Sawbridgeworth, and Ware.)

Flea market first and third Saturday of every month from 10 a.m. to 4 p.m. at the Corn Exchange on Fore Street in the town centre. Admission is 10p, free to persons over 65. All types of used items and antiques are offered at this rather general market: furniture, bric-a-brac, tools, clothes, jewellery, brass, and other similar items. Parking is available at the Gascoyne Way Car Park. Access by public transport by train to Hertford East station and by bus to the bus station, both within walking distance of the Corn Exchange. Organised by Alan J. Barrett Fairs, Glenroy, Paynes Lane, Nazeing, Waltham Abbey, Essex EN9 2GU, telephone (0992) 460929.

Norris & Duvall, Fine Art Auctions
Auctions of fine arts and antiques are held once
every month on a Thursday at 9.30 a.m. at
Castle Hall, Hertford, a large, relatively new hall
on the grounds of Hertford Castle (hall telephone
(0992) 589024). An annual schedule of auctions is
available upon request. Catalogues are issued at
least one week before the sale. Viewing is held
the Wednesday before the sale from noon to 7
p.m. and the morning of the sale. Bids may be
left or posted, or made by telephone. All bidders
not present must call the afternoon of the sale to
see if they have won. There is no buyer's
premium. All lots must be removed by 6 p.m. on
the day of the sale; if unable to this, arrange
removals before sale day with the auctioneers.

This auction house also holds weekly auctions
of all types of used goods, furniture, and
household items at its salesroom at Caxton Hill,
Hertford. No catalogues are issued for these
weekly sales. For exact sale dates and further
information, contact Norris & Duvall, 106 Fore
Street, Hertford, Hertfordshire SG14 1AH,
telephone (0992) 582249.

Hitchin, Hertfordshire

Antiques and collectables market every Friday
from about 8.30 a.m. until 4.30 p.m. at
Churchgate in the town centre. This is a small
regional market, with about 40 vendors of odds
and ends, used items, and collectables. In addition, the 20-stand West Alley Antiques Market
takes place every Tuesday and Saturday. Access
by car to the centre of Hitchin. Access by train
from Kings Cross (London) or by bus on the London Country bus lines to Hitchin. Organised by
the Market Office, 22 Churchgate, Hitchin,
Hertfordshire SG5 1DN, telephone (0462) 56202.

Holker, Cumbria

"The Holker Hall Antiques Fair" one weekend
(usually third but may vary from year to year) in
November at Holker Hall. This is a regional fair,

offering all types of good quality antiques. All items are vetted by outside experts. The dateline is 1885 to 1920 depending on the particular type of item. Admission is £2.50, but free to members of the antiques trade with a business card. For exact dates and further information, contact Robert Bailey Antique Fairs, 1 Roll Gardens, Gants Hill, Ilford, Essex 1G2 6TN, telephone 01-550-5435.

Holmfirth, West Yorkshire

(Please also see Uppermill.)

Flea market and collectors' fair several Saturdays a year (dates vary) from 9.30 a.m. to 5 p.m. at the Civic Hall. At least 60 vendors offer all types of collectables, bric-a-brac, and antiques. For exact sale dates and further information, contact Panda Promotions, 24 Westgate, Honley, Huddersfield, West Yorkshire HD7 2AA, telephone (0484) 666144.

Hornchurch, Essex

"Antique & Collectors' Fair" one Sunday in October (varies from year to year) at the Hornchurch Sportcentre, Harrow Lodge Park, from 10.30 a.m. to 5 p.m. Some 200 stalls are offer all types of antiques and collectables. Organised by Bartholomew Fayres, Executive House, The Maltings, Station Road, Sawbridgeworth, Hertfordshire CM21 9JX, telphont (0279) 725809 and 725699.

Horsham, West Sussex

(Please also see Haywards Heath.)

Denham Auction Galleries
Auctions are held the first and third Wednesday of every month at the galleries. On the first Wednesday, lower quality antiques are offered, plus pine furniture. On the third Wednesday, good antique furniture plus silver, pictures, and clocks,

and other good antiques are offered. Most sales have over 500 lots. Previews are the Tuesday before the sale. The buyer's premium is 10%. The sales site and further information are available from Garth Denham & Associate, Horsham Auction Galleries, The Carfax, Horsham, West Sussex, telephone (0403) 43837.

Hove, East Sussex

(Please see Brighton, East Sussex.)

Huddersfield, North Yorkshire

Eddisons Auctioneers
Sales every fortnight on Wednesdays at the salesrooms in High Street. Items include antique, modern, and reproduction furnishings and effects, consisting of 400 to 600 lots. Viewing is Tuesdays prior to sales (Mondays for the trade). Quarterly catalogue sales are held for antique furniture, silver, pictures, and jewellery. For information and schedules, contact Raymond Butterworth, Eddisons, 4/6 High Street, Huddersfield, North Yorkshire HD1 2LS, telephone (0484) 533151, telex 55169 EDDLDS G.

Hull, Humberside

H. Evans & Sons, Auctioneers
Sales of antiques once every three months, general household effects every two to three weeks, usually on Tuesdays, at the St. James Auction Rooms, St. James Street. Viewing is the Monday prior to sale. Catalogues are £1.20 to £1.50 for antique sales and 50p for general household sales. Car parking is at the rear of the auction rooms. Information from H. Evans & Sons, 1 Parliament Street, Hull, Humberside HU1 1AR, telephone (0482) 23033.

Huntingdon, Cambridgeshire

Antiques fair third Friday to following Sunday of May at Huntingdon Racecourse (racetrack) along A1 about one mile west of Huntingdon station. Ample parking for cars. This fair prohibits all reproductions and items made after 1920. Organised by Christina Page Fairs, telephone (0223) 211736.

Antiques fair fourth Saturday to following Monday of May from 10 a.m. to 5 p.m. at Hitchingbrooke House, a major stately home southwest of the town on A141. About 110 dealers and a few collectors (including much furniture) show their wares. In the vicinity, follow the yellow AA signs to the fair. Parking is available on the grounds. Organised by Crown Antiques Fairs, 55 Barton Road, Cambridge, Cambridgeshire CB3 9LG, telephone (0223) 353016.

Hurst Green, Lancashire

(Please also see Preston.)

"The Lancashire Antiques and Interior Design Fair" the first weekend of November (Friday from 11 a.m. to 9 p.m., Saturday and Sunday from 10 a.m. to 6 p.m. at Stonyhurst College, just north of the village. This event mixes antiques with a few modern items for interior design purposes. All types of antiques are sold, including furniture, silver, clocks, paintings and prints, and other items. All items are vetted. The general dateline is 1880. This is a good regional fair. Admission is £2, accompanied children free. Access by car on A59 east from Junction 31 on M6, then to Billington, north on B6246 for 3 miles, then west on B6243 to Hurst Green. Free parking is available. There is no convenient public transport. Organised by Castle Fairs, telephone (0937) 845829. For exact dates and further information, contact Robert Soper, Castle Fairs, Bowcliffe Road, Bramham, Wetherby, West Yorkshire, telephone (0937) 845829.

Hythe, Kent

(Please also see Folkestone.)

Butler & Hatch Waterman, Auctioneers
This country auction house holds monthly auctions, usually on a Wednesday (call for exact date and time). Auctions include antiques, silver, and miscellaneous items. For further information contact Butler & Hatch Waterman, 86 High Street, Hythe, Kent, telephone (0303) 66023.

Ilkley, West Yorkshire

(Please also see Harrogate and Leeds.)

"The Kings Hall & Wintergardens Antiques Fair" held at the last weekend of August at Kings Hall. This regional fair offers good quality antiques, including Persian rugs, glass, porcelain, jewellery, silver, and other objets d'art. All items are vetted by outside experts. The dateline is 1885 to 1920 depending on the particular type of item (for example, furniture 1885, paintings 1920). Admission is £2.50, but free to members of the antiques trade with a business card. Free parking is available. Access by public transport to Ilkley station, then walk or take a taxi. For exact dates and further information, contact Robert Bailey Antiques Fairs, 1 Roll Gardens, Gants Hill, Ilford, Essex IG2 6TN, telephone 01-550 5435.

Dacre, Son & Hartley Auctions
Auctions are held every Wednesday at 10 a.m. at The Victoria Hall Saleroom, Little Lane, Ilkley. Each sale includes between 400 and 500 lots of antique and used goods, including pottery and porcelain, miscellaneous items and books, silver, silver plate, and jewellery, rugs, clocks, and furniture. Viewing is held the Tuesday before the sale. Bidders must register with the office before bidding. Smoking is prohibited permitted on the premises. There is no buyer's premium. Purchases must be paid for and removed within two days of the sale. Catalogues (which often include

some photographs of the best items) are available about two weeks before the sale, cost £2. A free auction schedule is available upon request. Telephone and posted bids can be left with the management by known bidders. Access is from London (King's Cross) to Leeds, change at Leeds to Ilkley, and walk from the station. Parking is available near the sale room. For further information and exact schedule, contact Dacre, Son & Hartley, Victoria Hall, Little Lane, Ilkley, West Yorkshire LS29 8EA, telephone (0943) 600655, fax (0943) 816086.

Ipswich, Suffolk

Phillips in Ipswich
Auctions are held on Thursdays approximately every two weeks at 11 a.m. at Dover House, Wolsey Street. Most auctions are specialized (for example "Silver and Jewellery" or "Victoriana"). Inspections are held the day before and morning of the sale. Catalogues are issued approximately two weeks before every sale, and cost from £1 to £2. Bids may be left, posted, or made by telephone. The buyer's premium is 10%. Information can be obtained from Phillips in Ipswich, Dover House, Wolsey Street, Ipswich, telephone (0473) 55137.

Kendal, Cumbria

Street market every Monday, Wednesday, and Saturday from early morning to early afternoon in the centre of this town at the entrance to the beautiful Lake District. A number of dealers offer small antiques, collectables, and junk on Monday, where they congregate in the Market Hall. Other days offer all types of new and used goods as well as food in the Market Square as well as the hall. A book fair is held in mid-July at the same location.

Kettering, Northamptonshire

Antiques market every Wednesday at the Market Place in the town centre. This market is long-established, and a good number of dealers and collectors regularly buy and sell all types of antiques, collectables, and bric-a-brac. Parking in the immediate area can be difficult.

Kingston-upon-Hull, Humberside

(Please see Hull.)

Kingston-upon-Thames, Surrey

Hogg Robinson Auctioneers
General sales three times a month, antiques and fine art sales once a month, on Thursdays, at the saleroom, rear of 82 Eden Street. General sales begin at noon, and viewing is on Wednesdays from 2 p.m. to 8 p.m. and Thursdays from 9 a.m. to noon before the sales. Catalogues are 30p and available on viewing days. Antiques and fine art sales are at 10 a.m., with viewing on Tuesdays (2 p.m. to 8 p.m.) and Wednesdays (9 a.m. to 5 p.m.) and Thursday mornings before the sales. Catalogues are 70p and available a week before each auction. Buyer's premium is 10%. Parking is available at the cattle market car park five minutes walk from the saleroom. Access from London is on the Sheperton line from Waterloo Station. For details, contact Mrs. C. Shaw, Hogg Robinson, 82a Eden Street, Kingston-upon-Thames, Surrey KT1 1DV, telephone 01-541 4139, fax 01-541 1360.

Kinver, West Midlands

(Please also see Birmingham.)

Antique fairs first Sunday of every month from 10 a.m. to 5 p.m. at the Kinver Community Centre in the centre of Kinver village. Approximately 40 dealers and amateurs sell antiques and collectables of all types, plus modern paintings. The third Sunday of the month, this same site is a large book fair with books, postcards, postage stamps, and records. No early admission for dealers is allowed. Access by car only; no public transport is convenient. Organised by Waverly Fairs, Boreley Cottage, Boreley, Near Ombersley, Worcester, telephone (0205) 620697.

Kirkby Lonsdale, Lancashire

James Thompson, Auctioneers
Monthly two-day sales of antique and reproduction furniture, glass, silver, and china, usually on Wednesday, and five sales a year of watercolours and oil paintings. Sales at the saleroom and the Royal Barn saleroom. Viewing is held Tuesdays before the sales. For details, contact James Thompson, 64 Main Street, Kirkby Lonsdale, Lancashire LA6 2AJ, telephone (0468) 71555.

Knowle, West Midlands

(Please also see Birmingham.)

Phillips Midlands
Auctions are held at least three Wednesdays per month at 11 a.m. Sales are specialized into subjects such as "Paintings and Drawings", "Victoriana", and "Fine Furniture". Catalogues are issued at least two weeks before each sale, and cost £1.50 to £2.50. Viewing is held two days before and morning of the sale. Bids may be left, posted, or telephoned. The buyer's premium is 10%. Access by car on M42 to Junction 2, then on A41 to Knowle. For exact sale dates and further information, contact Phillips Midlands, The Old House, Station Road, Knowle, Solihull, West Midlands B93 0HT, telephone (056) 456151.

Knutsford, Cheshire

"Tatton Park Antiques Fair" held twice a year, four days early in March and four days near the end of September, at Tatton Park, an 18th-cen-

tury historic estate. Only the finest quality antiques are shown. All items are vetted by
Sotheby's, Christie's, and Phillips specialists, or
officials from BADA or LAPADA. The dateline is
1860. These are major antique fairs. Admission is
£2.50, but free to members of the antiques trade
with a business card. Access by car on M6 to
Junction 19, then north on A530 past Mere village, then right on A50. Access by public
transport is inconvenient at best. For exact dates
and further information, contact Robert Bailey
Antiques Fairs, 1 Roll Gardens, Gants Hill, Ilford, Essex IG2 6TN, telephone 01-550 5435.

Lakenheath, Suffolk

Antique and collectors' fair one Sunday in
February, April, June, October, and December
(exact day varies) at American Elementary
School (opposite Gate 2) within the base housing
area of RAF Lakenheath, near Brandon. There
are 65 stalls, and the fair is open to the public.
Parking is free. For information, contact Mrs.
Lorna Quick, Four Seasons Fairs, 6 Post Office
Lane, Glemsford, Sudbury, Suffolk CD1O 7RA,
telephone (0787) 281855.

Lamport Hall, Northamptonshire

Antiques fair last weekend of May at Lamport
Hall, a stately historic house. Access by A 508
about 9 miles north of Northampton, then follow
signs to the hall. Organised by Prestige Promotions, telephone (0533) 56045.

Lancing, Sussex

(Please also see Brighton.)

Collectables market most Thursdays from 8.30
a.m. to noon at the Parish Hall. This is a regular,
local market in an antiques-rich area. Organised
by Shirley Mostyn, Mostyn Fairs, 64 Brighton
Road, Lancing, Surrey, telephone (0903) 752961.

"Drive-in Antiques Market" usually the third Wednesday of May, August and September from 8 a.m. to 2.30 p.m. at Lancing Beach Green. Outside spaces only—no indoor area. Admission free, parking 50p, bus stop on line from Brighton across the street.

Leamington Spa, Warwickshire

Black Horse Agencies—Locke & England, Fine Arts Auctioneers
Auctions every Thursday (except on holidays) at Walton House, 11 Parade, Leamington Spa. Preview Wednesdays 5 p.m. to 7 p.m. for general household sales, and 10.30 a.m. to 7 p.m. for fine art sales (once a month). Items include Jacobean, Georgian, Victorian, Edwardian, and contemporary furniture, clocks, rugs, silver, jewellery, porcelain, and paintings. Catalogues are £1 for general sales and £1.50 for fine art sales. The buyer's premium is 5%. Parking is available in large public car parks nearby. For information, contact Locke & England, 18 Guy Street, Leamington Spa, Warwickshire CV32 4RT, telephone (0926) 27988, fax (0926) 450242.

Leeds, West Yorkshire

Flea market and collectors' fair several times per year on Saturdays from 9.30 a.m. to 5 p.m. at Queens Hall. All types of antiques and bric-a-brac is offered. This is a large indoor regional fair with as many as 500 vendors. Admission is 50p. Parking is available at a charge. Organised by Panda Promotions, 24 Westgate, Honley, Huddersfield, West Yorkshire HD7 2AA, telephone (0484) 666144.

Phillips in Leeds
Auctions are held most (but not all) Wednesdays at the salerooms on East Parade. Auctions are specialized into various subjects, such as "Silver and Jewellery", "Clocks and Watches", and "Art Nouveau and Art Deco". Catalogues are issued at least two weeks before each sale. Bids may be left or made by post or telephone. The buyer's

premium is 10%. Sales are held at and further information is available from Phillips in Leeds, 17a East Parade, Leeds, West Yorkshire LS1 2BU, telephone (0532) 448011.

Phllips in Morley
Auctions are generally held every fortnight on a Tuesday, consisting of Victorian and reproduction furniture, household effects, and, occasionally, pianos at the Fountain Street Auction Rooms. Catalogues are available prior to sale. For details, contact Phillips in Morley, 20 Fountain Street, Morley, Leeds, West Yorkshire LS27 9EN, telephone (0532) 523888.

Leicester, Leicestershire

"Annual Leicester Antiques Fair" third Thursday to Saturday of February at Moat House Hotel in the Oadby district of Leicester, about 3 miles south of the city centre on A6. This is a long-established regional fair. All vendors are antiques dealers, and most items are furniture. The dateline is 1890. Organised by Tony Keniston, Hopton Castle, Craven Arms, Shropshire SY7 0QJ, telephone (05474) 356.

Heathcote Ball & Co. Fine Art Auctioneers
Sales of general antiques, furniture, pictures, objets d'art, silver, and porcelain on a Thursday every five to six weeks at the Auction Room, five minutes from the centre of Leicester (opposite Holiday Inn). Sales begin at 10.30 a.m., and viewing is day before and morning of sale. Catalogues are £2 to £3. Parking is available at nearby national car park, and the British Rail station is about half a mile away. For information, contact Heathcote Ball & Co., Fine Art Auctioneers, Castle Auction Rooms, 78 St. Nicholas Circle, Leicester, Leicestershire LE1 5NW, telephone (0533) 526789.

Letchworth, Hertfordshire

(Please also see Hitchin and Luton.)

Antique and collectors' fair five Sundays per year (usually but not always the last Sunday of the month) from 10.30 a.m. to 5 p.m. in the Functions Suite at The Broadway Hotel on The Broadway (hotel telephone (04626) 685661). This is a small regional fair, with about 60 stalls at each fair. Admission is 40p, 20p for children, but this fair is free to members of the antiques trade. Access by car from the A1 to Letchworth, then follow the signs to the fair. Parking is free at the hotel. For exact fair dates and further information, contact Bartholomew Fayres, Executive House, The Maltings, Station Road, Sawbridgeworth, Hertfordshire CM21 9JX, telephone (0279) 725809.

Antiques and collectors' fair Sunday during May Bank Holiday Sunday (but may change), July, and September, 11 a.m. to 5 p.m., at Plinston Hall. Car parking is on the site. Organised by Herridges Antiques & Collectors Fairs Limited, Chanctonbury, 8 Kimbolton Avenue, Bedford, Bedfordshire MK40 3AD, telephone (02234)45725

Lewes, East Sussex

(Please also see Brighton.)

Gorringe's Auction Galleries
This general auction house sells all types of antiques furniture, china, glass, silver, jewellery, pictures, and rugs at three-day sales (Tuesday to Thursday) held about every six weeks. Previews of sales items are held the Friday and Saturday before the sale from 10 a.m. to 5 p.m. Information and sale site is Gorridge's Auction Galleries, 15 North Street, Lewes, East Sussex BN7 2PD, telephone (0273) 472503 and 427382.

Lewes Auction Rooms
Another auction house offers antiques every six weeks on Thursday, and bric-a-brac, furniture,

and used goods every Monday at the sale rooms on Garden Street. There is no buyer's premium. Free car parking is available. For information contact Julian Dawson, Lewes Auction Rooms, 56 High Street, Lewes, East Sussex, telephone (0273) 478221

Wallis & Wallis, Auctioneers
This specialist auction house has nine auctions per year of militaria, arms, armor, and coins and medals. Information is available from Wallis & Wallis, 7-9 West Street, Lewes, East Sussex BN7 2NJ, telephone (0273) 473137, fax (0273) 476652, telex 896691 TLXIR G. The sales are held at the West Street Auction Gallery.

Leyland, Lancashire

Warren & Wignal, Limited, Auctioners
Sales every Wednesday at 10 a.m. at The Mill, Earnshaw Bridge, Leyland Lane. Viewing is on Tuesdays from 9 a.m. to 7 p.m. General antiques are on sale every third Wednesday, otherwise the goods offered are mainly household furniture and effects. Catalogues are 75p. Access by car on M6 to Junction 28 from M6. There is ample car parking. Access by rail on the Glasgow line to Leyland. For information, contact Warren & Wignall Limited, The Mill, Earnshaw Bridge, Leyland Lane, Leyland, Lancashire PR5 3PH, telephone (0772) 453252 and 451430.

Lingfield, Surrey

"Wakefield Ceramic Fairs", for two days at end of April and first of May and one late in September at The Pavilion, Lingfield Park. There are from 40 to 60 stands. There is an identification service for members of the public and collectors to bring porcelain for free evaluation. For details and exact dates, contact Fred Hynds, Wakefield Ceramics Fairs, 1 Fountain Road, Strood, Rochester, Kent ME2 3SJ, telephone (0634) 723461.

Liverpool, Merseyside

"Paddy's Market", common name for St. Martin's Market, Monday to Saturday (Friday and especially Saturday best) from early morning until early afternoon on Great Homer Street, about half a mile north of the Lime Street station. This boisterous street market is a combination of new and used, collectables, clothes, furniture, and other odds and ends. Access by public transport from the city centre on Bus 101; free parking is available but sometimes difficult on streets surrounding the market. Organised by Liverpool City Council Markets Department, St. Martin's Market, Great Homer Street, Liverpool, Merseyside L5 3LQ, telephone (051) 207 0601.

Outhwaite & Litherland, Fine Art Auctioneers
Fine art and antique auctions monthly, usually the last Wednesday of month, at 1030 a.m. at the Kingsway Galleries, Fontenoy Street (telephone (051) 236 6561). Viewing two days prior to the sale. Catalogues are £1.50. Weekly sales of general items, shipping goods, and antiques on Tuesdays at 10.30 a.m.; catalogues 20p. Parking in a private car park. The mainline Lime Street station is close by. For information, contact Outhwaite & Litherland, Office 3, 43 Hoghton Street, Southport, Merseyside, telephone (0704) 38489.

Llangefni, Gwynedd (Wales)

Morgan Evans & Co. Ltd., Auctioneers
Auctions are held on the last (or occasionally next to last) Wednesday of each month at 10.30 a.m. at the salerooms. Previews are held on the Monday before the sale from 10.30 a.m. to 12.30 p.m. and 2 to 6 p.m., and the morning of the sale. Auctions consist of several hundred lots, including furniture, china and pottery, glassware (including crystal), paintings and prints, rugs, metalware (all types—silver, silver plate, gold, brass, iron) and miscellaneous items. Catalogues are issued several weeks before the sale. Bids may

may be left, posted, or made by telephone
(saleroom direct line is (0248) 355). Buyers
receive the next six catalogues free, postpaid.
There is no buyer's premium. All purchases must
be paid for and removed by the end of the second
working day after the sale. This new saleroom is
in a far corner of Britain; as a result, Welsh
woodwork and other items can be found. Access
by car across on A5 toward Holyhead; then take
A6114 toward Llangefni. Free parking is available at the saleroom. Access by public transport
can be difficult; the nearest main railway stations are at Bangor and Holyhead, though the
nearest one is at Llanfair. Sales are held at and
further information is available from Morgan
Evans & Co. Ltd., 28/30 Church Street, Llangefni, Gwynedd, telephone (0248) 723303.

Llangybi near Usk, Gwent

Antiques fair, third Sunday of every month from
11 a.m. to 5 p.m. at the Cwrt Bleddyn Hotel in
the village of Llangybi. This regional fair is of
good quality; several dozen dealers show wares.
Reproductions must be clearly marked. Items offered include small furniture, brass, copper,
postcards, and other miscellaneous items. Admission is 30p, trade free. Free parking is available
at the hotel; no public transport is available (no
service to this location on Sunday). Organised by
Doug Burnell-Higgs, Isca Fairs, 10 Norman
Street, Caerleon near Newport, Gwent NP6 1BB,
Wales, telephone (0633) 421527.

London

*(Please also see Beaconsfield, Beckenham, Bex-
leyheath, Crayford, Croydon, Epping, Epsom,
Greenwich, Harlow, Harrow, Hornchurch,
Loughton, Redhill, Romford, Stanmore, Waltham
Abbey, Weybridge, and Windsor.)*

Dozens of markets of all types exist throughout
London: fruit and vegetable markets, wholesale
markets, clothes markets, even a gardening
market. They do not have any items of interest to

antique collectors and dealers, or only a very few such items. These markets are not discussed in this book even though those such as Petticoat Lane may be world-famous for other reasons.

These markets include: Bayswater Road, Balham, Battersea High Street, Berwick Street, Brixton, Broadway, Chapel Market, Chiswick, Chrisp Street, Church Street, Columbia Road, Exmouth, Hampstead, Hoxton Street, Lansbury, Leadenhall, Leather Lane, London Bridge, Middlesex Street (Petticoat Lane), Mile End Waste, Queens Market, Roman Road, Shepherd's Bush, Southwark, Strutton Ground, Tower Bridge Road, Watling, Whitechapel Road, Whitecross Street, and Woolwich.

Note: The number in parentheses immediately after the market, fair, or auction pinpoints its location on the London city maps on pages 162-165 or London region map near the end of the book. Numbers 1-30 are regularly-held markets on the city map, 40-60 are major antiques fairs on the city map, and 60-99 are auction houses on the city map. All numbers over 100 are on the London Home Counties map on pages 246 and 247, since they lie outside the central part of the city.

Regularly-held Antiques and Flea Markets

Bell Street Market (1) every Saturday from 9 a.m. to mid afternoon on Bell Street, just off Edgware Road and Marylebone Road, NW1. This is a small market with assorted odds and ends, including old clothes, broken-down furniture, bric-a-brac, and junk. Access by car to Marylebone (don't go up on the motorway) and look for parking on the side streets. Access by Underground to Edgware Road (District, Metropolitan, and Bakerloo Lines) or bus lines 6, 7, 8, 15, 16, 18, 27, 36, and 136.

Bermondsey Street Antiques Market (2) every Friday morning year round beginning at 6 a.m. and going until 2 p.m. It takes place on a square at the corner of Bermondsey Street and Long Lane, SE1. This is London's best antiques market and offers the best selection of good-quality items. There are few reproductions or modern craft work. Items offered include lots of silver, furniture, odds and ends, some pottery, some porcelain, glass and crystal. Get there early, and bring a flashlight! The antique-dealer buyers have picked over the market by about 7.30 a.m. Several permanent indoor antiques markets face the square. Access by Underground from London Bridge station (Northern Line), south on Bermondsey Street, or Borough station (Northern Line), east on Long Lane to the market, or by night bus N47 to Tower Brige Road, or N89 to London Bridge Station. For further information, contact the Consumer Services Division, London Borough of Southwark, 23 Harper Road, London SE1 6AW, telephone 01-403 5867.

Camden Antiques Market (3) every Thursday from 7 a.m. to 1 p.m. at the corner of Camden High Street and Buck Street in Camden Town, NW1. This market offers antiques and collectables, as well as new and used clothes. Access by car to Camden Town. Parking can be very difficult in this area. Access by Underground to Camden Town (Northern or Piccadilly Lines) or any of the many buses to Camden Town. Information from ABC, 15 Flood Street, Chelsea, London SW3, telephone 01-351 5353.

Camden Lock and the Stables (4) every Saturday and Sunday from 8 a.m. to late afternoon at Camden High Street and the Grand Union Canal, NW1. The Camden Lock part of this market is one of the best bric-a-brac and crafts fairs in London. As you cross the bridge over the canal, on the left is a jumble of hundreds of stands. Behind them, old mill buildings are the locations of craftsmen and some antique dealers. Jugglers and musicians entertain in one of the most pleasant and touristy London markets. The Stables, a five-minute walk further on Camden High Street past where it turns into Chalk Farm Road, is a major source of collectables, Victoriana, and some of the best Art Deco items found in Britain. In these old converted stables, several hundred vendors offer all types of items,

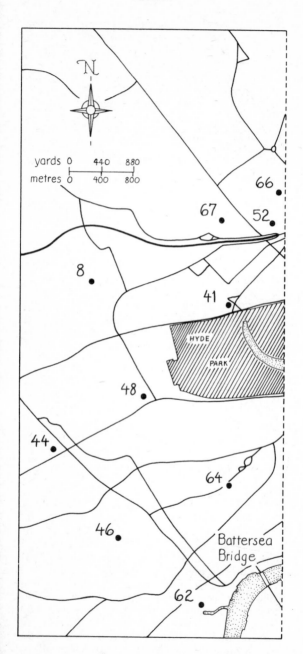

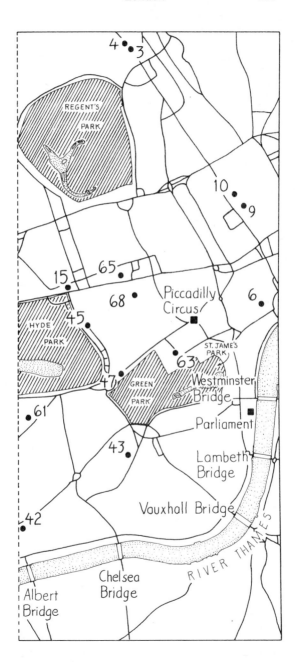

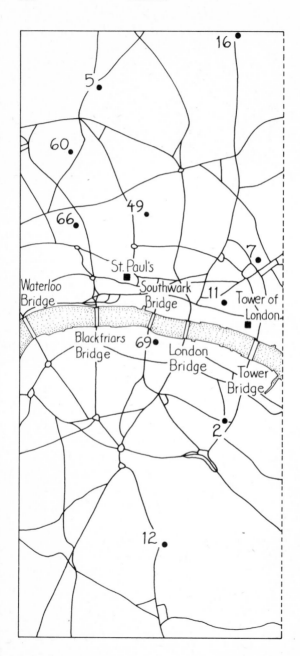

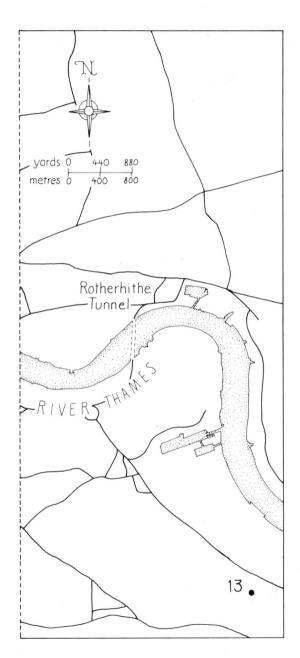

N

yards 0   440   880
metres 0   400   800

Rotherhithe
Tunnel

RIVER THAMES

13

but few new items or reproductions. Access by car to Camden Town; parking is easier to find along Chalk Farm Road and the Stables than near Camden Lock. Access by car to Camden Town. Parking can be very difficult in this area. Access by Underground to Camden Town Station (Northern or Piccadilly Lines) or any of the many buses to Camden Town.

Camden Passage (5) every Wednesday from 7 a.m. to mid afternoon and every Saturday from 7 a.m. to 5 p.m. (some dealers open later) on Camden Passage, N1. Camden Passage is a narrow pedestrian-only lane (actually named Islington High Street) behind Upper Street from Duncan Street to Essex Road.

A number of vendors offer all types of small antiques, collectables, and bric-a-brac on tables along the lane and its warren-like side alleys, and in some of the buildings converted into semi-permanent markets. In addition, a number of full-time shops and galleries offer some of the finer pieces of furniture, paintings, and objets d'art to be found. This is one of the more exclusive and most expensive markets in London. Access by car to Islington. Parking in the area can be almost impossible, though the car park on Duncan Street offers a large number of spaces. Access by Underground to Angel station (Northern Line), or on bus lines 4, 19, 30, 43, 73, 171, 171A, 277, and 279.

Clapham Collectors' Fair (100) first Saturday of every month from 10 a.m. to 5 p.m. at the Contact Centre, Hambalt Road, Clapham Park, SW4. This is a small fair of bric-a-brac and odds and ends. For information contact 01-622 4200.

Covent Garden Antiques Fair (6) every Monday from 6.30 a.m. to 4.30 p.m. on the east and south side of Covent Garden and the Jubilee Market, also on the south side, WC1. This is one of the best weekly fairs in London, and many regulars at the Bermondsey Street market can be found here Monday. Many are situated in the cavernous open building on the south side of the Covent Gardens market buildings. Most tourists don't arrive until about 9 a.m., but the bustle begins among the dealers at dawn. Organised from Sherman & Waterman Associates, 12/13 Henrietta Street, Covent Garden, London WC2E 8LH, telephone 01-240 7405.

Maridale Fairs also has an indoor antiques fair every Sunday from 10 a.m. to 5 p.m. and every Monday from 7.30 a.m. to 4.30 p.m. at 38 King Street, to the west of the Covent Gardens buildings. Information from Maridale Antique & Collectors Fairs, 9 Mill Ridge, Edgware, Middlesex, England, telephone 01-958 8354.

Access by car to Covent Garden area is easy before 7.30 a.m., and some free parking is available on the surrounding streets, but cars must be removed by 9 a.m. Access by Underground to Covent Garden station, on the Victoria Line. Any bus to Cambridge Circus or Holborn is within walking distance of Covent Garden.

Cutler Street Antiques Market (7) every Sunday from 6 a.m. to 2 p.m. on Goulston Street (near Aldgate), EC1. This market specializes in silver, gold, jewels, and coins. The early hours are when a large number of dealers come to buy; many of the items later turn up at the Silver Vaults, Portobello Road, or Camden Passage. By 8.30 or 9 a.m., the dealers are set up for the tourists. Prices increase, though the best items have long gone. This long-established market moved in 1985 from a courtyard off Cutler Street. Parking is difficult in this neighborhood after about 7 a.m. since the large Petticoat Lane and other markets take place in this area. Access by Underground to Aldgate East, and walk to the north. A large number of bus lines pass nearby, but few operate during the early hours of this market. Organised by ABC, 15 Flood Street, Chelsea, London SW3, telephone 01-351 5353.

Deptford market (13) every Friday from 8 a.m. to about noon on High Street and Douglas Way, SE8. The antiques and bric-a-brac are at the west end of the market on Douglas Way, past the fruit and vegetable vendors. While most of the items are junk, occasional treasures can be found, such as early 19th-century crystal port decanters, battered but solid oak chairs, and

similar types of used items. This market is totally away from the tourist and antiques orbit and
is refreshingly unpretentious. Access by Underground to New Cross station (Metropolitan Line),
walk north a short way to Douglas Way, then
turn right. The market is halfway down the
street.

Kingsland Waste market (16) every weekday but
really worthwhile only early on Saturday morning from dawn to about 9.30 a.m. along
Kingsland Road, E8. This market offers all types
of merchandise—food and new items as well as
antiques and junk—but on Saturdays, the used-
furniture merchants and used-bicycle sellers arrive in force. True bargains can be found by those
who are both early and knowledgeable. Access by
car to Kingsland Road; early arrivals will be
rewarded by nearby street parking, but later arrivals will have to walk a short way. Access by
British Rail to Dalston Junction from Camden
Road or on bus lines 22, 22A, 30, 38, 48, 67, 78,
149, 243, 243A, and 277.

Portobello Road market (8) every Saturday from
6 a.m. to 5 p.m. on Portobello Road and some
side streets, W10 and W11. Without doubt, this
is the most famous antique market in Britain.
The market stretches for almost a quarter of a
mile from Chepstow Villas under the Westway
motorway to Monroe Mews and takes in several
side streets, numerous warren-like warehouses
and buildings, and any nook that is available.
Unfortunately, though it is the most famous and
there are hundreds of dealers offering immense
quantities of all types of items, it is over-
touristed, and prices sometimes seem to be sig-
nificantly higher for equivalent items than at
other markets. In fact, a number of Portobello
Road dealers can be found bidding at various
auctions during the week and at Bermondsey on
Friday morning to obtain stock to resell to the
tourists on Saturday. Also, at this market,
reproductions and some arts-and-crafts items are
offered. During the week and on Saturdays as
well, a fruit, vegetable, fish, and meat market
takes place about midway through the antiques
market—which then picks up on the other side of

the fish. Access by Underground to Notting Hill Gate station (Central, Circle, and District Lines) and walk one block up Pembridge Road, then to the left along Portobello Road until arriving at the market, or to Ladbroke Grove station (Metropolitan Line), walk east under the Westway to Portobello Road. Most but not all of the market is to your right. Access by bus on lines 7, 15, 15A, 28, 31,52, and 52A.

Putney Flea Market (101) every Saturday from 8.30 a.m. to mid afternoon on Putney Hill near Upper Richmond Road, SW15. This small market has about 30 vendors of old clothes, mismatched china, bric-a-brac, and junk. Parking in the area can be difficult, since the Lacey Road Car Park is a general Saturday market as well. Access by Underground to East Putney station (District Line), or by bus lines 13, 30, 37. 74, and 85.

Sclater Street market (14) every Sunday from 4.30 a.m. (5 a.m. in winter) until mid afternoon on Sclater Street, Cheshire Street, and surrounding lanes, E1. This market is also called Brick Lane, Club Row, or Cheshire Street. This is the quintessential Sunday market to make true finds of antiques, collectables, and other items. Beginning at 4.30 a.m., all types of antiques and collectables come out of battered doctors' bags, cars, cardboard boxes, and other anonymous containers. This market seems to be one of the places that antiques and other interesting items first surface, and at a lower price than later. Because of its rather early hour, only dealers looking for stock and dedicated collectors come to this market. The main part of this early market is on Cheshire Street, which is a continuation of Sclater Street. Later in the morning, a regular market with cheap clothes, car parts, food, and other items engulfs this early morning market. Street parking is easy until about 7 a.m. After that, it rapidly becomes difficult, then almost impossible. Access by Underground (after 6 a.m. only) to Shoreditch station (Central Line), then walk north over the tracks on Brick Lane to Sclater Street and Cheshire Street. Access by bus on lines 8, 8A, and 78 after 6 a.m., or night bus N83 or N11 to Bethal Green Road.

Streatham Antiques Market (102) every Tuesday from 8 a.m. to 2 p.m. at the United Reformed Church Halls on Streatham High Road, Streatham, SW16. This is a smaller but regular market for minor antiques and collectables. Access by Underground to Tooting Bec station (Northern Line) and walk east on A214. Organised by Ray Ratcliff, London, telephone 01-764 3602.

Antiquarian book fair (9) second Sunday of every month in the assembly rooms of the Hotel Russell on Russell Square (telephone 01-837 6470). The fair is open on Sunday from 2 to 7 p.m. and Monday from 10.30 a.m. to 7 p.m. Once a year, in June the fair runs a whole week (two fairs back-to-back) from 10.30 a.m. to 7 p.m., and is much larger than usual (about 200 vendors) and includes a third day. Access by Underground to Russell Square station (Piccadilly Line), walk one block to the hotel at Russell Square. Access by bus on lines 68, 77, and 77A. Parking is difficult and expensive, though there are some parking meters on surrounding streets and cars may be parked at the hotel. Organised by the Provincial Booksellers Fairs Association, P.O. Box 66, Cambridge, Cambridgeshire CB1 3PD, telephone (0223) 240921.

"Bloomsbury Fair" (10) postcard, cigarette card, and printed ephemera fair the last Sunday of every month from 10 a.m. to 4 p.m. at the Bloomsbury Crest Hotel on Coram Street, just north of Russell Square, W1 (hotel telephone 01-837 1200). This is a long-established specialists' fair; more than 100 dealers offer all types of ephemera. Admission is 35p. Parking is available at the hotel or in a car park across the street. Access by Underground to Russell Square station (Piccadilly Line) and walk left to Russell Square and then right along Woburn Place, or on bus lines 77, 77A, and 188. Organised by IPM Promotions, 2 Frederick Gardens, Brighton, Sussex BN1 4TB, telephone (0273) 675757, or in London at 62 Greyhound Hill, Hendon, London NW4, telephone 01-203 1772.

"London City Book Market", (11) an antiquarian book fair the third Tuesday of most months at St. Olaves Parish Hall from 10.30 a.m. to 6 p.m., in Mark Lane, EC3. Access by car is difficult at best and parking is almost impossible. A parking garage is near the Tower of London. Access by Underground to Tower Hill station, then walk west to Mark Lane. Organised by the Provincial Booksellers Fairs Association, P.O. Box 66, Cambridge, Cambridgeshire CB1 3PD, telephone (0223) 240921.

Westmoreland Road (12) used goods and bric-a-brac market every Sunday from 8 a.m. to noon on Westmoreland Road, SE17. About 70 vendors offer all types of used goods and junk. This is a market at which finds can be made, including beat-up Victorian furniture and other neglected but restorable or salvageable items. It is also a good market for those unwilling to arrive by dawn. Access by car to Elephant and Castle, then southeast along Walworth Road to Westmoreland Road (Walworth Road changes its name to Camberwell Road near the market). Street parking is available to early arrivals. Access by Underground to Elephant and Castle station (Northern and Bakerloo Lines), or by bus lines 12, 35, 40, 42, 45, 46, 68, 171, 176, 184, and 185A.

Antiques Fairs

These markets are held irregularly, but are often the largest specialized markets in the London area, and some include museum-quality antiques offered by the top dealers as well as large markets with all types of bric-a-brac, antiques, and collectables.

"The Alexandra Palace Antique and Collectors Fair" (103) five times a year (mid January, early March, mid May, mid September, and early November) from noon (members of the antiques trade 10.30) until 6 p.m. at the Great Hall, Alexandra Palace, Wood Green, London N22. Admission at 10.30 is £3 and an antiques trade business card required; at noon the general public is admitted for £1.50. All children with adults are free. This is one of the largest fairs in London; more than 700 stands offer all types of items. No reproductions or new work may be offered. Free parking is available on the grounds. Access by British Rail from Kings Cross to Alexandra Palace station, then by free bus to the fair, or by underground (Piccadilly line) to Wood Green then W3 bus. Organised by Pig & Whistle Promotions, 53 Muswell Ave., London N10 2EH, telephone 01-883 7061.

"West London Antiques Fair" (48) held the second Wednesday to following Sunday of January and August from 11 a.m. to 8 p.m. (Sunday 11 a.m. to 6 p.m.) at Kensington Town Hall on Hornton Street, W8. This is a good fair, with about 90 stands. All types of items are offered, from small pieces of jewellery to large furniture. However, coins, medals, stamps, and militaria are prohibited. The dateline is 1870, except jewellery, textiles, and collectables 1900, and paintings 1920. All items are vetted, and reproductions and modern works are prohibited. Admission is £3, which includes a catalogue. Members of the antiques trade are admitted free with a business card. Access by car to Kensington High Street. Parking on the street is often difficult, but there is a car park under the library in the Kensington Town Centre. Access by Underground to Kensington High Street, and then walk across the street past the library to Kensington Town Hall. Many buses from all over London stop in front of the Underground station and library. For further information, contact Penman Antiques Fairs, P.O. Box 114, Haywards Heath, West Sussex, RH16 2YU, telephone (04447) 2514 and 4531.

"The London Decorative Arts Fair" (40) four times a year, usually the end of March, June, September, and December from 11 a.m. (trade 9.30) to 4.30 p.m. at the Westminster Exhibition Centre, Vincent Square, SW1. About 150 dealers of Art Nouveau, Art Deco, and modern works show their items, for one day only. Organised by Bagatelle Fairs, London, telephone 01-391 2339.

"The International Silver & Jewellery Fair & Seminars" (47) held four days during April (exact dates vary from year to year) at the Park Lane Hotel, Piccadilly, London W1 (hotel telephone 01-499 6321). This fair includes not only excellent examples of vetted sterling silver and jewellery, but also seminars and lectures by well-regarded experts. Entry to the sale is £5, and an illustrated catalogue is £4. Lectures are £10 for the first one and £7 for the following ones. Access by car is to Piccadilly; street parking is difficult to nonexistent, but cars may be parked at the hotel. Access by Underground to Hyde Park Corner or Green Park, then walk along Piccadilly to the hotel. Organised by Brian & Anna Haughton, ICF&S Ltd., 3B Burlington Gardens, Old Bond Street, London W1X 1LE, telephone 01-734 5491.

"The Chelsea Antiques Fair" (42) second Tuesday to third Saturday (11 days) of March and September from 11 a.m. to 8 p.m. (5 p.m. Saturday and closed Sunday) at Chelsea Old Town Hall, Kings Road at Sydney Street, SW3 (Old Town Hall telephone 01-351 9152). These fairs are high points of the British antiques fair circuit and are older, well-established fairs. All types of items are shown, from small items such as jewellery, glass, coins, and medals, to paintings and a large selection of furniture. The dateline for furniture is 1830; for most other items 1851; and for paintings, jewellery, and rugs, 1889. All vendors are professional dealers. All items are vetted, and new work, reproductions, and over-restored items are prohibited. Admission is £3.50, which includes an illustrated catalogue. There is no reduction or free admission for the trade. Access by car is easy, and the fair is AA signposted. Parking, however, is difficult, since there is no on-site parking, and unoccupied street spaces are scarce. Access by Underground to Sloane Square or South Kensington, then walk. Bus lines 11, 19, 22, and 49 stop in front of the exhibition hall. For further information, contact Penman Antiques Fairs, P.O. Box 114, Haywards Heath, West Sussex RH16 2YU, telephone Lindfield (04447) 2514 and 4531.

"The Westminster Spring Antiques Fair" (43) held in late April. This is a relatively new antiques fair held near Victoria station. All antiques will be vetted, and furniture has an 1830 dateline and most other items have an 1860 dateline. Admission is £2.50, which includes a catalogue, but members of the antiques trade are admitted free. Contact the organiser to find the exact location and for further details. Organised by Penman Fairs, P.O. Box 114, Haywards Heath, West Sussex RH16 2YU, telephone Linfield (04447) 2514.

"The Syon Park Antiques Fair" (105) held one weekend in February at Syon Park in west London near Kew Bridge. (This fair will not be held in 1989, however.) This is a major antiques fair. Only the best antiques may be offered; items found include clocks, furniture, silver, porcelain and pottery, paintings, and other items too numerous to mention. All items are vetted before the sale by experts from Christie's, Phillips, or Bonhams. Admission is £2.50. (In addition to the fair, Syon Park also has an excellent transport museum and an Adam-designed house.) Access by car to Syon Park along A315 (follow Kew Bridge Road west from Kew Bridge) to the park. Parking is available. Access by bus lines 117, 203, 237, 267, and E2 to Syon Park stop. Organised by Robert Bailey, 1 Roll Gardens, Gants Hill, Ilford, Essex 1G2 6TN, telephone 01-550 5435.

"The Fine Arts & Antiques Fair" (44) for two weeks in June at the Grand Hall, Olympia Exhibition Centre, Hammersmith Road, W14. This is a major antiques event with more than 300 dealers exhibiting; all items are vetted. Hours are 2 p.m. to 8 p.m. the first day and 11.30 a.m. to 8 p.m. weekdays, to 6 p.m. weekends. Access by Underground to Olympia Kensington and walk south and across the road to the entrance. Pay parking available in a car park behind the Centre. Organised by Philbeach Events Ltd., Earls Court Exhibitions Centre, Warwick Road, London SW5, telephone 01-370 8205, fax 01-244 7617, telex 919746 ENCANDO G.

"The Grosvenor House Antiques Fair" (45) for 10 days in early to late June (usually about the 10th to 20th) at the Grosvenor House Hotel in the Great Room. Hours vary: opening night is 5 to 8 p.m., others are 11 a.m. to 8 p.m. or 11 a.m. to 6 p.m. These fairs are some of the very highest peaks of the British antique fair circuit; well worth attending. All items are vetted and all sellers are antique dealer members of the British Antique Dealers Association. Only the finest antiques, almost all of museum quality, are shown and offered. Admission and catalogue are £3. Held at the Grosvenor House Hotel, Park Lane, in Mayfair just east of Hyde Park and between Mount Street and Grosvenor Street. Pay parking is available in Reeves Mews across the street. Access by Underground to Marble Arch station on Central Line, then walk, or any bus to Marble Arch/Oxford Street and walk. Organised by Ann Rudd and Elaine Dean, British Antique Dealers Association, 20 Rutland Gate, London SW7 1BD, telephone 01-581 0373.

Antique and collectors' fair (39), Sundays three times a year from 10.30 to 5 p.m. at Royal Free Hospital, Recreation Centre, Fleet Road Entrance, Hampstead, London NW3. Exact dates vary; contact the organiser for details. More than 100 stands offer all types of antiques and collectables. Organised by Bartholomew Fayres, Executive House, The Maltings, Station Road, Sawbridgeworth, Hertfordshire CM21 9JX, telephone (0279) 725809 and 725699.

"The International Ceramics Fair and Seminar" (47) the second weekend of June (Friday to following Monday) from 11 a.m. to 8 p.m. at the Park Lane Hotel, Piccadilly, London W1, telephone 01-499 6321. This fair not only has vetted ceramics of all types (Chinese, European porcelain, other types of ceramics) but also lectures by internationally known specialists in the field of ceramics. Entry for the public and antiques trade as well is £5, and an illustrated catalogue is £4. Lectures are £10 for the first and £7 for additional ones. Access by car to Piccadilly; street parking is difficult to nonexistent, but cars may be parked at the hotel. Access by Underground to Hyde Park Corner or Green Park, then walk along Piccadilly to the hotel. Organised by Brian & Anna Haughton, ICF&S, 3B Burlington Gardens, Old Bond Street, London W1X 1LE, telephone 01-734 5491.

"The London Arms Fair" (46) last Friday and Saturday of September at the London West Hotel, Lillie Road, SW6. This is one of the oldest regular fairs for antiques, armour, assorted militaria, and books. Admission is £3 on Friday and £2 on Saturday. Access by Underground to West Brompton (District Line) then walk west a short way on Lillie Road. Access by car to the hotel, where limited parking is available. Access by bus on lines 30, 264, and 283. Hotel telephone is 01-385 1255.

"The National Antique & Collectors' Porcelain, Pottery, and Glass Fair" (41) the third Sunday of September from 11 a.m. to 6 p.m. at the Park Court Hotel, 75 Lancaster Gate, Bayswater W2. The title of this specialists' fair is self-descriptive. Programmes and admission is 75p or £1. Organised by London House, 271-273 King Street, London W6, telephone 01-741 8011. This hotel is occasionally used for other one-day fairs. Information is available from the hotel 01-402 4272. The site is halfway between the Queensway and Lancaster Gate Underground stations on the north side of Bayswater Road. Access by bus on any line along Bayswater Road (12, 28, 88). Parking in this area can be difficult.

"The Olympia Decorative & Antiques Fair" (44) for five days in October at Olympia Exhibition Centre, Hammersmith Road, W14. This exhibition is comprised of vetted antiques displayed in room settings by more than 180 exhibitors. Access by Underground to Olympia Kensington and walk south a short way to Hammersmith Road, then west to the Centre. Pay parking available in a car park behind the Centre. Organised by Philbeach Events Ltd., Earls Court Exhibitions Centre, Warwick Road, London SW5, telephone 01-370 8205, fax 01-244 7617, telex 919746 ENCANDO G.

"The Park Lane Hotel Antiques Fair" (47) first week of October. This is another of the famous fairs held in posh hotels. Only beautiful, perfect antiques are shown at this exclusive fair. Organised by the Park Lane Hotel Antiques Fair, London House, 271-273 King Street, London W6 9LZ, telephone 01-741 8011.

This hotel is frequently used by other organisers for one-day antique fairs. Examples include a fair the third weekend of September, sponsored by Century Antiques Fair Ltd., 58 Mill Lane, London NW6 1N3, telephone 01-794 3551. The schedule of coming events can also be obtained from the hotel, telephone 01-499 6321. Access by Underground to Green Park, then walk along Piccadilly toward Hyde Park to Park Lane.

"Kensington Antiques Fair" (48) early in November at the New Town Hall, Hornton Street, Kensington W8. All antiques are vetted and the dateline is 1840. Admission is charged to all and includes a catalogue. Parking, for which a charge is made, is available in the Town Hall buildings. Access by Underground to Kensington High Street, then walk north on Hornton Street. Access by bus to Kensington High Street. Organised by Roger Heath-Bullock, Cultural Exhibitions Ltd., 8 Meadrow, Godalming, Surrey GU7 3HN, telephone (04868) 22562.

"The Chingford Antique and Collectors Fair" (106) is held three Saturdays and from 10.30 a.m. to 4 p.m. at the Chingford Assembly Hall, The Green, Station Road, Chingford, in the northeast part of London. About 80 dealers of antiques and collectables offer all types of items. Admission is 50p, but accompanied children and members of the antiques trade are free. Access by car from A104 to Woodford, then left to Chingford. This fair is signposted. Access by train to Chingford station from Liverpool Street (only about 10 miles). Access by bus on lines 69, 97, 235, and 313 to Chingford station. Chingford station is on Station Road. For exact dates and further information, contact Bartholomew Fayres, Executive House, The Maltings, Station

Road, Sawbridgeworth, Hertfordshire CM21 9JX, telephone (02779) 725809 and 725699.

"The City of London Antiques Fair and International Art Fair" (49) held the last Wednesday to Saturday of November from 11 a.m. to 8 p.m. (Saturday closing at 4 p.m.) at the Barbican Centre Exhibition Hall, across Beech Street from the Barbican Centre, EC2. This is a large, quality fair of more than 150 dealers of furniture, clocks, textiles, glass and crystal, silver, and quantities of furniture, and 100 art dealers. The dateline for furniture is 1850; for some other items 1860; jewels, textiles, and collectables 1900, and paintings 1920. All items are vetted. Admission, which includes an illustrated catalogue, is £5 for both fairs together. Readmission is free. There is no discount or free admission for members of the antiques trade. Access by car is easy: follow signs to Barbican Centre, and use Barbican Car Parks 2 and 3 off Silk Street, or 4 and 5 off Beech Street. A charge is made for parking, and street parking is virtually unavailable. Access by Underground to Barbican (the nearest), Moorgate, or St. Paul's station. Many buses stop in front of the Exhibition Hall, including 4, 9, 11, 21, 43, 76, 141, 279a, and 502. Organised by Penman Antiques Fairs, P.O. Box 114, Haywards Heath, West Sussex RH16 2YU, telephone (04447) 2514 and 4531.

"Wanstead Antique & Collectors Fair" (103) twice a year from 10.30 a.m. to 4 p.m. at Wanstead Leisure Centre (Alan Hearn Hall), Redbridge Lane West, Wanstead, London E11. THere are more than 80 stalls. Organised by Bartholomew Fayres, Executive House, The Maltings, Station Road, Sawbridgeworth, Hertfordshire CM21 9JX, telephone (0279) 725809 and 725699.

"Wakefield Ceramics Fair" (15) three days in June at the Cumberland Hotel, London W1. There are from 40 to 60 stands. There is an identification service for members of the public and collectors to bring porcelain for free evaluation. For details, contact Fred Hynds, Wakefield Ceramics Fairs, 1 Fountain Road, Strood,

Rochester, Kent   ME2 3SJ, telephone (0634) 723461.

Auctions

London is the auction centre of Britain; the major houses are listed here in alphabetical order. Be sure to contact them before planning to attend a sale, both to obtain catalogues (where one is issued) and to be sure that the auction will be held as scheduled.

Bainbridges Auctioneers and Valuers (160)

Auctions of all types of items, including antiques and art, are held about every six weeks at the Great Barn, Bury Street, Ruislip, Middlesex. For further information and sales calendar, contact Bainbridges Auctioneer, St. Johns Yard, St. Johns Parade, Mattock Lane, Ealing, London W13, telephone 01-840 7177.

Bloomsbury Book Auctions (60)

This auctioneer, a specialist in books and other papers, holds 22 auctions per year, with at least 400 lots in each auction. Auctions are held on Thursdays at 11 a.m. in their salesrooms and offices. Catalogues are available about three or four weeks before the sale for £3.50 each.

Viewing is held on Tuesday from 9.30 a.m. to 5 p.m., Wednesday from 9.30 a.m. to 8 p.m., and the morning of the sale. Bids may be left, posted, or telephoned. Bidders should register with the office before bidding. The buyer's premium is 10%. All bids must be paid for and purchases removed within five days. Access by car towards Finsbury Town Hall on Rosebery Avenue; the Finsbury Car Parks are nearby, for which a charge is made. Access by Underground to Angel (Northern Line) and walk south on St. John Street, then left on Rosebery Avenue to Hardwick Street, or by buses 19, 38, 153, 171, 171A, 196, all of which run on Rosebery Avenue. Sales are held at and exact dates and further information is available from Bloomsbury Book Auctions, 3/4 Hardwick Street, London EC1R 4RY, telephone 01-833 2636, 833 2637, and 636 1945.

Bonhams Knightsbridge (61)

This is one of the most active auctioneers of antiques and collectables in London. Three to five sales per week are held at 11 a.m. and 2 p.m. at the salerooms on Montpelier Street, Knightsbridge. This Bonhams usually offers more expensive items than at Bonhams Chelsea (please see next entry). A free bi-monthly guide to "What's Going on at Bonham's" is available on request. All sales are specialized categories of antiques.

Every other Tuesday, sales of silver and plate are held at 11 a.m. Every other Thursday a sale of English and continental furniture is held at 2 p.m.

In addition to these sales, Bonhams holds regular theme sales, such as "Dogs in Art", which coincides with Drufts Week in February, and flower and garden pictures, which coincides with Chelsea Flower Show in May. Catalogues are available two weeks before each sale and cost from £3 to £5. Viewing is held three days before the sales from 8:45 a.m. to 6 p.m. (and until 8 p.m. on Mondays). Bids may be left, poste, or telephoned. The buyer's premium is 10%.

Access by car to Brompton Road, on the south side of Hyde Park. Street parking is difficult, but several car parks are located on Sloane Street. Access by Underground to Knightsbridge, then walk along Brompton Road to Montpelier Street, on the right.

Sales are held at and further information is available from Bonhams, Montpelier Street, Knightsbridge, London SW7 1HH, telephone 01-584 9161, fax 01-589 4072, telex 916477 BONHAMS G.

Bonhams Chelsea (62)

This is Bonhams workaday auction gallery. Three sales a week are held at newly refurbished gallery, one of several auction houses on Lots Road. Sales are specialized, and usually start on Tuesday at 11 a.m. for furniture and carpets, and every other Wednesday at 10.30 a.m. for pictures and at 2 p.m. for ceramics, glass, and decorative objects. Catalogues are issued in advance of every sale, and often cost 80p to £1. Viewing is on Monday from 8:45 a.m. to 7 p.m., Tuesday to

Friday from 8:45 a.m. to 5 p.m., and Saturday from 10.30 a.m. to 1 p.m. The buyer's premium is 10%. All items must be paid for and removed by 6 p.m. on the day after the sale to avoid storage charges of £1 per lot per day. Access by car to Chelsea Bridge, then continue along the north bank of the Thames until the main road turns north. Lots Road is straight ahead, and when it turns north, the auction houses are found 100 yards on. A car park is between Lots Road and Upcerne Road. Access by Underground to Fulham Broadway, walk to King's Road, then east to Lots Road, or take busses 11 or 22 to Kings Road, then walk south on Lots Road to the auction house.

Sales are held at and further information is available from Bonhams New Chelsea Galleries, 65-69 Lots Road, Chelsea, London SW10 0RN, telephone 01-351 0466, fax 01-351 7754, telex 916477 BONHAMS G.

Christie's St. James's (63)

This is the head office of Christie's, where the best items are offered, such as Old Master paintings that sometimes are sold at record prices, which are recorded as newspaper headlines. However, not all items sold here are that expensive. Sales are specialized by category. A schedule of sales, which are held frequently, is available upon request.

Catalogues are issued in advance of all sales, and cost from £1 to £5. Bidders are required to register before bidding. Bids may be left, or made by post or telephone.

Access by car is difficult, and is just south of Piccadilly, off St. James's Street. Parking is difficult to impossible in this area. Access by Underground to Green Park or (with a longer walk) Piccadilly Circus. St James's Street is across the street from the Royal Academy.

Sales are held at and further information is available from Christie's St. James's (formally known as Christie, Manson, & Woods Ltd.), 8 King Street, St. James's, London SW1Y 6QT, telephone 01-839 9060, fax 01-839 1611, telex 916429.

Christie's South Kensington (64)

This is Christie's workaday auction house. While the grand sales of famous art take place in the St. James's location, almost every day (except Sunday) at least one sale takes place. Many days, there are three or four. A catalogue is issued at least a week before every sale (charges vary, never free), viewing is the day before the auction and just before the auction. A calendar of forthcoming sales is issued by the Press Office, and is available free upon request. The buyer's premium is 10% of the hammer price. Bids may be left, or made by post or telephone. Buyers have up to two days after the sale to pay for purchases and remove them.

While exceptions to the following schedule take place, and there are many special sales, in general the schedule is as follows:

Monday: 2 p.m. Silver, 5.30 p.m. Wine

Tuesday: 2 p.m. Jewellery, also at 2 p.m. Pictures

Wednesday: 10.30 a.m. Carpets, 1 p.m. Furniture, 2 p.m. Watercolours and Drawings, Prints

Thursday: 10.30 a.m. Glass and Ceramics, 2 p.m. Oriental Art, or Ceramics of various origins

Friday: 2 p.m. Books and Maps

Sales are informal, though bidders should register and obtain a bidder's number before bidding.

Access by car to Old Brompton Road. Some street parking with meters is available on the surrounding streets, or for £1 per hour at the National Car Park nearby. Access by Underground to South Kensington station (Circle, District, or Piccadilly Lines), then walk southwest down Old Brompton Road, or take bus 30, which travels on Old Brompton Road.

Information is available from and auctions are held at Christie's South Kensington, 85 Old Brompton Road, London SW7 3LD, telephone 01-581 7611, telex 922061.

Glendining's (65)

This Phillips-affiliated auction house has auctions twice a month (except January and August) on Wednesdays. This house specializes in coins and medals. Catalogues are issued four weeks before the sale, and cost from £1 to £4. The buyer's premium is 10%. Sales are held at and further information can be obtained from Glendining's, Blenstock House, 7 Blenheim Street, New Bond Street, London W1Y 9LD, telephone 01-493 2445, fax 01-629 8876, telex 298855 BLEN G. (This is the same building as Phillips Blenstock House.)

Hatton Garden Auctions (66)

This auction house specializes in jewellery and silver. Auctions are held every Thursday 1.30 p.m. Catalogues are issued at least one week before the sale and are free. Viewing is held all week prior to the sale. Bids may be left, or made by post or telephone. The buyer's premium is 10%.

Access by car is difficult and parking almost impossible except at the car park on Hatton Gardens near Clerkenwell Road. Access by Underground to Chancery Lane station (Central Line) or Farringdon (Circle or Metropolitan Lines), or British Rail to Holborn Viaduct station. Hatton Gardens is a street running between Holborn Circus and Clerkenwell Road; the auction house is almost exactly at the midpoint.

Auctions are held at and further information can be obtained from Hatton Garden Auctions, 36 Hatton Garden, London EC1N 8HP, telephone 01-242 6452.

London Bridge Auctions (69)

Weekly auctions of odds and ends are held at 2 p.m. at the saleroom at 6 Park Street, SE1. Almost anything can turn up at these sales: furniture, silver, porcelain, clocks and watches, jewellery, pictures, and other odds and ends. Each auction includes over 500 lots, and the auction moves quickly. There are no catalogues issued in advance of the sale. Viewing is the Sunday of the sale from 10 a.m. to 2 p.m. There is no buyer's premium. All purchases must be paid for and removed on the day of the sale.

Access by car to Southwark Bridge; Park Street is the second cross street. Access by Underground (Northern Line) and British Rail to London Bridge Station, walk upstream along the viaduct to Park Street. Access by bus on 17, 44,

70, 95, 149, 184, and any bus to London Bridge Station.

Sales are held at and further information is available from London Bridge Auctions, 6 Park Street, off Stoney Street, Southwark, London SE1, telephone 01-407 9577.

Lots Road Galleries (62)

The most hurly-burly of the several auction houses on Lots Road holds auctions every Monday at 6 p.m. Auctions are not specialized and consist of all types of antiques and used items. The auction moves at a *very* rapid pace, with a new item approximately every thirty seconds. Register with the office and obtain a bidder's number before bidding. Viewing on Fridays from 9: a.m. to 3 p.m., and Saturday, Sundays from 10 a.m. to 1 p.m. and 10 a.m. to 6 p.m. on Monday. Telephone bids and left bids can be made; if so, bidding is started at half the left bid. The buyer's commission is 12%. Catalogues are free. Buyers have 24 hours to pay for and remove their purchases.

Access by car to Chelsea Bridge, then continue along the north bank of the Thames until the main road turns north. Lots Road is straight ahead, and when it turns north, the auction houses are found 100 yards on. Access by Underground to Fulham Broadway, walk to King's Road, then east to Lots Road, or take busses 11 or 22 to King's Road, then walk south on Lots Road to the auction site.

Sales are held at and information is available from Lots Road Galleries, 71 Lots Road, Worlds End, Chelsea, London, SW10 0RN, telephone 01-351 7771, 351 5784, and 2349.

Newington Green Auctions (161)

Auctions are held every Thursday evening at 6.30 p.m. at the auction salesroom in the northern suburb of Stoke Newington. All types of antiques, including gold, silver, clocks, paintings, old furniture, and (if in good condition) some modern furniture is auctioned. Catalogues are issued the day before the sale, consisting of conditions of sale and a simple listing of 200 or more lots; there is no charge for the catalogue. Viewing takes place on Wednesday and Thursday before the sale. Bids may be left, posted, or telephoned. The buyer's premium is £2 per lot. No items may be removed before the end of the sale. Payment and removal must be completed by the close of business the following Tuesday. Access by Underground isn't convenient (nearest station is Manor House, and walk down Green Lanes). Access by bus to Stoke Newington is on lines 141 and 171A. Parking is on the street, sometimes difficult to find.

Sales are held at and further information is available from Newington Green Auctions, 55 Green Lanes, London N16 4TD, telephone 01-246 4222.

Phillips at Blenstock House (65)

The headquarters of the third largest auction house in Britain, Blenstock House is at the end of Blenheim Street, a small alley off New Bond Street. Regular auctions are held daily Monday to Friday. Items to be sold can be seen on Saturday from 8.30 a.m. to noon and on Sunday from 2 p.m. to 5 p.m., in addition to the day of each sale.

Weekly sales: Monday at 11 a.m., antique furniture, rugs, ceramics, glass, and art objects; Tuesday at 11 a.m., antique furniture, carpets, bronzes, and works of art; Wednesday at 11 a.m., alternating weekly between European ceramics and glass and Oriental works of art; Thursday at 11 a.m., postage stamps and sometimes paper money; Friday at 11 a.m., antique and modern silver. Viewing for these sales is two days prior.

There are regular (but not weekly) specialised sales of pictures held on Tuesdays at 11 a.m.; watercolours, drawings, and print sales on Mondays at 11 a.m. or 2 p.m.. Jewellery sales are held on most Tuesdays at 1.30 p.m. In addition, there are specialised sales are held every Thursday at 11 a.m. or 2 p.m. and include art nouveau, arms and armour, books and manuscripts, clocks, and musical instruments.

Catalogues vary in price from £1.20 to £10. The buyer's premium is 10%. Bids may be left or made by post or telephone. Payment and removal of purchases must be made within two working days.

Access by car is difficult, and parking is virtually impossible. The nearest underground parking is at Cavendish Square. Access by Underground to Bond Street or Oxford Circus (Central or Jubilee Lines), or any bus going to Oxford Street.

Sales are held at and further information is available from Phillips Blenstock House, 7 Blenheim Street, New Bond Street, London W1Y 0AS, telephone 01-629 6602, fax 01-629 8876, telex 29855 BLEN G.

Phillips Marylebone (66)

This is another Phillips auction house and the only auction rooms devoted entirely to selling pictures. Sales are held every Friday at 11 a.m., with quarterly specialist sales of old masters, prints, 19th-century continental, and modern British in the afternoon at 2 p.m. Viewing is on Thursday from 9 a.m. to 7 p.m. and the morning of the sale from 9 a.m. to 10 a.m. Most pictures can be bought for between £20 to £2,000. There are also occasional sales devoted to decorative picture frames. Catalogues are £1.20. Buyer's premium is 10%.

The saleroom is close to the West End and street parking is difficult in the neighborhood; the nearest car park is on Broadley Street, off Edgware Road. Access by Underground to Marylebone station then walk west a short way to Lisson Grove. Access by bus to Marylebone station and walk, or bus 159 to Lisson Grove.

Sales are held at and further information is available from Phillips Marylebone, Hayes Place, Lisson Grove, London NW1 6UA, telephone 01-723 2647,

Phillips West 2 (67)

The collectors' centre and textile deparments are based on Phillips West 2. Collectors' sales are held every Wednesday at noon. Items range from lead soldiers, toys and dolls to scientific instruments, pianos, photographica, postcards and sporting items, rock and pop memorabilia to classic and vintage cars.

There are 11 textile sales a year which include costumes, embroidery, and lace and four sales of fans. These are held on Wednesdys or Thursdays.

Furniture sales, held every Thursday at 10 a.m., include antique and modern furniture, porcelain, and objects. Specialised sales of pianos and keyboard instruments are held four times a year.

Viewing is Wednesday from 9 a.m. to 7 p.m. Catalogues are issued before the sales, usually for £1. The buyer's premium is 10%.

Access by public transport to Paddington station, then walk.

Sales are held at and further information is available from Phillips West 2, 10 Salem Road, London W2 4BU, telephone 01-221 5303.

Sotheby's (68)

This is the headquarters of the Sotheby's auction house, specializing in fine arts and the best antiques. This is the location of some of the sales that shatter world records for paintings. A free schedule of sales is available upon request. Viewing is held several days before every sale. Catalogues are issued before every sale. The buyer's premium is 10%. Parking in this area is almost impossible at any time.

Access by Underground to Bond Street (Central or Jubilee Lines) or any of the buses along Oxford Street.

Sales are held at and further information is available from Sotheby's, 34-5 New Bond Street, London W1A 2AA, telephone 01-493 8080, fax 01-409 3100, telex 24454 SBPLON G.

Southgate Antique Auction Rooms (163)

This auction of antiques and collectables and a few modern items takes place in the northern suburbs of London every Friday at 6.30 p.m. Catalogues (which are short descriptions of the items) are issued the day before the sale. Viewing is held Friday from 10 a.m. until the sale begins.

Sales consist of over 500 lots, and they move very rapidly through jewellery and silver, then bric-a-brac, glass, ands porcelain, paintings and drawings, and furniture. Bids may be left or telephoned. There is a 10% buyer's premium, but no commission to vendors. All items must be paid for within two days and removed by Monday evening following the sale.

Access by car north of London on Green Lanes
(A105) to Southgate Town Hall. Free parking is
available at the auction. Access by bus on lines
29, 123, green bus 735, and at night on bus N29.

Sales are held at and further information is
available from Southgate Antique Auction
Rooms, Rear of Southgate Town Hall, Green
Lanes, Palmers Green, London N13, telephone
01-886 7888.

Indoor, Permanent Antiques Markets

A number of antiques markets are open most
weekdays, and include large collections of
dealers with all types of items. They're included
because they are indoors, open most days,
though not antiques fairs as generally under-
stood. These markets' locations are not shown on
the maps.

Alfie's Antique Market, 13-25 Church Street,
London NW8, telephone 01-723 6066. Open
Tuesday to Saturday from 10 a.m. to 6 p.m.
About 90 dealers. Nearest Underground station:
Edgware Road or Marylebone.

Antiquarius Antiques Market, 135 Kings Road,
Chelsea, London SW3, operated by ABC, 15
Flood Street, Chelsea, London SW3, telephone
01-351 5353, open Monday to Saturday from 10
a.m. to 6 p.m. About 200 stands. Nearest Underground station: Sloane Square.

Bermondsey Antique Market and Antique Hyper-
Market, Long Lane at Bermondsey Street, London SE1, operated by ABC, 15 Flood Street,
Chelsea, London SW3, telephone 01-351 5353,
open Monday to Friday 7 a.m. to 5 p.m. (note:
Bermondsey Antique Market only open Friday
from 5 a.m. to 2 p.m.). Nearest Underground station: Tower Bridge.

Bond Street Antique Centre, 124 New Bond Street, London W1, operated by ABC, 15 Flood Street, Chelsea, London SW3, telephone 01-351 5353, Open Monday to Saturday from 10 a.m. to 5:45 p.m. About 25 dealers. Nearest Underground station: Bond Street.

Chelsea Antiques Market, 253 Kings Road, London SW3, telephone 01-352 1424 or 352 9695. Open Monday to Saturday from 10 a.m. to 6 p.m. Nearest Underground station: Sloane Square.

Chenil Galleries, 181 Kings Road, London SW3, operated by ABC, 15 Flood Street, Chelsea, London SW3, telephone 01-351 5353. Open Monday to Saturday from 10 a.m. to 6 p.m. About 45 dealers. Nearest Underground station: Sloane Square.

Earlham Street, London WC2. Open Monday to Saturday from 9 a.m. to 5 p.m. Nearest Underground station: Covent Garden.

Grays Antique Market, 58 Davies Street, London W1, telephone 01-629 7034. Open Monday to Friday from 10 a.m. to 6 p.m. Several hundred dealers. Nearest Underground station: Bond Street.

Grays Mews Antique Market, 1-7 Davies Mews, London W1, telephone 01-629 7034 and 629 7036. Open Monday to Friday from 10 a.m. to 6 p.m. Nearest Underground station: Bond Street.

London Silver Vaults, Chancery Lane, London WC2, telephone 01-242 3844. Open Monday to Friday from 9 a.m. to 5.30 p.m. and Saturday from 9 a.m. to 12.30 p.m. The most amazing and largest quantity of silver for sale. Nearest Underground station: Chancery Lane.

Long Ashton, Avon

(Please see Bristol.)

Lostwithiel, Cornwall

Jefferys, Auctioneers & Estate Agents
Auctions are held every other Wednesday at
10.30 a.m. at the salerooms at 5 Fore Street.
Auctions include antiques, collectables, and
other used goods. These can be good country auctions, since this is in an out-of-the-way corner of
Britain. No catalogues are issued. Inspection is
held on Tuesday before the sale during normal
business hours, and on Wednesday morning. The
buyer's premium is 5%. Bids may be left, posted,
or telephoned, but references (such as a banker)
are required. Access by car is on A390 to
Lostwitheil. Free parking is available all around
the town. Access by train to Lostwithiel, then
walk across the bridge and take the first left. The
auction rooms are almost straight ahead. Auctions are held at and further information is available from Jefferys, The Auction Rooms, 5 Fore
Street, Lostwithiel, Cornwall PL22 0BP,
telephone (0208) 872245.

Loughton, Essex

(Please also see Epping, Harlow, and London.)

Antique and collectors fair held four Bank
Holiday Mondays per year (third Monday of
April, first and fourth Monday of May, and last
Monday of August) from 10 30 a.m. to 5 p.m. at
the Loughton Methodist Hall on High Road. This
is a small fair with about 35 dealers offering
mainly small items on tables. Access by car on
High Road (A104) directly to the hall. Access by
bus on line 20 and Green Lines 201, 250, and 501
from London, or by British Rail to Loughton station from Liverpool Street station, also in London. For further information, contact Bartholomew Fayres, Executive House, The Maltings, Station Road, Sawbridgeworth, Hertfordshire CM21 9JXZ, telephone (0279) 725809
and 725699.

Luton, Bedfordshire

(Please also see Hatfield, Hitchin, Letchworth, and Tring.)

Antique and collectors fair five Sundays a year from 10.30 a.m. to 5 p.m. at the Putteridge Recreation Centre on Putteridge Lane, Stopsley, along A505. This is a good-sized regional fair with about 100 stands. Admission is 60p, but accompanied children are free. Entrance is free to members of the antiques trade who enter between 9 and 10.30 a.m. Access by car is on A505, 2 miles north from Luton towards Cambridge. The fair is signposted, and there is free parking. This fair is not easily accessible by public transport. For further information, contact Bartholomew Fayres, Executive House, The Maltings, Station Road, Sawbridgeworth, Hertfordshire CM21 9JX, telephone (0279) 725809 and 725699.

Lyndhurst, Hampshire

(Please also see Brockenhurst, Ower, and Southampton.)

Antiques and collectors' fair two weekends (Saturday and Sunday) per year at the Lyndhurst Park Hotel. This is a good regional fair with all types of antiques and collectables shown. The dateline is 1930. Admission is 50p. Free parking is available at and near the hotel. For exact dates and further information, contact Kingston Promotions, 157 Plymouth Drive, Hill Head, Fareham, Hampshire PO14 3SN, telephone (0329) 661780.

"Wakefield Ceramics Fair" in mid May at the Lyndhurst Park Hotel. There are from 40 to 60 stands. There is an identification service for members of the public and collectors to bring porcelain for free evaluation. For information, contact Wakefield Ceramics Fairs, 1 Fountain Road, Strood, Rochester, Kent ME2 3SJ, telephone (0634) 723461.

Maidstone, Kent

B.J. Norris, Auctioneers
Auctions are held every other Thursday at 10.30
a.m. at the Agricultural Hall at Maidsone
Market (Agricultural Hall telephone (0622)
58705). This is an auction of all types of items:
antiques and newer furniture, collectables, and
other odds and ends. There is no buyer's
premium. No catalogues are issued in advance of
the sale. Viewing is held the morning of the sale
from 8 a.m. to 10 a.m. For further information,
contact B.J. Norris, Auctioneers, The Quest,
West Street, Harrietsham, Kent, telephone
(0622) 859515 and (0860) 819335.

Malvern, Worcestershire

Antique fair Sundays in early February, March,
April, June, July, and August, mid September,
and late November from 10.30 a.m. to 4.30 p.m.
at the Exhibition Hall, Three Counties Show
Ground, Malvern. There are more about 100
stands at this fair. Admission is 50p. Access on
M50 to Junction 1, then follow signs. Organised
by KS Fairs, Evergreen Productions, P.O. Box 58,
Weston-Super-Mare, Avon BS22 8ER, telephone
(0934) 683648.

Manchester, Greater Manchester

(Please also see Stretford.)

Capes Dunn & Company Fine Art Auctioneers
Specialized antiques auctions are held most
Mondays and Tuesdays of the year, with each
auction focusing on a particular type of goods,
such as antique furniture, bronzes and small
sculpture, paintings and watercolours, jewellery,
sterling, glass, ceramics, carpets, musical instruments, and books. Catalogues are issued for the
antique sales, priced £1. In addition, used and
household goods are held every Monday year
round. Previews are held the Monday before the
sale from 10 a.m. to 4 p.m. Most auctions consist

of 100 to 500 lots. There is a 10% buyer's premium. Bids may be left or telephoned if the bidder is known to the auctioneers. Access by public transport by rail to Oxford Road or Manchester Piccadilly Road stations, or by bus on Oxford Road or Princess Street. There is no on-site parking, and street parking may be difficult to find, since the auctions are in central Manchester.

In addition, this firm holds bi-annual gala evening auctions in the spring and autumn of high quality items at selected venues. Contact the Auction Galleries for details.

Sales are held at and additional information can be obtained from Capes Dunn & Company, 38 Charles Street, Manchester M1 7DB, telephone (061) 273 1911 and 273 6060.

Prudential Fine Art Auctioneers
Sales held on Wednesdays and Thursdays at Trinity House, with viewing one or two days prior. Items offered include fine art, antiques, old and modern furniture, and effects. There is a 10% buyer's premium. Catalogues vary in price from 50p to £5. Trinity House is six miles north of the city centre, with parking nearby. Sales are held at and additional informaation can be obtained from Prudential Fine Art Auctioneers, Trinity House, 114 Northenden Road, Sale, Manchester, Greater Manchester M33 3HD, telephone (061) 962 9237.

Margam, West Glamorgan (Wales)

"Antique Dealers' Fair of Wales" third weekend of May (Friday 11 a.m. to 8 p.m., Saturday and Sunday 11 a.m. to 6 p.m.) at Margam Castle in the Orangery, a stately home. This is one of the best antique fairs in Wales. All items are vetted. The dateline is 1880, though a very few more recent pieces are accepted. Food is available on the site. Access by car on M38 to Junction 49, then south to the castle on A48. Free parking is available on the grounds. Nearest railway station is 3 miles away in Port Talbot. For further information and exact sale dates, contact Robert Soper, Castle Fairs, Bowcliffe Road, Bramham,

Wetherby, North Yorkshire, LS23 9JS, telephone
(0937) 845829.

Margate, Kent

Stewart, Gore, Auctioneers and Valuers
Auctions every four to six Thursdays (varies),
starting at 9 a.m., are held at the Salerooms,
Clifton Place, Margate. All types of items are of-
fered—modern, antique, and in between. For
exact sale dates and further information, contact
Stewart, Gore, 102 Northdown Road, Margate,
Kent, telephone (0843) 221528.

Marlborough, Wiltshire

"Oxfam Antiques Fair" second Friday and Saturday of May at the Town Hall in the Marlborough
town centre. Friday the hours are 11 a.m. to 8
p.m., and Saturday hours are 10 a.m. to 5 p.m.
No train service is available; parking is available
on nearby streets and carparks. For further information contact Mrs. L. Smith, Marlborough &
District Oxfam Committee, 27 Oxford Street,
Ramsbury,   Marlborough,   Wiltshire   SN8,
telephone (0672) 20354.

Hamptons Pocock & Lear Auctioneers
Auctions of antiques are held the first Wednesday of every month at 10 a.m., and of used goods
in general and garden furniture on the second
Wednesday of every month at 10 a.m. at the
Marlborough   Salerooms   at   the   auctioneers'
premises. Catalogues are issued about two weeks
before the antiques sale. Previews are held the
Tuesday before the auction from 9 a.m. to 7 p.m.
and from 9 a.m. on the sale day. Auctions consist
of up to 1000 lots. There is no buyer's premium.
Bids may be left or telephoned if the bidder is
known to the auctioneers. Purchases must be
removed by 5 p.m. on the Thursday after the
sale, or storage charges of £1 per day will accrue.
There is no easy access by public transport to
Marlborough. Parking is available on High
Street, the George Lane car park, or in the
Waitrose car park in front of the saleroom. Sales

are held at and further information can be obtained from Hamptons Pocock & Lear, 20 High Street, Marlborough, Wiltshire SN8 1AA, telephone (0672) 55181, fax (0672) 55882.

Middlesbrough, Cleveland

Flea market and collectors' fair several times per year on several Saturdays at the Town Hall on Albert Road. This is a large indoor regional fair in an out-of-the-way part of England. All types of antiques, collectables, and bric-a-brac are offered. Parking (charge) is available a little way east on Corporation Road. Admission is 50p. Access by rail to Middlesbrough, then walk about 200 yards on Albert Street. Exact dates and further information are available from Panda Promotions, 24 Westgate, Honley, Huddersfield, West Yorkshire HD7 2AA, telephone (0484) 666144.

Midhurst, West Sussex

King & Chasemore (incorporating G. Knight & Son) Auctions
Auctions are held every six weeks on a Thursday (call for exact schedule) at the saleroom on Bepton Road, Midhurst. The sales include antiques, reproductions, miscellaneous collectables, and ordinary household items. For information and exact dates, contact King & Chasemore, West Street, Midhurst, West Sussex GU29 9NG, telephone (073081) 2456.

Mildenhall, Suffolk

Antique and collectors' fair Sundays in January, April, September, and October from 11 a.m. to 5 p.m. at the Bob Hope Recreation Centre, RAF Mildenhall. There are 70 stands. Admission is free and parking is available. For information and exact dates, contact Lorna Quick, Fourseason Fairs, 6 Post Office Lane, Glemsford, Suffolk CO10 7RA, telephone (0787) 281855.

Minehead, Somerset

Gribble Booth & Taylor, Auctioneers
Sales are held every three weeks on Thursdays
at 10.30 a.m. at the Mart Road Salesrooms,
Minehead (telephone (064) 3646). There are
usually 600 to 700 lots. No buyer's premium is
charged. Items are mostly general furniture, including antiques and modern items. Viewing is
held on the day before the sale from 9 a.m. to 4
p.m., and bids may be left with the sale porter.
Catalogues are available on request. Parking is
available nearby. For further information, contact Gribble Booth & Taylor, 32 The Avenue,
Minehead, Somerset TA24 5AZ, telephone (0643)
2281, fax (0643) 7523.

Mundford near Brandon, Suffolk

Antiques fair first Saturday, Sunday and Monday of May (Bank Holiday) from 10 a.m. to 4 p.m.
at Lyford Hall in Mundford, about 2 miles north
of Brandon and 5 miles northwest of Thetford.
This regional fair has about 70 stands, mostly
dealers. In the area, follow the yellow AA signs to
the fair. Organised by Crown Antiques Fairs, 55
Barton Road, Cambridge, Cambridgeshire CB3
9LG, telephone (0223) 353016.

Nately Scures near Hook, Hampshire

Antiques fair last Sunday of every month at the
Basingstoke Country Hotel on A30 west of Hook.
This show has about 40 dealers, mostly of small
items including silver, linens, crystal, porcelains,
and prints. Organised by Stagecoach Antique
Fairs, telephone (0628) 23970.

Newark, Nottinghamshire

Antique & Collectors' Fair the last Tuesday of
February, second Tuesday of June, third Tuesday
of August and last Tuesday of October at the
Newark & Nottinghamshire Showground from 8

a.m. (7 a.m. with an antique dealer business card). More than 1000 stands are at every show, as many as 2000 in October, making these some of the largest one-day shows in Britain. Tens of thousands of visitors crowd the grounds. Access by car: follow yellow AA signs to the free car parking area, or take chartered buses from London (call 01-249 4050 for information). These shows offer shipping services from small consignments to shipping containers. All types of items, including a lot of furniture, are represented at this show. Admission is £2 before 9 a.m., £1 after. Organised by Geoffrey Whitaker Antique Fairs, 25B Portland Street, Newark, Nottinghamshire NG24 1LP, (0636) 702326.

Newcastle-upon-Tyne, Tyne and Wear

Tynemouth Flea and Antique Market, held every Saturday from April to October at the Tynemouth Metro station, in Tynemouth, five miles east of the city centre. This market is a general market with a fair representation of antiques, bric-a-brac, collectables, and just plain junk. Access by Metro to the Tynemouth station; free parking is available in the area. Organised by Newcastle City Council, Estate & Property Department, Civic Centre, Newcastle-upon-Tyne, Tyne and Wear, telephone (091) 232 8520.

Flea market every other Saturday, year round, at the Guildhall, Quayside, Newcastle-upon-Tyne. This is a general market with good quantities of antiques, bric-a-brac, and other miscellaneous odds and ends. This indoor market is accessible by public transport, but parking in the area is difficult. Information available from the Newcastle City Council, Estate & Property Department, Civic Centre, Newcastle-upon-Tyne, Tyne and Wear, telephone (091) 232 8520.

"The Newcastle-upon-Tyne Antiques Fair" during the first week in May for four days at the Holiday Inn Hotel on the Great North Road (hotel telephone (091) 365432). This is one of the major fairs of top-quality antiques in northern England. All types of antiques are offered, including furniture, silver, porcelain and pottery, paintings, and other items. All items are vetted by Phillips and Bonhams experts. The dateline is 1860. Admission is £2.50. Parking is available in the park. For exact dates and further information, contact Robert Bailey Antiques Fair, 1 Roll Gardens, Gants Hill, Ilford, Essex 1G2 6TN, telephone 01-550 5435.

Newcastle-under-Lyme, Staffordshire

Antique and junk market every Tuesday from 8 a.m. until early afternoon in the town centre. All types of items are available, with an emphasis on small items. Most markets have from 40 to 70 stands. Information from Alan Kipping, Wonder Whistle Enterprises, 1 Ritson Road, London E8, telephone 01-249 4050.

Antiques Fair one day twice a year at the end of April and beginning of September from 10 a.m. to 5 p.m. at the Sports Centre at Keele University west of the city on A525. This site is also used for crafts fairs. For exact dates and further information, contact the Sports Centre, Keele University, Newcastle-under-Lyme, Staffordshire, telephone (0782) 621111.

Newton Abbot, Devon

"Giant Antiques & Collectors' Fair" third Wednesday and Thursday of March, June, and September at the racecourse along the river. This is a regional fair. Admission is charged, but parking is free. Organised by Gerry Mosdell, West Country Antiques & Collectors Fairs, The Dartmoor Antiques Centre, off West Street, Ashburton, Devon, telephone (0364) 52182.

Michael J. Bowman, Auctioneer
Auctions are usually held on the third or fourth Friday of every month at 11 a.m., often at the Chudleigh Town Hall. Auctions include antiques and used goods, including appliances(!), books, pictures, glass, ceramics and porcelains, clocks and jewelry, furniture, and miscellaneous items.

Catalogues are available before the sale, price 40p. No items can be taken until the sale is over, but all items must be paid for and removed the day of the sale. The buyer's premium is 5%. Bids can be left, mailed, or telephoned, but a banker's reference or deposit may be required. For further information and exact sale dates, contact Michael J. Bowman, Auctioneer, 6 Haccombe House near Netherton, Newton Abbot, Devon TQ12 4SJ, telephone (0626) 872890.

Northampton, Northamptonshire

"The Castle Ashby Antiques Fair" held five days in late August at Castle Ashby, a Tudor historic home east of the city. Only top-quality antiques are offered, including furniture, silver, porcelain and pottery, paintings, and other items. All items are vetted by experts from BADA or LAPADA. The dateline is from 1885 (furniture) to 1920 (artwork). Admission is £2.50. Access by car on A428. Free parking is available on the grounds. For exact dates and further information, contact Robert Bailey Antiques Fair, 1 Roll Gardens, Gants Hill, Ilford, Essex 1G2 6TN, telephone 01-550 5435.

Lowery Antique Auctions
Sales approximately every two months on the premises, 24 Bridge Street, Northampton, or at the owner's premises or in local villages. Catalogues are £1, including postage. For details, contact Lowery Antique Auctions, 24 Bridge Street, Northampton, Northamptonshire NN1 1NT, telephone (0604) 21561.

Heathcote Ball & Co., Fine Art Auctioneers
Sales of general antiques, including furniture, pictures, objets d'art, silver, and porcelain are held every 10 to 12 weeks on Fridays at 10.30 a.m. at the Albion Auction Rooms. Viewing is the day before from 10 a.m. to 4 p.m. and the morning of the sale. Catalogues are £1 to £2.

Also, there are general household goods sales every other Saturday at 10.30 a.m. (no catalogues). Viewing is the day before from 1 p.m. to 5 p.m. The buyer's premium is 7-1/2% at the antiques sales and and 10% at the general household sales. Bids may be left or made by post or telephone. Storage charges may be levied for lots not cleared withing seven days of sale. Lots purchased in the general sale must be cleared by 12.30 p.m. the following Monday. The Auction Room is five minutes walk from the city centre, with a car park less than a minute a away. The British Rail station is about half a mile away. For information, contact Heathcote Ball & Co., Albion Auction Rooms, Commercial Street, Northampton, Northamptonshire NN1 1PJ, telephone (0604) 22735.

Norwich, Norfolk

Antiques and collectables market most (but not every) Wednesdays from 9.30 a.m. to 3.30 p.m. in the cloisters at St. Andrews Hall on George Street in the city centre. The number of vendors varies; all types of antiques are offered. There is no admission fee, but there is access for the disabled. Parking (pay) is available behind the hall off Elm Hill. For information, contact Mr. A. Bailey, Cloisters Antique Market, St. Andrews Hall, Norwich, Norfolk, telephone (0603) 628477.

Nottingham, Nottinghamshire

Neales of Nottingham, Auctioneers
Sales of antique and modern silver, jewellery and bijouterie, European and Oriental ceramics and glass, and Oriental works of art are held Thursdays, bi-monthly, at 10.30 a.m. Sales of paintings, drawings, prints, books, oriental carpets and rugs, metalwork, weapons, and selected English and continental furniture and works of art are held on Fridays, bi- monthly, at 10.30 a.m. Viewing for both sales is the Sunday prior to the sale from 2 p.m. to 5 p.m., the Tuesday prior to the sale from 10 a.m. to 8 p.m., and the morning of the sale from 9 a.m. Catalogues are £3.50, £4 by post.

Sales of postcards, cigarette cards, autographs, manuscripts, and ephemera are held on Thursday and Friday every six weeks at noon.

Viewing is Wednesday prior to the sale from 10 a.m. to 5.30 p.m. and the morning before the sale from 9 a.m.

Collective sales of antique, reproduction and later furnishings, shipping goods, and decorative items are held every Monday. Viewing is Saturday prior to the sale from 9 a.m. to 12.30 p.m. and the morning of the sale from 9 a.m.

The buyer's premium is 10%. Sales are held at and information is available from Neales of Nottingham, 190-192 Mansfield Road, Nottingham, Nottinghamshire, NG1 3HX, telephone (0602) 624141, fax (0602) 607456.

Orsett, Essex

"Bank Holiday Antiques Drive-in and Country Fair" first weekend of May (Bank Holiday) at Orsett Hall near Orsett. Access from A13 east from London to Orsett. Organised by Stephen Charles, Basildon, telephone (0268) 774977.

Ower, Hampshire

(Please also see Brockenhurst, Lyndhurst, and Southampton.)

Antiques and collectors' fairs one Sunday of every other month (exact day varies) at the New Forest Moat House Hotel on A31 in Ower. This is a small, regional fair. Most items are small; there's not much furniture. The dateline is 1930. Free parking is available on the grounds. For exact dates and further information, contact Kingston Promotions, 157 Plymouth Drive, Hill Head, Fareham, Hampshire PO14 3SN, telephone (0329) 661780.

Oxford, Oxfordshire

Phillips in Oxford
Auctions of all types of antiques and collectors' items take place almost every week at the three salerooms. Sales of Victoriana take place every three weeks at 10 a.m. on Tuesdays; furniture,

usually at 11 a.m. on first the Thursday of every
month except January and August; and paintings, rugs, silver, jewellery, books, and wine
every three months. A free schedule of sales is
available upon request. Catalogues are issued
before every sale, priced between £1 and £2.50.
Viewing is held on Saturday morning and the
day before for Victoriana sales and for two days
before the sale on all other sales from 9 a.m. to 5
p.m. and the day of the sale from 9 a.m. Bids may
be left or made by post or telephone. The buyer's
premium is 10%. All purchases must be paid for
and removed within two days unless otherwise
arranged. The salerooms are on the west side of
Oxford, a few hundred yards toward the city
centre from the British Rail station. Some free
parking is available on the street in front of the
saleroom, and more is available (for a charge) at
the car park at the east end of Park End Street.
Sales are held at and further information is
available from Phillips in Oxford, 39 Park End
Street, Oxford, Oxfordshire OX1 1JD, telephone
(0865) 723524, fax (0865) 791064.

Par, Cornwall

Phillips in Cornwall
Each month there is a major auction at the Cornubia Hall salerooms and each fortnight a sale of
Victorian and later items, including shipping
goods. On alternate months, the sale is spread
over two days and includes ceramics, glass, silver, silver-plated items, jewellery, bijouterie, pictures, carpets, clocks, metalware, and period furniture. The other monthly sales are one-day
events of ceramics, glass, clocks, metalware, and
furniture. Every three months there is a
collectors' sale of books, postcards, cigarett cards,
dolls, teddy bears, soldiers and other toys and
models, coins, and medals. Catalogues are priced
from £1.50 to £3.50. Sales usually begin at 10.30
a.m. There are three viewing days before each
sale, with one until 7 p.m. Bids may be left or
made by post or telephone. For further information and exact sale dates contact Phillips in
Cornwall, Cornubia Hall, Par, Cornwall PL24

2AQ, telephone (072681) 4047, fax (072681) 7979.

Pattingham, West Midlands

Antique fair last Sunday of February, April, October, and December. This is a new, small antique fair with about 30 dealers. Organised by Waverley Fairs, Boreley Cottage, Boreley near Ombersley, Worcester WR9 0HS, telephone (0205) 620697.

Peterborough, Cambridgeshire

"International Antiques and Collectors' Fair" last Tuesday of September at the East of England Showground along the A1 road. Hundreds of stands inside, plus trucks and outdoor spaces. This large fair is one of the largest autumn fairs and has many services, including food, packing and shipping services, and money exchange. Open to members of the antiques trade at 6.30 a.m. and to the public at 8 a.m., and closes at 4 p.m. Admission is £1. Parking is free. Organised by Crown Antiques Fairs, 55 Barton Road, Cambridge, Cambridgeshire CB3 9LG, telephone (0223) 353016.

Petworth, West Sussex

(Please also see Billingshurst.)

"The Petworth Antiques Fair" New Year's weekend, weekend at end March, first of April, and the first weekend of September at Seaford College near Petworth village. This is a good regional fair of good-quality antiques, including furniture, silver, jewellery, porcelain, paintings and prints, and other items. All items are vetted. The dateline is from 1885 (furniture) to 1920 (paintings and ceramics). Admission is £2.50, free to members of the antiques trade with a business card. Access is only by car. Parking is available at the fair. For exact dates and further information, contact Robert Bailey Antiques

Fairs, 1 Roll Gardens, Gants Hill, Ilford, Essex
1G2 6TN, telephone 01-550 5435.

Plymouth, Devon

Plymouth flea market every Bank Holiday
weekend at the Guildhall at Royal Parade and
Armada Way. This is a regional fair with all
types of collectables, some antiques, and a bit of
junk. Admission 35p. Organised by P. Smith, 87
Pembroke Street, Sevon Port, Plymouth,
telephone (0752) 668837. Another organiser uses
this location at irregular but approximately
monthly intervals. For further information, contact A. Robins, Chapel Cottage, Cubert, near
Newquay, Cornwall, telephone (0637) 830566.
Parking at this location is available in the adjoining council car park.

Michael Newman Fine Art Auctioneer
Sales of antiques and objets d'art are held the
first Tuesday of each month at 10 a.m. Viewing is
on the Saturday prior to the sale from 9 a.m. to
noon, Monday prior to the sale from 9 a.m. to 1
p.m. and 2.15 p.m. to 5 p.m., and on the morning
of sale from 9 a.m. to 10 a.m. Coins, medals, and
tokens are offered three Fridays a year (in April,
August, and December) at 6 p.m., and on view on
the previous day from 9 a.m. to 5 p.m. and on the
day of sale from 9 a.m. Pictures, prints, and
maps are offered three Wednesdays a year (in
February, June, and October) at 2.30 p.m., and
on view on Tuesday prior to the sale from 9 a.m.
to 1 p.m. and 2.15 p.m. to 5 p.m. and on the
morning of sale from 9 a.m. to 2.30 p.m. Books,
manuscripts, postcards, and ephemera are offered three Wednesdays a year (in March, July,
and November) at 10.30 a.m., and are on view on
Tuesday prior to the sale from 9 a.m to 1 p.m.
and 2.15 p.m. to 5 p.m. and on the morning of
sale from 9 a.m. to 10.30 p.m. Twelve-month's
catalogues range in price from £3 to £18, depending on categories requested. The buyer's
premium is 10%. Car parking is available at
Drake Circus multi-storey car park about 200
yards away. Sales are held at and information is
available from Michael Newman Fine Arts Auc-

tioneer, Kinterbury House, St. Andrew's Cross, Plymouth, Devon PL1 2DG, telephone (0752) 669298.

Phillips in Plymouth
Sales of pictures, fine furniture, jewellery, silver, works of art, and ceramics are held every four to six weeks on Wednesdays at 11 a.m. Preview days are the Monday prior to the sale from 9 a.m. to 5 p.m. and and Tuesday prior to the sale from 9 a.m. to 7 p.m., and also the morning of the sale. Catalogues vary from £1.50 to £3. Victoriana sales of general furnishings and household items of Victorian, Edwardian, and later items are held every fortnight on a Tuesday at 11 a.m. Preview day is the Monday prior from 9 a.m. and 7 p.m., and also the morning of the sale. Catalogues are £1. The buyer's premium is 10%. Car parking is limited. Sales are held at and information is available from Phillips in Plymouth, Armada Street, North Hill, Plymouth, Devon PL4 8LS, telephone (0752) 673504.

Portishead, Avon

(Please also see Bristol and Yatton.)

Antiques and collectors' fair at usually on the last Sunday of five months of the year and Bank Holiday Monday in May and August from 10 a.m. (9 a.m. for members of the antiques trade) to 5 p.m. at Somerset hall. This is a local fair, with some antiques and collectables. Admission is 25p, but is free to accompanied children. Access from M5 Junction 19, then on A369 to Portishead. A large car park is available at the fair. Access by rail to Portishead, then walk. For further information, contact the organiser at Yatton (0934) 838187.

Portsmouth and Southsea, Hampshire

(Please also see Botley, Chichester and Southampton.)

Antiques and collectors' fair the third Sunday of March, May, July, September, and November from 11 a.m. to 6 p.m. at the Guildhall in the city centre. This is a regional fair of antiques and collectables. Admission is 30p, but accompanied children are free. Access by car to any of the car parks in the city centre. Access by train to Portsmouth station, then walk about 100 yards south to the Guildhall. (The Tourist Information Centre is also in the Guildhall Square.) For further information, contact Kingston Promotions, 157 Plymouth Drive, Hill Head, Fareham, Hampshire PO14 3SN, telephone (0329) 661780.

Antiques and collectors' fair the first, second, or (most often) third Sunday of February, April, June, August, October, and December from 11 a.m. to 6 p.m. at the Crest Hotel on Pembroke Road in Southsea, about half a mile east of the Hoverport (hotel telephone (0705) 827651). This is a fair of regional interest. There is a good amount of silver, porcelain, and pottery, but little furniture or other large items. Admission is 30p, but accompanied children are free. Parking is available at or near the hotel. For exact dates and further information, contact Kingston Promotions, 157 Plymouth Drive, Hill Head, Fareham, Hampshire PO14 3SN, telephone (0329) 661780.

Preston, Lancashire

(Please also see Charnock Richard and Hurst Green.)

"Collectors' Market and Boot Sale" every Tuesday and Thursday from 8 a.m. to early afternoon (official closing 4 p.m.) under the old but open-air covered markets in the town centre. Up to 300 sellers of used goods and miscellaneous items sell all types of items. No new items are allowed in the Car Boot section of the market. Don't confuse this with the new items at the Monday, Wednesday, Friday, and Saturday market in the same location or the new, adjacent indoor marketplace just to the north! Access by public transport or walk to the city centre to the Head Post Office. Street parking is difficult or almost impossible, though there are pay car parks on Lancaster

Road and Ringway. Organised by Hoyle's Markets, telephone (0153) 725788.

"The Hoghton Tower Antiques Fair" last weekend of February and first weekend of December. This is a good-quality regional fair in a relatively depressed area. Only antiques dealers may sell, and all items are vetted. The dateline is from 1885 (furniture) to 1920 (pottery and paintings). Admission is £2.50 for the public but free to members of the antiques trade with a business card. Parking is available at the fair. For exact dates and further information, contact Robert Bailey Antiques Fairs, 1 Roll Gardens, Gants Hill, Ilford, Essex IG2 6TN, telephone 01-550 5435.

Redhill (near Reigate), Sussex

(Also please see Epsom.)

Antiques and collectors' fair the second Sunday of every month from 10 a.m. to 5 p.m. at Lakers Hotel, Redstone Hill, Redhill, Surrey. Access by train to Redhill, or drive. Organised by Ray Ratcliff, telephone 01-764 3602.

Retford, Nottinghamshire

(Note: this town is shown on some maps as "East Retford".)

Henry Spencer & Sons Ltd., Fine Art Auctioneers Auctions are held twice a year at 10 a.m. at the company's saleroom. A free schedule is available upon request. Most sales are specialized: for example, silver, silver plate, jewellery, and watches, or furniture, or pictures and paintings. Catalogues are issued at least one week before the sale, price from £1 to £3, and by annual subscription. Viewing is held the day before the sale from 10 a.m. to 3 p.m. Bids may be left, posted, or telephoned. The buyer's premium is 10%. Cars may be parked for £1 per day. Access by train to Retford from Kings Cross in London, then walk to the saleroom. Sales are held at and further information is available from Henry Spencer & Sons Ltd., 20 The Square, Retford, Nottinghamshire DN22 6DJ, telephone (0777) 708633, fax (0777) 709299.

Ringwood, Hampshire

Antique and Collectors' Fair last Sunday of every month (except June, July, and August) from 10.30 a.m. to 5 p.m. at the Crown Hotel. This small regional fair of approximately 20 stands offers small antiques and bric-a-brac. Parking is free; admission is 20p. Organised by Linda Forster, Forest Fairs, 28 Glenwood Road, West Moors, Dorset, telephone (0202) 875167.

Antique and collectors' fair on Easter Monday, Spring Bank Holiday (last Monday of May), August Bank Holiday Monday (last Monday of August) at the Avon Country Club. This is a moderately-sized regional fair with antiques and collectables. The dateline is around 1930, but this is not always monitored by the organisers. For further information, contact Kingston Promotions, 157 Plymouth Drive, Hill Head, Fareham, Hampshire PO14 3SN, telephone (0329) 661780.

Ripon, North Yorkshire

Flea market and collectors' fair on several Sundays (about six to eight weeks apart) from 9.30 a.m. to 5 p.m. at the racecourse southeast of town on B6265. This is a large regional fair, offering all types of collectables. Admission is 50p. Exact dates and further information are available from Panda Promotions, 24 Westgate, Honley, Huddersfield, West Yorkshire HD7 2AA, telephone (0484) 666144.

Romford, Essex

(Please also see London.)

Antique market as part of a gigantic market held on Wednesday, Friday, and especially Saturday from early morning until mid afternoon at the Market Place. This large market draws people from a large area. The general market is held in the Market Place, but the antiques market is held on North Street, outside the main market area. Dealers offer antiques, bric-a-brac, and reproductions in abundance. Access by car from London on A12. Parking is available in four large car parks. Access by British Rail to Romford station from Bethnal Green, or bus lines 66, 66A, 248, and 252.

Rotherham, South Yorkshire

Flea market and collectors' market on several Saturdays per year from 9.30 a.m. to 5 p.m. at Clifton Hall. This is a regional fair with all types of items. Admission is 50p. Exact dates and further information are available from Panda Promotions, 24 Westgate, Honley, Huddersfield, West Yorkshire, HD7 2AA, telephone (0484) 666144.

"The Ridings Antiques and Interior Design Fair" the third weekend of September (Friday 11 a.m. to 8 p.m., Saturday and Sunday 11 a.m. to 6 p.m.) at Wentworth House, a palatial 18th-century stately home. This is a very good regional antiques fair. All items are vetted. The dateline is 1880, though a very few more recent pieces are accepted. Access by car on M1 to Junction 35, then north on local roads to Wentworth House. Free parking is available on the grounds. Nearest railway station is 3 miles away in Rotherham. For further information and exact sale dates, contact Robert Soper, Castle Fairs, Bowcliffe Road, Bramham, Wetherby, North Yorkshire LS23 9JS, telephone (0937) 845829.

Royal Leamington Spa, Warwickshire

(Please see Leamington Spa, Warwickshire.)

Royal Tunbridge Wells, Kent

(Please see Tunbridge Wells, Kent.)

Rye, East Sussex

Prudential Fine Art, Auction & Estate Offices
Auctions of antiques and fine art are held the
first Friday of each month at 10 a.m. Previews
are held the afternoon before the sale from 1 to 5
p.m. The sales are held at the Rye Auction Galleries, Cinque Ports Street. For information, contact Prudential Fine Art Auction & Estate Offices, Cinque Ports Street, Rye, East Sussex,
telephone (0797) 222124.

St. Ives, Cambridgeshire

(Please also see Huntingdon.)

Antiques and collectors' fair, five per year,
January 1 and 2, Easter Sunday and Monday,
second May Bank Holiday, August Bank Holiday
Sunday and Monday, and the third weekend of
November, most days from 11 a.m. to 5 p.m.) at
St. Ives recreation centre (telephone (0480)
63028). These are good regional fairs. All types of
collectables and other items are offered. The
dateline is 1930. Admission is 50p, but free to the
antiques trade. This fair is signposted, and parking is available nearby. Organised by Herridges
Antiques & Collectors Fairs, Chanctonbury, 8
Kimbolton Avenue, Bedford, Bedfordshire MK40
3AD, telephone (0234) 45725.

Prudential Fine Arts Auctioneers
Antique auctions are held every four weeks on
Tuesday at 10 a.m.; previews are held the Saturday before the sale from 9 a.m. until noon, and
Monday from 9 a.m. to 5 p.m. Catalogues are
issued and usually cost £1. Auctions include all
types of antiques, including silver, paintings, furniture, glass, and ceramics. There are also sales
of household items and used items every other
Saturday at 10 a.m.; no catalogues are issued
and viewing is the morning of the sale from 9

a.m. There is no buyer's premium. Bids may be left or posted but must be in writing. No personal cheques are accepted without a bank guarantee or a credit card. Sales are held at and further information is available from Prudential Fine Arts Auctioneers, St. Ives Auction Rooms, The Market, St. Ives, Cambridgeshire PE17 4JA, telephone (0480) 68144.

Salisbury, Wiltshire

Antique market every Tuesday in the hall of the United Reformed Church in Fisherton Street only a few blocks from the famed cathedral. This market is as much a rummage sale as an antique market; therefore, finds can be made, but lots of uninteresting items must be looked at as well. Parking is available in the car park north of the church, more easily accessible from Churchill Way West.

"The Wilton House Antiques Fair" held one weekend in mid March. This is a good-quality regional fair on the grounds of a historic stately home; only antiques dealers may sell, and all items are vetted. The dateline is from 1885 (furniture) to 1920 (pottery and paintings). Admission is £2.50, but is free to members of the antiques trade with a business card. For exact dates and further information, contact Robert Bailey Antiques Fairs, 1 Roll Gardens, Gants Hill, Ilford, Essex 1G2 6TN, telephone 01-550 5435.

Wooley & Wallis Auctioneers
Antique furniture sales are held monthly on Thursdays and feature European porcelain and glass, Oriental furniture and works of art, eastern carpets and rugs, and textiles. General household sales are held fortnightly on Fridays. There are quarterly sales on Wednesdays of plated items and silver and jewellery, objets of vertu, and of selected oil paintings and watercolours. Catalogues are £3. Parking on the premises is limited, but there is a large public car park at the city centre. Hourly trains run from London. Sales are held at and information

is available from Wooley & Wallis, The Castle Auction Mart, Salisbury, Wiltshire SP1 3SU, telephone (0722) 411422.

Sandwich, Kent

(Please also see Deal.)

"Riverside Annual Bank Holiday Boot Fair", held on Bank Holiday Sunday afternoon and Monday from 10 a.m. to 5 p.m. at Gazen Salts. This is a large regional boot fair. Admission is 25p per person. Thousands of cars can be parked in the nearby car park. Organised by East Kent Fairs, 201 London Road, Dover, Kent CT17 0TF, telephone (0304) 201644.

Sawbridgeworth, Hertfordshire

(Please also see Epping, Harlow, Hatfield, Hertford, and Ware.)

Antiques and collectors' fair five Saturdays per year from 10.30 a.m. to 4 p.m. at the Memorial Hall, The Forebury. This is a local fair, with about 40 dealers of antiques, collectables, and other odds and ends. Admission is 50p. Parking is available near the hall. For further information, contact Bartholomew Fayres, Executive House, The Maltings, Station Road, Sawbridgeworth, Hertfordshire CM21 9JX, telephone (0279) 725809 and 725699.

Scarborough, North Yorkshire

Ward Price & Co.
Sales of general household furnishings and effects are held fortnightly at the Royal Auction Rooms, 14-15 Queen Street. Specialist catalogue sales are also held at regular intervals. For exact dates and futher information, contact Ward Price & Co., 14-15 Queen Street, Scarborough, North Yorkshire YO11 1HQ, telephone (0723) 353581.

Sevenoaks, Kent

Prudential Fine Art Auctioneers
Fine arts and antique auctions are held every six
weeks on Wednesdays at the Argyle Salerooms,
Argyle Road, Sevenoaks. Each sale contains
about 1000 lots. The buyer's premium is 10%.
For further information, contact Prudential Fine
Art Auctioneers, 49 London Road, Sevenoaks,
Kent TN13 1AR, telephone (0732) 740310

Sheffield, South Yorkshire

Flea market and collectors' fair several Saturdays per year from 9.30 a.m. to 5 p.m. at Roxy's
Disco. All types of antiques and collectables are
offered at this indoor fair, for which admission is
charged. Over 150 vendors usually offer their
goods. Admission is 50p. Exact dates and further
information are available from Panda Promotions, 24 Westgate, Honley, Huddersfield, West
Yorkshire HD7 2AA, telephone (0484) 666144.

A.E. Dowse & Son Fine Art Auctioneers
Monthly sales are held for general antiques,
fortnightly for household items, and quarterly
sales of fine arts and also of diecast and tinplate
toys. Viewing is the day or morning prior to
sales. Sales are held at and information is available from A.E. Dowse & Son Fine Art Auctioneers, Cornwall Galleries, Scotland Street,
Sheffield, South Yorkshire S3 7DE, telephone
(0742) 725858.

Shepton Mallet, Somerset

(Please also see Wells.)

"Annual Summer Antiques Fair and Drive-in"
second Tuesday of September at the Royal Bath
& West Showground south of the town on A371.
There are 750 stands. Parking is available on the
grounds, but this fair is not accessible by public
transport. Organised by Ms. Anne Stroud, Merlin

Fairs, Will-o-the-Wisp, Moorland near Bridgwater, Somerset, telephone (0278) 691616.

"Antiques & Collectors' Fairs" usually held the
fourth weekend of April and the third weekend of
November from 10 a.m. to 5 p.m. at the Royal
Bath and West Showground south of the town on
A371. These are good indoor regional fairs, with
all types of antiques and collectables. Dateline is
1930. Admission is £1, free to members of the
antiques trade. Free parking is available on the
grounds, but this fair is not accessible by public
transport. Organised by Ms. Anne Stroud, Merlin
Fairs, Will-o-the-Wisp, Moorland near Bridgwater, Somerset, telephone (0278) 691616.

Sherborne, Dorset

Phillips in Sherborne
Auctions are held every other Tuesday at 10 a.m.
at the salerooms. Each auction is a specialized
category, such as "Victorian Furniture",
"Ceramics", or "Victoriana". A catalogue is published several weeks before each sale, and usually costs £1 to £2. Viewing is held the day before
the sale and on the morning of the sale. Bids may
be left, posted, or telephoned. The bidder's
premium is 10%. For further information, contact Phillips in Sherborne, Long Street Sale
Rooms, Long Street, Sherborne, Dorset DT9 3BS,
telephone (0935) 815271, fax (0935) 816416.

Shiplake, Oxfordshire

Duncan Vincent Fine Art Auctioneers
Collective antiques sales are held one Thursday
a month (except February, June, August, and
November) at Shiplake Memorial Hall at 10 a.m.
Viewing is from noon to 6 p.m. on the day before
the sale and rom 8.30 a.m. to 9.30 a.m. on the
day of xsale. Admission is by catalogue, £1.25
(admits two). Memorial Hall is off A4155 six
miles northeast of Reading. Parking on the road
across from the Hall. An Alder Valley bus service
is a few minutes walk. For exact dates and further information, contact Duncan Vincent Fine

Art Auctioneers, 105 London Street, Reading, Berkshire RG1 3LF, telephone (0734) 589502 and 594748.

Shrewsbury, Shropshire

"Annual Shropshire Antiques Fair" second Tuesday to Thursday of February and July from 11 a.m. to 9 p.m. at the Lion Hotel, Wyle Cop (hotel telephone (0743) 52107). Only antiques (dateline 1890) may be sold and all purchases carry a money-back guarantee of authenticity. Admission is charged. This is a large, well-established antiques fair. Organised by Tony Keniston, Hopton Castle, Craven Arms, Shropshire SY7 0QJ, telephone (05474) 356.

South Darenth, Kent

Kent Sales Auctioneers
Sales of militaria, including guns, swords, uniforms, Nazi items, Japanese items, Eastern and ethnic items, medals, and badges, are held every six weeks on Wednesdays. Preview days are on the Saturday and Monday prior to the sale and on sale day between 11 a.m. and 2 p.m. Catalogues are £22 per annum. Car parking is available, and the Farningham Road railway station is close by, with trains hourly from London (Victoria station). For dates and information, contact Kent Sales, "Giffords", Holmesdale Road, South Darenth, Kent DA4 9AF, telephone (0322) 864919, telex 896691 KENT SALES G.

Southampton, Hampshire

(Please also see Winchester.)

"Annual Stamp and Postcard Fair" first Sunday of May from 11 a.m. to 5 p.m. at Southampton Guildhall. This is the largest stamp and postcard fair in the region, with more than 60 vendors. Free parking is available next door in the car park. For further information, contact Ron Emmott Productions, 2 Fourways, Church Hill, West

End, Southampton, Hampshire SO3 3AU, telephone (0703) 474862.

"Special Summer Antique Event" second Sunday of June from 11 a.m. to 5 p.m. at Southampton Guildhall. This is a large indoor event with antiques of all types, including silver, brass, clocks, porcelain and pottery, and other items, but not much furniture. Admission is 35p. Free parking is available next door in the car park. For further information, contact Ron Emmott Productions, 2 Fourways, Church Hill, West End, Southampton, Hampshire SO3 3AU, telephone (0703) 474862.

"Antique and Bric-a-Brac Marquee" first weekend of July (Friday, Saturday, Sunday) on the Southampton Common about one mile north of the city centre on The Avenue. This is a large regional fair, with hundreds of vendors of antiques, collectables, and just bric-a-brac and junk. Parking is available nearby. For further information, contact Ron Emmott Productions, 2 Fourways, Church Hill, West End, Southampton, Hampshire SO3 3AU, telephone (0703) 474862.

"Collectorama" second Sunday of October from 11 a.m. to 5 p.m. at Southampton Guildhall. This is an event for collectors of all types of things, from antiques to corkscrews. Admission is 35p. Parking is available next door in the car park. For further information, contact Ron Emmott Productions, 2 Fourways, Church Hill, West End, Southampton, Hampshire SO3 3AU, telephone (0703) 474862.

Stafford, Staffordshire

"Stafford Giant Antique Fairs" three-day fairs held six times per year (February, April, June, August, August, and December) from 10 a.m. to 5 p.m. at Bingley Hall at the Country Showground, A518 Weston. There are also three one-day "Giant Antique and Collectors Fairs" in March, July, and November from 9.30 a.m. to 4 p.m. at the same Hall. These are large regional fairs, with between 300 and 500 stalls at each. All types of items are available. The dateline is

1930; new items and reproductions are prohibited. Admission is £1, or 50p for people over 65. Shipping company representatives are available at these fairs. The County Showground can be reached by from Junction 14 of the M6. A large free car park is on the showgrounds. This fair is not easily accessible by public transport, but trains from London (Euston) go to Stafford. Organised by Bowman Antiques Fairs, P.O. Box 37, Otley, West Yorkshire LS21 3AD, telephone (0943) 465782 or (0532) 843333.

Stamford, Lincolnshire

Antiques and collectors' fair, four per year, third Saturday and Sunday of February, second Saturday and Sunday of April, second Saturday and Sunday of August, and third Saturday and Sunday of October (Saturday from 10 a.m. to 5 p.m. and Sunday from 11 a.m. to 5 p.m.) at the Stamford Boys Public School. This is a good regional fair, with all types of small antiques and collectables. The dateline is 1930. Admission is 50p, but free to members of the antiques trade. The fair is signposted and parking is available nearby. Organised by Herridges Antiques & Collectors Fairs, Chanctonbury, 8 Kimbolton Avenue, Bedford, Bedfordshire MK40 3AD, telephone (0234) 45725.

Stanmore, Middlesex

"Antique & Collectors Fair" one Sunday in December from 10.30 a.m. to 5 p.m. at The Royal National Orthopædic Hospital, Louis Fleischmann House, Brockley Hill, Stanmore. There are more than 70 stalls. For information, contact Bartholomew Fayres, Executive House, The Maltings, Station Road, Sawbridgeworth, Hertfordshire CM21 9JX, telephone (0279) 725809 and 725699.

Stevenage, Hertfordshire

(Please also see Luton.)

"Antique & Collectors Fair" three Saturdays a
year from 10.30 a.m. to 4 p.m. at Stevenage Moat
House Hotel, High Street, Old Town, Stevenage
(hotel telephone (0438) 359111). There are more
than 40 stalls. For information and exact sale
dates, contact Bartholomew Fayres, Executive
House, The Maltings, Station Road, Sawbridgeworth, Hertfordshire CM21 9JX, telephone
(0279) 725809 and 725699.

Stockport, Cheshire

(Please also see Manchester.)

Burlings St. Mary's Auction Rooms
Auctions are held every other Tuesday at 11 a.m.
at the Auction Rooms. Auctions include antiques,
secondhand goods, and bric-a-brac of all types.
Viewing is Monday before the sale from noon to
7 p.m. Buyer's premium is 10% including VAT.
Free parking is available on the site. Access by
train to Disley railway station. Sales are held at
and further information is available from
Andrew McCann, Burlings St. Mary's Auction
Rooms, Buxton Old Road, Disley, Stockport,
Cheshire SK12 2BB, telephone (0663) 64854.

Stockbridge, Hampshire

(Please also see Salisbury.)

"Antique and Collectors' Fair" occasionally on
Saturday from 2 p.m. to 6 p.m. at Marsh Court
School. This is a very small local sale, with 15 to
20 stands. Free parking is available. Organised
by Linda Forster, Forest Fairs, 28 Glenwood
Road, West Moors, Dorset, telephone (0202)
875167.

Stratford-Upon-Avon, Warwickshire

Bigwood Auctioneers Ltd.
Auctions are held every Friday at 11 a.m. at the salerooms. These sales are specialized: silver, furniture, and books are some categories. Catalogues are issued in advance of all sales and cost £2. Viewing is held the two days before each sale from 9 a.m. to 5.30 p.m. Sales are held at and further information is available from Bigwood Auctioneers Ltd., The Old School, Tiddington, Stratford-upon-Avon, Warwickshire CV37 7AW, telephone (0789) 69415, fax (0789) 292686.

Stretford, Greater Manchester

(Please also see Manchester.)

Antiques fair first Friday, Saturday, and Sunday of May (Bank Holiday) at the Stretford Sports Centre, near Junction 7 of the M63 motorway, along Chester Road, A5067. Organised by Dualco Promotions, telephone (061) 766 2012.

Sudbury, Suffolk

Antiques fair second Saturday and Sunday of May at the Sudbury Town Hall. Follow the yellow AA signs to the fair. Organised by Crown Antiques Fairs, 55 Barton Road, Cambridge, Cambridgeshire CB3 9LG, telephone (0223) 353016.

Swindon, Wiltshire

Allen & Harris—The Planks Salerooms
Auctions of used items and other odds and ends, including quantities of furniture, are held every Saturday at 10 a.m. The last Saturday of every month, an antique and collector's auction is held at 10.30 a.m. In addition, specialist sales of period furniture, silver, and fine art are held bimonthly. Viewing for all sales is held on the day before the sale from 1 p.m. to 7 p.m. Catalogues

are available (usually £2) for antique and collector's sales only. A free schedule of all auctions is available upon request. Bids may be left, posted, or telephoned if you're known to the auctioneers. The buyer's premium is 5%. The auction rooms are in the centre of the Old Town; parking is available across the street in a car park. Information is available from and sales are held at the Allen & Harris—The Planks Salerooms, Old Town, Swindon, Wiltshire SN3 1QP, telephone (0793) 615915.

Tarporley

(Please see Beeston.)

Tatton Hall near Knutsford, Cheshire

(Please also see Knutsford.)

"The Tatton Park Antiques Fair" first week of October at Tatton Park (a historic house). On most days, the fair is open from 11 a.m. to 9 p.m. This is a good regional fair, with approximately 120 dealers. This fair prohibits new work and reproductions. Access by car: M6 to Junction 19, then follow yellow AA signs to the fair. Parking is available on site. Organised by Robert Bailey Antiques Fairs, 1 Roll Gardens, Gants Hill, Ilford, Essex IG2 6TN, telephone 01-550 5435.

Taunton, Somerset

"Taunton Antiques Fair" held on a Friday and Saturday in September, from 2 p.m. to 8 p.m. the first day and 10 a.m. to 5 p.m. the second day, at The County Hotel, Taunton (hotel telephone (0823) 87651). Organised by Gerry Mosdell, West Country Antiques & Collectors Fairs, The Dartmoore Antiques Center, off West Street, Ashburton, Devon TQ13 7DV, telephone (0364) 52182.

"Taunton Antiques Centre", with 85 independent dealers, is open every Monday, including Bank

Holidays, from 9 a.m. to 4 p.m. Admission is free. Car parks are nearby and some parking is available on the premises. For information, contact Michael Carter, Taunton Antiques Centre, 27-29 Silver Street, Taunton, Somerset TA1 3DH, telephone (0823) 289327.

Tenterden, Kent

Butler & Hatch Waterman, The County Group, Auctioneers
The second Thursday of most months, this auction house sells between 500 and 700 lots of antiques of all types, including furniture, silver, and other miscellaneous items. The auction room is behind the firm's offices. Previews are held the Sunday from 10.30 a.m. to 4 p.m. and Tuesday from 9.30 a.m. to 4 p.m. before the sales. Catalogues are sold (price varies), available the Friday before the sale. Mail bids and left bids may be made. Information is available from and sales are held at the Butler & Hatch Waterman, The County Group, Auctioneers, 102 High Street, Tenterden, Kent, telephone (05806) 3233.

Torquay, Devon

Antiques and collectors' fair the first Sunday of every month at the Belgrave Hotel on Seafront (hotel telephone (0803) 28566). These are regularly held regional fairs. All vendors are dealers. Admission is charged. Organised by Westfairs, P.O. Box 43, Weston-super-Mare, Avon BS23 2DS, telephone (0934) 33596.

"Antiques & Collectors Fair" one Thursday in October from noon to 7 p.m. at the English Riviera Conference Centre, Torquay. There are more than 100 stands, and admission is 60p. For information, contact Kay Crisp, KS Fairs, Evergreen Promotions, P.O. Box 58, Weston-super-Mare, Avon BS22 8ET, telephone (0934) 636648.

Bearne's Auctioneers
Auctions are held two or three times per month, either on Tuesdays, Wednesdays, or Thursdays

at the saleroom and offices. Auctions consist of specialized items, such as paintings and prints, jewellery and silver and silver plate, furniture and miscellaneous items, or ceramics and glass. A free schedule of sales is available upon request. Catalogues are issued several weeks before the sale, and cost from £1 to £3. Viewing is held the two (business) days before the sale from 9.30 a.m. to 5 p.m. and the morning of the sale. Bids may be left, or made by post or telephone. The buyer's premium is 10%. All purchases must be paid for and removed within two working days of the sale, but no purchases can be taken until the end of the sale. Access by car is on A380 from Newton Abbot. On Avenue Road, take the second right past the Torre Station, and then go to "Rainbow", which is at the top of the drive. Free parking is available at the salerooms. Access by train to Torquay station, then left along Falkland Road to Avenue Road, then left past Mill Lane. (While it can be walked, it is much quicker by taxi.) For exact schedule and further information, contact Bearne's Auctioneers, Rainbow, Avenue Road, Torquay, Devon TQ2 5TG, telephone (0803) 296277.

Tring, Hertfordshire

Brown & Merry Ltd., Auctioneers
Auctions are held every two weeks on Saturdays at 10 a.m. at the Saleroom, Cattle Market, Brook Street, Tring. About 1,000 lots are offered, including antiques, silver, porcelain, painting, furniture, and used goods that are not antique. Formal catalogues aren't issued, but printed sheets of items are available a few days before the auction. Viewing is the Friday before the sale from 2 to 6 p.m. and Saturday from 8.30 until the sale begins. Bids may be made by telephone if you leave your name, address, and a telephone number where you can be reached. Payment must be made by Monday after the sale. Free parking is available at the site. Further information and exact sale dates are available from Brown & Merry Ltd., 41 High Street, Tring, Hertfordshire HP23 5AP, telephone (044282) 6446, fax (044282) 7743.

Truro, Cornwall

"Truro Antiques, Collectors' & Book Fair" two
days in April, mid-August, and late September–
early October at the conference hall in City Hall.
Hours on the first day are 2 to 8 p.m., other days
10 a.m. to 5 p.m. This is a local fair, but sometimes interesting pieces surface. All vendors are
dealers. Organised by Gerry Mosdell, West
Country Antiques & Collectors Fairs, The
Dartmoor Antiques Centre, off West Street, Ashburton, Devon, telephone (0364) 52182.

Tunbridge Wells, Kent

Bracketts Auctions
Weekly auctions are held on Friday at the Royal
Sussex Assembly Rooms, The Pantiles,
Tunbridge Wells. All types of items are sold in
rapid succession, many for only a few pounds.
Both antiques and modern items are sold.
Previews are held Thursday and early Friday
morning before the sale. For information contact
Bracketts, 27-29 High Street, Tunbridge Wells,
Kent, telephone (0892) 33733.

*Black Horse Agencies—Geering & Colyer, Auc-
tioneers*
Every two months, always on a Wednesday, this
firm auctions off more than 400 lots of fine art,
including painting, sculpture, prints, and similar
items. Since this is a specialized auction house,
no other items are offered. Previews and sales
are held at the Winston Mnor (telephone (0892)
652772). For information and catalogues, contact
Black Horse Agencies—Geering & Colyer, Highgate, Hawkhurst, Cranbrook, Kent TN18 4AD,
telephone (05805) 3181.

Wakefield, Kent

"Ceramics Fair" first weekend of May (Bank
Holiday) at the Greenway on London Road (A20),
West Malling, about 2 miles west of Maidstone.
Ceramics and glass only, all before 1920. About

50 dealers from all over Britain sell at this fair, which is one of the largest for ceramics and glass. An expert identification service is available. Admission to the public is £1. Organised by Wakefield Antiques Fairs, 1 Fountain Road, Rede Court, Rochester, Kent, telephone (0634) 723461.

Wallington, Surrey

(Please also see Croydon and London.)

Wallington Missionary Auctions
Two-day auctions are held, on a Thursday and Friday, of March, April, June, September, November, and November-December at 7.30 p.m. at Crusader Hall, Stanley Park Road, Wallington, Surrey SM5 4PP. Though these sales are somewhat smaller than many others, they are of interest because of being held in the evening. They offer jewellery, silver, clocks, and other antiques and collectables. Viewing is held the Wednesday evening prior to the sale, and all day Thursday. Catalogues are available several days before the sale, and cost 25p. For further information, contact Wallington Missionary Auctions, Crusader hall, Stanley Park Road, Wallington, Surrey, telephone 01-647 8437.

Waltham Abbey, Essex

(Please also see Epping, Harlow, Hatfield, Hertford, London, and Loughton.)

Antique and collectors' fair six Sundays a year (usually second Sunday of April, June, August, October, and November, but check with the organiser) from 10.30 a.m. to 5 p.m. at Waltham Abbey Town Hall, on Highbridge Street. This is a local fair, with about 50 vendors of all types of small antiques and collectables, but little furniture. Admission is 40p, children 20p, but the fair is free to members of the antiques trade. The fair is signposted from Junction 25 of the M5 Orbital Motorway. Parking is available, not all free. Access is more difficult by public transport: train to

Cheshunt, then a long walk to Waltham Abbey. For further information, contact Bartholomew Fayres, Executive House, The Maltings, Station Road, Sawbridgeworth, Hertfordshire CM21 9JX, telephone (0279) 725809 and 725699.

Antique and collectors fair one Sunday in August from 10.30 a.m. to 4 p.m. at the Waltham Abbey Sports Centre, Broomstick Hall Road. There are about 80 stalls. Organised by Bartholomew Fayres, Executive House, The Maltings, Station Road, Sawbridgeworth, Hertfordshire CM21 9JX, telephone (0279) 725809 and 725699.

Ware, Hertfordshire

(Please also see Epping, Hatfield, Hertford, Waltham Abbey, and Ware.

"Fanhams Halls & Gardens Fair" first Friday, Saturday, and Sunday of May (Bank Holiday) from 11 a.m. to 5 p.m.; the trade is admitted from 10 a.m. (card or other proof required). Held at Fanhams Hall in the town. Antiques and collectors items, none from after 1930. Access by A10 north from London, and follow yellow AA signs in the area, or by rail to Ware. Organised by Chilterns Fairs, Chorleywood, telephone (0928) 2144.

Wareham, Dorset

S.W. Cottee & Son, Auctioneers
Auction every other Tuesday at the Wareham Markets Sale Rooms on East Street in the town centre. This country auction offers various used goods and antiques, but auctions are not further specialized. No catalogues are issued; inspection is the day before the sale from 1 to 5 and 6 to 8 p.m. and immediately before the sale. Bids can be left or made by post, but not by telephone. Access by car or train to Wareham. Sales are held at and further information is available from S.W. Cottee & Son, Wareham Markets Sale Rooms, East Street, Wareham, Dorset BH20 4NR, telephone (09295) 2826.

Wellington, Somerset

Wellington Salerooms, Auctioneers
Sales of general shipping furniture and effects
are held fortnightly and of selected antiques
every six to eight weeks. Catalogues are 20p.
There is a 10% buyer's premium. Parking is
within 100 yards of the salerooms. Sales are held
at and further information, including sale dates,
is available from Wellington Salerooms, Clifton
House, Mantle Street, Wellington, Somerset,
telephone (082347) 4815.

Wells, Somerset

(Please also see Shepton Mallet.)

Antique and collectors' fair held the last Saturday of every other month from 9 a.m. to 5 p.m. at
the Wells Town Hall. These are small, local fairs,
offering collectables and antiques. Admission is
free. Organised by Tony Weekes, Pickwick Fairs,
Shepton Mallet, telephone (0749) 3595 (evenings
only).

Wem, Shropshire

Wright-Manley Auctioneers
Collective antique and modern furniture sales
are held on one Saturday in February and May
and two in October at the Wem Market Hall on
High Street. There is no buyer's premium. For
exact dates and further details, contact Wright-
Manley Auctioneers, 2 High Street, Wem, Shropshire SY4 5AA, telephone (0939) 32471.

Weston-super-Mare, Avon

(Please also see Bristol and Portishead.)

Prudential Fine Art Auctioneers
Auctions are held every other Tuesday at 11 a.m.
at the auctioneers' offices on Station Road. All
types of antiques, collectables, and used goods

are offered, including furniture, miscellaneous items, and some silver. A free calendar of auctions is available upon request. Catalogues are issued (price usually £1) about two weeks before the sale. Bids may be left, posted, or made by telephone. The buyer's premium is 10%. Sales are held at and further information is available from Prudential Fine Art Auctioneers, Station Road, Weston-Super-Mare, Avon BS23 1XU, telephone (0934) 33174.

Weybridge, Surrey

"Wakefield Ceramic Fair" one weekend in February at the Oatlands Park Hotel. There are from 40 to 60 stands. There is an identification service for members of the public and collectors to bring porcelain for free evaluation. Organised by Fred Hynds, Wakefield Ceramics Fairs, 1 Fountain Road, Strood, Rochester, Kent ME2 3SJ, telephone (0634) 723461.

Whitchurch, Shropshire

(Please also see Wem.)

Wright-Manley Auctioneers
Collective antique and modern furnitues sales are held on one Wednesday in February, April, July, September, and November at the Whitchurch Market Hall, 29 St. Mary's Street. For dates and details, contact Wright-Manley Auctioneers, 16 Watergate Street, Whitchurch, Shropshire SY13 1DX, telephone (0948) 2281.

Whitton, Middlesex

Antique and collectors' fair first Wednesday of every month year round from 10 a.m. to 4 p.m. and third Sunday of every month from 11 a.m. to 5 pm. at the Winning Post on Great Chertsey Road (A 316). Approximately 40 to 50 stalls of odds and ends and some local dealers. Admission is 15p. Information from Magna Carta Country Fayres, Slough, telephone (0753) 685098.

Wilton, Wiltshire

(Please also see Salisbury.)

"Wakefield Ceramics Fair" one weekend in November at Michael Herbert Hall. There are from 40 to 60 stands. There is an identification service for members of the public and collectors to bring porcelain for free evaluation. Organised by Fred Hynds, Wakefield Ceramics Fairs, 1 Fountain Road, Strood, Rochester, Kent ME2 3SJ, telephone (0634) 723461.

Winchester, Hampshire

(Please also see Southampton and Stockbridge.)

"Collectors' Spring Fair" second Sunday of May and "Collectors' Autumn Festival" from 11 a.m. to 5 p.m. at Winchester Guildhall near the cathedral on The Broadway. Antiques and collector's items, such as porcelain, gold, silver, brass, coins, stamps, linen and lace are offered, with the exception of large furniture. This large regional show includes three halls. No modern items or reproductions may be shown or sold. Admission is 40p. This organiser occasionally uses this hall for other, irregularly-held antiques fairs. Parking is available next to the Guildhall. For further information, contact Ron Emmott Productions, 2 Fourways, Church Hill, West End, Southampton, Hampshire SO3 3AU, telephone (0703) 474862.

Windsor, Berkshire

(Please also see Ascot.)

Antiques and collectables fair every Saturday from March to October from 8 a.m. to mid afternoon on Thames Avenue at River Street. This fair takes place inside and outside, and offers about 40 vendors of all types of antiques and collectables, but there are few if any large items. An overflow market sometimes takes place along the river, but there is little of interest in this part. Street parking is difficult in the immediate area, but a car park is across the street and a block away at Riverside station. Access by train to Windsor Central station, and walk toward the river.

Witham, Essex

"Antique & Collectors' Fair" three Saturdays a year from 10.30 a.m. to 4 p.m. at Witham Public Hall, Collingwood Road. There are more than 40 stalls. Organised by Bartholomew Fayres, Executive House, The Maltings, Station Road, Sawbridgeworth, Hertfordshire CM21 9JX, telephone (0279) 725809 and 725699.

Woking, Surrey

(Please also see Godalming and Guildford.)

Barbers Fine Art Auctioneers Ltd.
Auctions are held approximately every five weeks on Monday at 10 a.m. at the auctioneers' offices at the Mayford Centre. Auctions include all types of antiques, including silver, carpets, furniture, porcelain, glass, and other items. Viewing is held the Saturday and Sunday before the sale from 10 a.m. to 5 p.m. The buyer's premium is 10%. Bids may be left, posted, or made by telephone. Access by public transport is by train to Woking, then by taxi. Access by car is on A320 to Smarts Heath Road, then left into Mayford Centre. Free parking is available on the site. Sales are held at and further information is available from Barbers Fine Art Auctioneers Ltd., The Mayford Centre, Smarts Heath Road, Mayford Green, Woking, Surrey GU22 0PP, telephone (04862) 28939.

Wolverhampton, West Midlands

(Please also see Birmingham and Wombourne.)

"Wolverhampton Antiques, Crafts, and Collectors' Market" held every Tuesday, Wednesday, Friday, and Saturday at the Market Halls in the city centre. Approximately 20 to 50 dealers and collectors of all types of items are present. Parking is available in the council car park for 40p per day. Access by rail to Wolverhampton High Level station and walk or use the Town Centre Bus Service. Organised by the Wolverhampton Markets Department, 1st Floor, Heantun House, Salop Street, Wolverhampton, West Midlands WV3 0SH, telephone (0902) 21571 and 26528.

Wombourne, West Midlands

(Please also see Wolverhampton.)

Antiques fair every second Sunday of many (but not all) months from 10 a.m. to 5 p.m. at the Wombourne Community Centre, in the town centre. Parking is available on surrounding streets. This is a small, local fair, with not more than 40 vendors. A book fair is also held at the Community Centre on one Sunday in January, April, July, and October. Organised by Waverly Fairs, Boreley Cottage, Boreley near Ombersley, Worcestershire, telephone (0205) 620697.

Woodbridge, Suffolk

(Please also see Ipswich.)

Antique and collectors fair one Sunday in February, April, September, and November at the tactical operational base, Officer's Club, RAF Bentwaters. There are 60 stands. Admission and parking are free. Organised by Lorna Quick, Fourseason Fairs, 6 Post Office Lane, Glemsford, Suffolk CO10 7RA, telephone (0787) 281855.

Neal Sons & Fletcher

Auctions are held from time to time on Wednesday at 11 a.m. at the Theatre Street Saleroom. Catalogues are issued for all antiques sales, and usually cost £2. Viewing is held the Tuesday before the sale from 11.15 a.m to 4.30 p.m. and 6.30 to 8 p.m. For further information, contact Neal Sons & Fletcher, 26 Church Street, Woodbridge, Suffolk, telephone (03943) 2263.

Woodcote, Oxfordshire

Duncan Vincent, Fine Art Auctioneers

Collective antiques auctions are held on one Thursday in May and one in October at the Village Hall. The buyer's premium is 7- 1/2%. For dates and further information, contact Duncan Vincent, 105 London Street, Reading, Berkshire RG1 3LF, telephone (0734) 589502 and 594748.

Woodford Green, Essex

(Please also see Epping, London, Loughton, and Waltham Abbey.)

Antique and collectors' fair held five Saturdays a year from 10.30 a.m. to 5 p.m. at the Sir James Hawkey Hall, Broadmead Road. This is a local fair of about 80 dealers of small antiques, bric-a-brac, and collectables. A small admission fee is charged, but entry is free to members of the antiques trade. Access by car from London to Woodford on A121 (High Road) to Broadmead Road. Access by bus on line 275 and by British Rail from Liverpool Street station to Woodford station. For further information, contact Bartholomew Fayres, Executive House, The Maltings, Station Road, Sawbridgeworth, Hertfordshire CM21 9JX, telephone (0279) 725809 and 725699.

Worcester, Hereford & Worcester

Andrew Grant, Fine Art Auctioneers
Auctions are held six times per year at 11.30 a.m.
at the Grandstand, Worcester Racecourse, north
of the city on A449. Auctions include all types of
antiques and collectables, including sterling,
jewellery, books, glass, paintings and drawings,
glass, porcelain, pottery, and furniture.
Catalogues are issued two weeks before the sale;
usual price is £2. Viewing is the day before the
sale from 3 to 7 p.m. and two hours before the
sale begins. There is no buyer's premium. Bids
can be left, posted, or telephoned, but a 25%
deposit may be required. All items must be paid
for and removed on the day of the sale. Payment
can be made while the auction is still in progress.
Access by car to the racecourse on A38, then
towards the river on Castle Street. Park on the
site. Access by train to Foregate station, Worcester, then walk to the racecourse on Foregate
and Castle Street. For further information, contact the auctioneer at the office: Andrew Grant,
Fine Art Auctioneers, 59/60 Forgate Street, Worcester, Hereford & Worcester, telephone (0205)
52310. On sale dates, call (0905) 25970.

"Wakefield Ceramics Fair" one weekend in October at The Dyson Perrins Museum. There are
from 40 to 60 stands. There is an identification
service for members of the public and collectors
to bring porcelain for free evaluation. Organised
by Fred Hynds, Wakefield Ceramics Fairs, 1
Fountain Road, Strood, Rochester, Kent ME2
3SJ, telephone (0634) 723461.

Worksop, Nottinghamshire

"The Welbeck Abbey Antiques Fair" on the first
weekend in July. This is a regional fair of good-
quality antiques, including furniture, silver,
jewellery, porcelain, paintings and prints, and
other items. All items are vetted. The dateline is
from 1885 (furniture) to 1920 (paintings and
ceramics). Admission is £2.50 for the public, but
free to members of the antiques trade with a
business card. Organised by Robert Bailey An-

tique Fairs, 1 Roll Gardens, Gants Hill, Ilford, Essex IG2 6TN, telephone 01-550 5435.

Worthing, West Sussex

(Please also see Brighton.)

Worthing Antiques Fair, first Wednesday of every other month from June to December from 8 a.m. to 2.30 p.m. at the Worthing Pier Pavilion on the shore. This local fair usually has about 60 vendors. Free to members of the antiques trade, 30p to others. Parking available on the street, about half a mile south of the central station. Organised by Mostyn Fairs, 64 Brighton Road, Lancing, Sussex, telephone (0903) 752961.

F. H. Ellis & Sons, Auctioneers

Auctions are held three Mondays per month (usually first, third, and fourth, though this can vary) at the auctioneers' office. Each sale consists of a miscellaneous collection of about 400 lots of all types. Previews are held the Saturday before the sale. Sales are held at and further information is available from F. H. Ellis & Sons, 44-46 High Street, Worthing, West Sussex, telephone (0903) 38999.

Fox & Sons Worthing Auction Galleries

Auctions are held some Tuesdays (check for exact schedule) at the galleries. Sales consist of about 400 lots of various modern and antique furniture, and whatever else is brought in. Previews take place Saturday morning and Monday before the sale. Sales site and further information are available from Fox & Sons, 31 Chatsworth Road, Worthing, West Sussex, telephone (0903) 205565.

Wrotham Heath, Kent

"Nepicar Farm Boot Sale" the first Sunday of each month fronm March through December from 10 a.m. to 5 p.m. Admission is 50p, children free. Parking is free. In addition, an auto jumble is held on a Saturday in the spring and autumn at the same site, from 9 a.m. to 5 p.m. Admission is £1.50, children 50p. The Farm is on A25 between Maidstone and Sevenoaks. For exact dates and further information, contact Nepicar Farms, Wrotham Heath, Sevenoaks, Kent TN15 7SR, telephone (0732) 883040.

Yatton, Avon

Antique and bric-a-brac fair the last Saturday of every month from 10 a.m. to 4 p.m. at the Yatton Village Hall. This is a small local fair. For further information, contact Kay Crisp, Evergreen Promotions, 118 Main Road, Cleeve, Bristol, Avon BS19 4PN, telephone (0934) 833629.

Yelverton, Devon

"Dartmoor Antiques, Collectors and Book Fair" one Sunday from May through December from 10.30 a.m. to 5 p.m. at the Moorland Links Hotel (telephone (0822) 852245), 2 miles south of the town on A386. Organised by Gerry Mosdell, West Country Antiques and Collectors Fairs, the Dartmoor Antiques Center, off West Street, Ashburton, Devon TQ13 7DV, telephone (0364) 52182.

York, North Yorkshire

(Please also see Castle Howard.)

Flea market and collectors' fair several times a year (often last Saturday of the month) from 9.30 a.m. to 5 p.m. at the Racecourse Grandstand about one mile south of the railway station between Bishopsgate Road and Tadcaster Road (A1036). This is a regional fair with up to several hundred vendors of all types of items. Admission is 50p. Exact dates and further information are available from Panda Promotions, 24 Westgate, Honley, Huddersfield, West Yorkshire HD7 2AA, telephone (0484) 666144.

"Annual York Antiques Fair" held the last Thursday to Saturday of October from 11 a.m. to

8 p.m. and "York Summer Antiques Fair" last Thursday to Saturday of June from 11 a.m. to 8 p.m. at the DeGrey Rooms, next to Theatre Royal (returns in 1990 to Assembly Rooms in Blake Street, hall telephone (0904) 24604). These are long-established, high-quality regional fairs. Only dealers may sell, and all items sold carry a money-back guarantee of authenticity. Admission is charged. Parking is available at a car park within five minutes walk. For further information, contact Tony Keniston, Hopton Castle, Craven Arms, Shropshire SY7 0QJ, telephone (05474) 356.

"York Antiques Centre" is a building full of antiques dealers open Monday to Saturday at 2 Lendal, York.

Markets, Fairs, and Auctions in Scotland

Edinburgh, Lothian

(Please also see Queensferry.)

"Ingliston Saturday Market" held every Saturday from dawn or 6 a.m. (whichever is earlier) at Ingliston Field, about 5 miles east of Edinburgh on A8. This large open-air market is held adjacent to the airport. A large (approximately 40-foot) painted gorilla is found on the grounds, and is visible from the road. This market has large quantities of new items. In many ways Ingliston resembles a street market, with clothes and new items, but there is also lots of junk and collectables. Parking is available on the grounds, for which a fixed fee is charged. Access by bus to Ingliston.

"Edinburgh Annual Antiques Fair" last Tuesday to Thursday of each July and the "Edinburgh Winter Antiques Fair" is held Friday to Sunday in mid November from 11 a.m. to 8 p.m. at the Roxburghe Hotel, 38 Charlotte Square (telephone (031) 225 3921). Be sure to confirm dates and times! Only dealers may sell, and offer various items from before 1890. All purchases are guaranteed to be as described. Organised by Tony Keniston, Hopton Castle, Craven Arms, Shropshire SY7 0QJ, telephone (05474) 356.

"Scottish Antiques Fair" is held each April at Roxburghe Hotel, 38 Charlotte Square (telephone (031) 225 3921). One of Scotland's premier antiques fairs, it has mainly pre-1830 antiques and is vetted. Confirm the exact dates. Organised by Tony Keniston, Hopton Castle, Craven Arms, Shropshire SY7 0QJ, telephone (05474) 356.

Phillips Scotland, Fine Art Auctioneers
Auctions of household and used goods are held nearly every Friday and some Wednesdays at 11 a.m. at the offices and sale rooms. No catalogues

are issued for these sales.

Catalogues are issued at least one week in advance for all specialized sales, price usually £1, but sometimes as much as £3. Specialized sales include "Victoriana","Silver & Plate","Coins", "Furniture", "Oil Paintings", etc.

Viewing is held the day before and morning of the sale. Bids may be left, posted, or telephoned. The buyer's premium is 10%. Street parking (metered) is difficult but available, and a parking structure is found at St. James Centre a few minutes away. Access by train to Waverley station and walk up to the north a little past Princes Street, then left on George Street. Sales are held at and further information is available from Phillips Scotland, Fine Art Auctioneers, 65 George Street, Edinburgh, Lothian EH2 2JL, telephone (031) 225 2266.

Glasgow, Strathclyde

(Please also see Edinburgh and Hamilton.)

"The Barrows", also called "The Barras", every weekend from just after dawn in summer (or 6 a.m. in winter) until mid afternoon in the market area between London Road and Gallowgate. This is a large outdoor and indoor general market, with a large number of vendors of collectables, junk, and antiques. The antiques and collectables tend to be on the eastern part of the fair. Several blocks are closed off for the day. Some old warehouse buildings have been converted into halls of antique dealers. This market has one of the best potentials for making finds in all of Britain. Parking is difficult on market days but can be found on the streets to the west and east. A few vacant lots are turned into car parks for the weekend; a fee is charged.

Christie's and Edmiston's Ltd.
The Scottish branch of Christie's holds frequent sales of all types of antiques and collectables. A schedule of sales is available on request. Catalogues are published for important sales and cost from £1 to £3. Sales are held at and further information is available from Christie's and

Edmiston's Ltd., 164-166 Bath Street, Glasgow, telephone (041) 332 8134, telex 779901.

Phillips Scotland, Fine Art Auctioneers
Auctions are held once in May, twice in June, and once in December at 10 a.m. and include antiques, silver, porcelain, painting, furniture (both antique and contemporary), carpets, and sculpture at the sale rooms in central Glasgow. In addition, several times a month, specialized sales are held of items including paintings, silver, jewellery, dolls, etc. A schedule of sales is free upon request. Catalogues are issued at least one week before each sale, price usually £1. Viewing is the day before the Tuesday sales from 9 a.m. to 5 p.m. and the morning of the sale, and two days before every special sale from 9 a.m. to 5 p.m. The buyer's premium is 10%. Payment must be made and all items removed by the end of the second working day after the sale. Bids may be left, posted, or telephoned. Parking is available at 50p. Access by public transport is by bus or train to Queen Street station or Central station and walk. Sales are held at and further information is available from Phillips Fine Art Auctioneers, 207 Bath Street, Glasgow G2 4HD, telephone (041) 221 8377, fax (041) 226 4441.

Sotheby's Scotland
Auctions are held three times a year in Scotland: Scottish paintings and watercolours and jewellery at the Royal Scottish Automobile Club; Scottish paintings and watercolours and silver at the Hopetown House, South Queensferry, at the end of April; and Scottish paintings, watercolours, jewellery, silver, and sporting guns at the Gleneagles Hotel in Perthshire. Catalogues are issued about two weeks before each sale and usually cost £5 to £25. Viewing is held two days before the sale and the morning of the sale. A free schedule of sales is available upon request. Bids may be left, posted, or telephoned. The buyer's premium is 10%. For sales dates and further information, contact Sotheby's Scotland, 146 West Regent Street, Glasgow G2 2RQ, telephone (041) 221 4817.

Hamilton, Strathclyde

L.S. Smellie & Son, Auctioneers
Every Monday at 10 a.m. all types of household
furnishings are auctioned in no particular order.
This is very much a country sale, with all types
of used goods and items, and antiques scattered
in. Items such as used toasters and children's
toys are sold as well as Victorian cases, silver
and silver plate, and all other types of items.
Easily portable items are sold before the furniture. Several dealers find much of their stock at
this auction. No catalogues are issued. Viewing
takes place the morning of the sale. Payment
must be made the day of the sale and all items
must be removed within two days. Specialized
sales of fine antique furniture, porcelain, jewellery, and carpets are held on the third Thursday
of February, May, August, and November, with
detailed catalogues available, price 50p. Viewing
is held the day before and the morning of the
sale. Sales are held at the salerooms, about a half
mile west of the city centre at Cattlemarket,
Lower Auchingramont Road, Hamilton, Strathc-
lyde, telephone (0698) 282007.

Kelso, Borders

Antiques fair twice a year (May Bank Holiday
Sunday and Monday and third weekend of Oc-
tober) at the Ednam House Hotel on Bridge
Street (hotel telephone (0573) 24168). This is a
small, local fair in an out-of-the-way corner of
Scotland. Free parking is available. Organised by
Borough Fairs, 83 Hunstanton Road, Old
Hunstanton, Norfolk, telephone (04853) 33732.

Queensferry, Lothian

(Please also see Edinburgh.)

"The Scottish Antiques and Interior Design Fair"
the second weekend of October (Friday 11 a.m. to
8 p.m., Saturday and Sunday 11 a.m. to 6 p.m.)
at Hopetoun House, an excellent early 18th-cen-
tury stately home, which Robert Adam

remodelled. This is one of the best Scottish regional antiques fairs. All items are vetted. The dateline is 1880, though a very few more recent pieces are accepted. Access by car on M9 to Junction 2, then east on A904 and local roads to Hopetoun House. Free parking is available on the grounds. Nearest railway station is 3 miles east in Queensferry. For further information and exact sale dates, contact Robert Soper, Castle Fairs, Bowcliffe Road, Bramham, Wetherby, North Yorkshire LS23 9JS, telephone (0937) 845829.

Perth, Tayside

"Perthshire Antiques Fair" the first Friday to Sunday in May and last weekend of September from 11 a.m. to 8 p.m. at the Station Hotel, Leonard Street (telephone (0738) 24141) across the street from the railwat station. All items are vetted and mainly pre 1890. Organised by Tony Keniston, Hopton Castle, Craven Arms, Shropshire SY7 0QJ, telephone (05474) 356 and 464.

Thomas Love & Sons Ltd., Auctioneers
Quarterly sales of period furniture, clocks, mirrors, ceramics, silver, metalware, pictures, collector's items, works of art, and rugs are held on Tuesdays in March, June, September, and December at the Auction Galleries, 52 Canal Street (telephone (0738) 24111). Catalogues are £2. Viewing is the day prior to sale. Weekly sales of Victoriana and household effects are held on Fridays, with viewing on Thursday. No catalogues are issued. There is no buyer's premium. Parking is available in car park opposite the saleroom. The railway station is 5 minutes walk. For information, contact Thomas Love & Sons Ltd., 6 South St. John's Place, Perth, Tayside PH1 5SU, telephone (0738) 24111.

Markets, Fairs, and Auctions in Northern Ireland

Belfast, County Antrim

"St. George's Variety Market" every Tuesday and Friday from 7 a.m. to 3 p.m. (more vendors on Friday) is held on May Street (postal district BT1). All types of bric-a-brac, junk, and new and used items are sold in a flea market atmosphere.

"Belfast Antiques Market" open most Saturdays from 10 a.m. to 5 p.m. an indoor private market offering furniture, small items, and bric-a-brac. The market is located at 126 Donegal Pass, Belfast, County Antrim BT7 1BZ, telephone (0232) 247372.

Antiques and collectables fair held the first Saturday of every month from 10.30 a.m. to 4 p.m. at the organiser's hall. For a schedule and further information, contact Antiques & Collectables Fairs, Hinghan Hall, 13 Botanic Avenue, Belfast, County Antrim BT7 1JG, telephone (0238) 528428.

"May Day Antiques Fair" the first of May at the Conway Hotel, 6 miles south on A1 (hotel telephone 0232) 612101. This is a local antiques fair with all types of small items. Admission is charged. Free parking is available at the hotel. Organised by Mrs. Winifred Bell, Johnston House, 14 Derriaghy Road, Lisburn, telephone (0846) 624412.

"Great Victoria Carousel" is a regular indoor building full of little antiques stands open Tuesday to Saturday from 11 a.m. to 5.30 p.m. Items offered include some furniture, bric-a-brac, books, paintings, and other odds and ends. The "Great Victoria Carousel" is located at 69a Great Victoria Street, Belfast, County Antrim BT2 7AF, telephone (0232) 230215.

Anderson's Auction Rooms
Auctions are held most Wednesdays at 11 a.m. at
the offices and salerooms. Items sold include furniture, jewellery, and other miscellaneous items.
Many items are Victorian or more recent. Viewing is held Tuesday from 9 a.m. to 8 p.m., and
Wednesday before the sale. Sales are held at and
more information is available from Anderson's
Auction Rooms, 28 Linenhall Street, Belfast,
County Antrim BT2 8BG, telephone (0232)
221401.

Kennedy Wolfenden, Fine Art Auctioneers
Auctions are held approximately every two
months at the auctioneer's salerooms and offices.
Items sold include furniture, silver, porcelain,
and jewellery. For auction schedule and
catalogues, contact Kennedy Wolfenden, Fine Art
Auctioneers, 218 Lisburn Road, Belfast, County
Antrim, BT9 6GD, telephone (0232) 681775.

Osborne King and Megran Auctions
Auctions are held quarterly, usually on the last
Wednesday of a month at the Gallery, Gilford
Castle, Gilford postal district BT63. Items include fine arts, furniture, and various types of
antiques including silver. Catalogues are issued
before the sale; minimum price is £1. For exact
sale dates and further information, contact Osborne King and Megran, 17 Castle Arcade, Gilford, BT63, telephone (0232) 240332.

Boardmills, County Down

Temple Auctions
Auctions are held every other Saturday beginning at 10 a.m. at firm's salerooms and offices.
Items sold include all types of fine arts and antiques. Viewing is on Friday from 9 a.m. to 9 p.m.
and Saturday before the sale begins. For further
information and exact sale dates contact Temple
Auctions Ltd., 133 Carryduff Road, Boardmills,
Lisburn, County Down BT27 6YL, telephone
(0846) 638777.

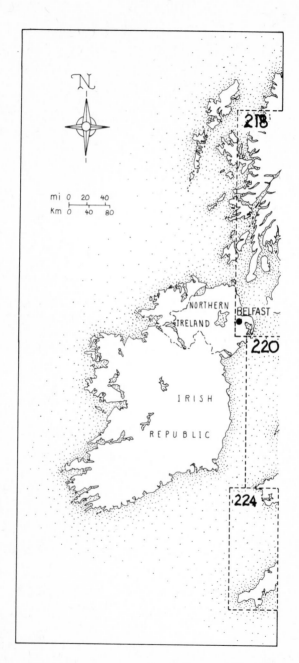

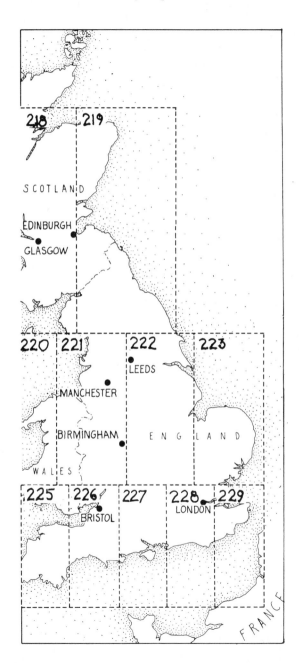

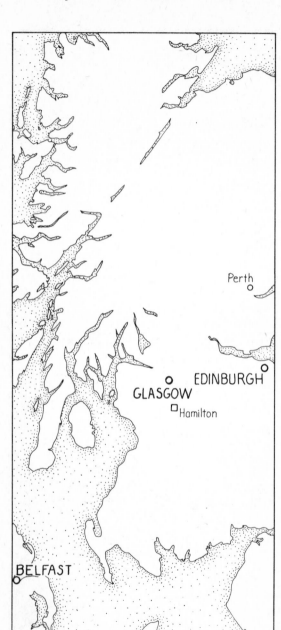

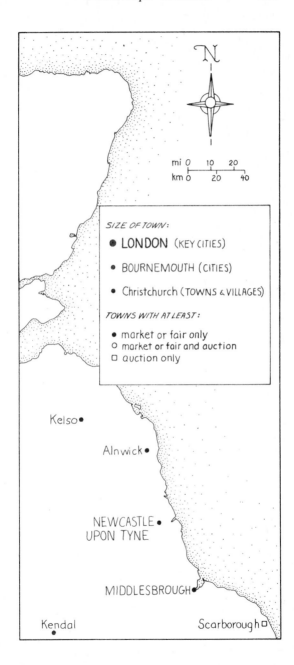

SIZE OF TOWN:

● **LONDON** (KEY CITIES)

● BOURNEMOUTH (CITIES)

• Christchurch (TOWNS & VILLAGES)

TOWNS WITH AT LEAST:

• market or fair only
○ market or fair and auction
□ auction only

Kelso•

Alnwick•

NEWCASTLE UPON TYNE•

MIDDLESBROUGH•

Kendal•

Scarborough□

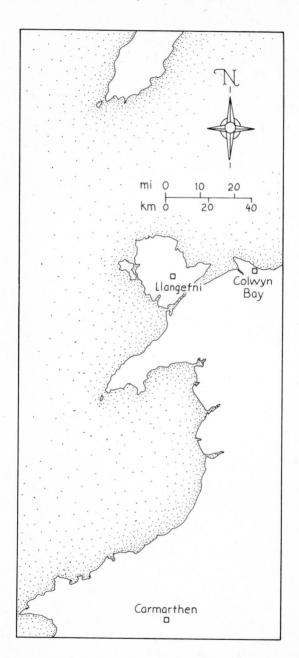

N

mi 0   10   20
km 0   20   40

Llangefni

Colwyn
Bay

Carmarthen

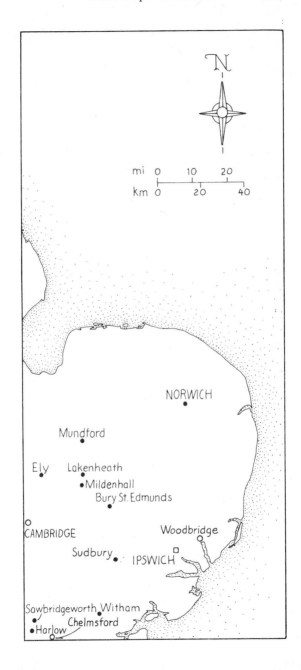

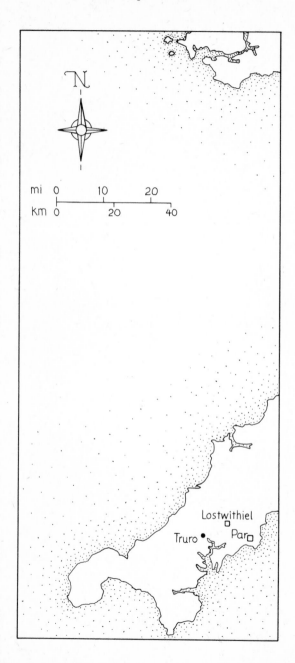

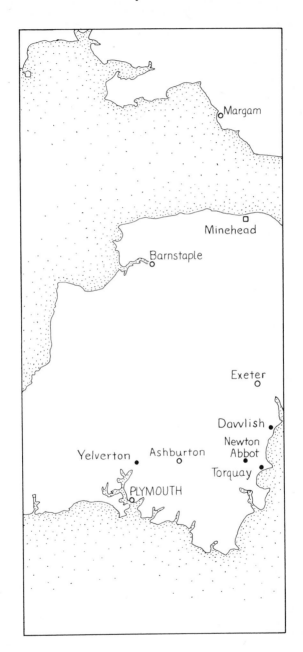

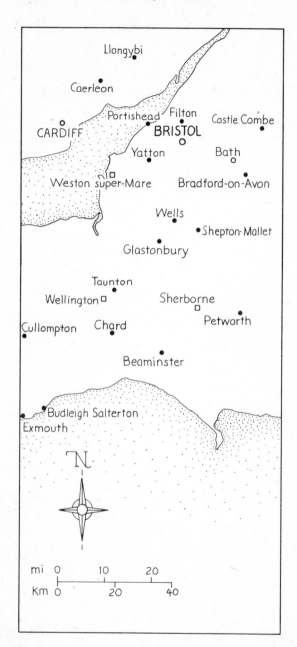

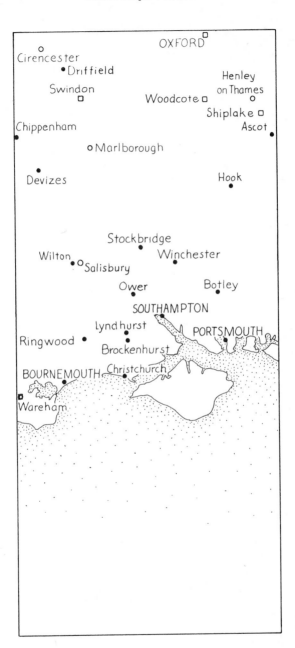

OXFORD

Cirencester

Driffield

Swindon

Henley on Thames

Woodcote

Shiplake

Chippenham

Ascot

Marlborough

Devizes

Hook

Stockbridge

Wilton Salisbury

Winchester

Ower

Botley

SOUTHAMPTON

Lyndhurst

PORTSMOUTH

Ringwood

Brockenhurst

BOURNEMOUTH Christchurch

Wareham

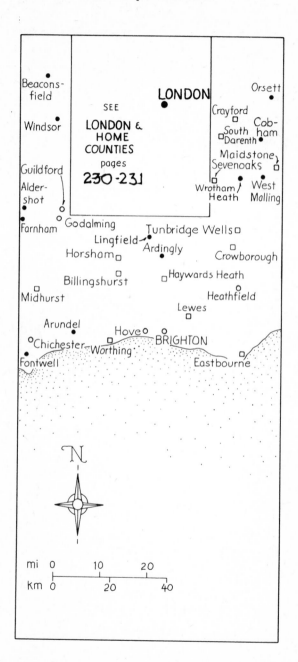

Beacons-
field

Windsor

SEE

LONDON

Orsett

LONDON &
HOME
COUNTIES
pages
230-231

Crayford

Cob-
ham
South
Darenth

Maidstone
Sevenoaks

Guildford

Alder-
shot

Farnham   Godalming

Wrotham
Heath

West
Malling

Tunbridge Wells

Lingfield
Horsham   Ardingly

Crowborough

Billingshurst

Haywards Heath

Midhurst

Heathfield

Lewes

Arundel

Hove

Chichester   Worthing   **BRIGHTON**

Fontwell

Eastbourne

N

mi 0   10   20

km 0   20   40

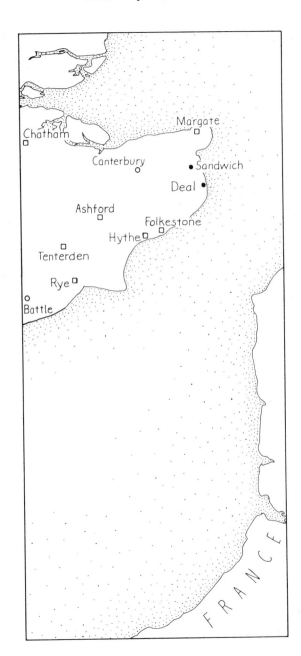

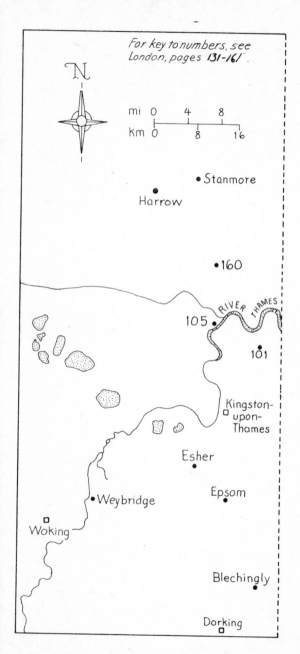

For key to numbers, see
London, pages *131-161*.

N

mi 0   4   8
km 0   8   16

● Stanmore

● Harrow

●160

RIVER THAMES

105 ●

101 ●

Kingston-
upon-
Thames ▫

Esher ●

Epsom ●

● Weybridge

▫ Woking

Blechingly ●

Dorking ▫

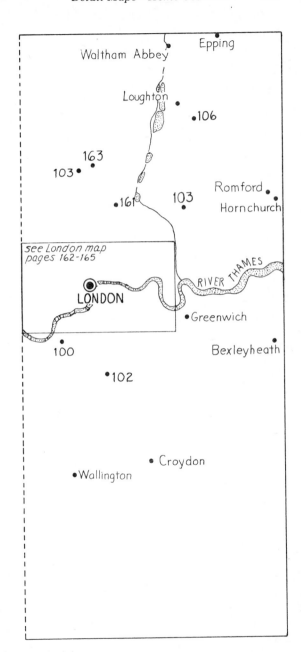

Index of Organisers

Organisers Without Mailing Addresses

Bagatelle Fairs, London, telephone 01-391 2339

Bray Enterprises, telephone (0883) 42561

Stephen Charles, Basildon, telephone (0268) 774977

Chilterns Fairs, Chorleywood, telephone (0928) 2144

Dualco Promotions, (Manchester area) telephone (061) 766 2012

Fair Organiser, Beaconsfield, telephone (04946) 5338.

Fair Organiser, London, telephone 01-657 7414

Fair Organiser, telephone (0423) 770385

Gamlins Exhibition Services, telephone (045) 285 2557

Mr. Gill, Illminster, telephone (04605) 2873

Granny's Attic Antique Fairs, Marlow, telephone (06284) 3658

Hallmark Antique Fairs, Keynsham, telephone (02756) 3795

Mr. Holley, Stalbridge, telephone (0963) 62478

Hoyle's Markets, telephone (0153) 725788

Jubilee Antiques Fairs, London, telephone 01-989 8693

LaChaise Antiques, telephone (0367) 20427

Libra Hall Fairs, telephone (0633) 422489

Magna Carta Country Fayres, Slough, telephone (0753) 685098

Midas Fairs, Beaconsfield, telephone (04946) 4170

Christina Page Fairs, telephone (0223) 211736

Tony Weekes, Pickwick Fairs, Shepton Mallet, telephone (0749) 3595

Prestige Promotions, telephone (0533) 56045

Ray Ratcliff, London, telephone 01-764 3602

Somerset & Avon Antique Fairs, telephone (0278) 784912

Stagecoach Antique Fairs, telephone (0628) 23790

Mrs. Jean Younger, Harpenden, telephone (05827) 61235

Organisers With Mailing Addresses

ABC, 15 Flood St., Chelsea, London SW3, telephone 01-351 5353

A.K. Fairs, 693 Stratford Road, Shirley, Solihull, West Midlands, telephone (021) 744 4385

Anglian Arts & Antiques, Linthorpe House, Station Road, Halesworth, Suffolk, telephone (09867) 2368

Antiques and Collectors Club, P.O. Box 14, Horley, Surrey, telephone (0293) 772206

Antiques & Collectables Fairs, Hinghan Hall, 13 Botanic Avenue, Belfast, County Antrim BT7 1JG, Northern Ireland, telephone (0238) 528428

Mrs. Winifred Bell, Antique and Collectors Fairs, Johnston House, 14 Derriaghy Road, Lisburn, Northern Ireland, telephone (0846) 624412

Antiques & Collectors Fairs, 17 Elm Close, Yatton nr. Bristol, Avon, telephone (0934) 838187

Antiques Forum Antiques Fairs, Flat 2—197 Maida Vale, London W9, telephone 01-624 3214

Antiques in Britain *(Please see Keniston.)*

Mr. A. Bailey, Cloisters Antique Mariet, St. Andrews Hall, Norwich, Norfolk, telephone (0603) 628477

Robert Bailey Antiques Fairs, 1 Roll Gardens, Gants Hill, Ilford, Essex IG2 6TN, telephone 01-550 5435

A.J. Barrett Fairs, Glenroy, Paynes Lane, Nazeing, Essex, telephone (0992) 460929

Jenny Scott, Bartholomew Fayres, The Maltings, Station Road, Sawbridgeworth, Hertfordshire CM21 9JX, telephone (0279) 725809 and 725699

Birmingham Markets Department, Manor House, 40 Moat Lane, Birmingham B5 5BD, telephone (021) 622 3452

Mrs. Irene Poulter, Borough Fairs, 83 Old Hunstanton Road, Old Hunstanton, Norfolk, telephone (04853) 2122

Miss Helen Bowman, Bowman Antique Fairs, P.O. Box 37, Otley, West Yorkshire LS21 1RA, telephone (0532) 843333 or (0943) 465782

Ann Rudd and Elaine Dean, British Antique Dealers Association, 20 Rutland Gate, London SW7 1BD, telephone 01-581 0373

British International Antiques Fair, Exhibitions & Events Division, National Exhibition Centre, Birmingham B40 1NT, telephone (021) 780 4171, fax (021) 780 2518

Canterbury City Council Amenities Department, Council Offices, Military Road, Canterbury, Kent CT1 1YU, telephone (0277) 763763

Castle Combe Circuit Ltd., Chippenham, Wiltshire SN14 7EY, telephone (0249) 782417

Robert Soper, Castle Fairs, Bowcliff Road, Bramham near Weatherby, North Yorkshire LS23 9JS, telephone (0937) 845829

Centre Crafts, 308A Station Road, Harrow, London, telephone (0923) 46559

Century Antiques Fair Ltd., 58 Mill Lane, London NW6 1N3, telephone 01-794 3551

Crown Antiques Fairs, 55 Barton Road, Cambridge, Cambridgeshire CB3 9LG, telephone (0223) 353016

Mrs. Kay Crisp *(Please see Evergreen.)*

Roger Heath-Bullock, Cultural Exhibitions Ltd., 8 Meadrow, Godalming, Surrey GU7 3HN, telephone (04868) 22562

Mr. R.F.J. Peck, Darent Antiques & Collectors Fairs, Whitestacks, Crockenhill Lane, Eynsford, Kent, telephone (0322) 863383

J.A. Day, 17 Elm Close, Yatton, Avon, telephone (0934) 838187

East Kent Fairs, 201 London Road, Dover, Kent CT17 0TF, telephone (0304) 201644

Ron Emmott, Ron Emmott Promotions, 2 Fourways, Church Hill, West End, Southampton, Hampshire SO3 3AU, telephone (0703) 474862

E & M Enterprises, 28 Nutbush Drive, Northfield, Birmingham B31 5SJ, telephone (021) 477 3143

Mrs. Kay Crisp, Evergreen Productions/Promotions, KS Fairs, P.O. Box 58, Weston-super-Mare, Avon BS22 8ER, telephone (0934) 836648

Falcon Fairs, Capp House, 96a Southend, Croyden, Surrey CR9 3SD

Linda Forster, Forest Fairs, 28 Glenwood Road, West Moors, Dorset, telephone (0202) 875167

Seasons Fairs *(Please see Mrs. Lorna Quick.)*

Mr. A. W. Garrett, The Old Court House, Upper Hardres, Canterbury, Kent, telephone (0227) 70437

Ken Graves Fairs, 75 Princes Avenue, Hedon, Hull, Humberside, telephone (0482) 896854

Bob Harris & Sons, 2071 Coventry Road, Sheldon, Birmingham, telephone (021) 743-2259

Heritage Antiques Fairs Harvey (Management Services) Ltd., P.O Box 149, London W9 1QN, telephone 01-624 1787

Herridges Antiques & Collectors Fairs Limited, Chanctonbury, 8 Kimbolton Avenue, Bedford MK40, telephone (0234) 45725

Hitchin Market Office, 22 Churchgate, Hitchin, Hertfordshire SG5 1DN, telephone (0462) 56202

Brian Haughton, International Ceramics Fair, 38 Burlington Gardens, Old Bond Street, London W1X 1LE, telephone 01-734 5491 and 02232

Doug Burnell-Higgs, Isca Fairs, 10 Norman Street, Caerleon, Gwent, Wales, telephone (0633) 421527

K.M. Fairs, 58 Mill Lane, London NW6 1NJ, telephone 01-794 3551.

KS Fairs *(Please see Evergreen.)*

Tony Keniston, Hopton Castle, Craven Arms, Shropshire SY7 0QJ, telephone (05474) 356 and 464

James Quigley, Kingston Promotions, 157 Plymouth Drive, Hill Head, Fareham, Hampshire PO14 3SN, telephone (0329) 661780

Brenda Lay, Dyke Farm, West Chiltington Road, Pulborough, West Sussex, telephone (07982) 2447

Liverpool City Markets Department, Edge Lane, Liverpool L13 2EP, telephone (051) 228 4741

London, Borough of Southwark, Consumer Services, 23 Harper Road SE1 6AW, telephone 01-403 5867

London House Fairs, 271-273 King Street, Hammersmith, London W6 9LZ, telephone 01-741 8011

Maridale Antique & Collectors Fairs, 9 Mill Ridge, Edgware, Middlesex, telephone 01-958 8354

Marlborough District Oxfam Committee, 27 Oxford Street, Ramsbury, Marlborough, Wiltshire SN8, telephone (0672) 20354.

Anne Campbell Macinnes, 9 George Street, Bath, Avon BA1 2EH, telephone (0225) 463727

Ms. Anne Stroud, Merlin Fairs, Will-o-the-Wisp, Moorland near Bridgwater, Somerset, telephone (0278) 691616

Bob Hopwood, Miniatura, 41 Eastbourne Avenue, Hodge Hill, Birmingham B34 6AR, telephone (021) 783 2070

M. Morris, M & S Fairs, 38 Oakwood Avenue, Southgate, London N14, telephone 01-440 2330

Shirley Mostyn, Mostyn Fairs, 64 Brighton Road, Lancing, Surrey, telephone (0903) 752961

The National Crafts Fair, 69 Church Road, Richmond, Surrey, telephone 01-940 4608

Nepicar Farm, Wrotham Heath, Sevenoaks, Kent TN15 7SR, telephone (0732) 883040

Newcastle City Council, Estate & Property Department, Civic Centre, Newcastle-upon-Tyne, Tyne and Wear, telephone (091) 232 8520

Northern Antiques Fair, Manor House, High Birstwith, Harrogate, North Yorkshire HG3 2LG, telephone (0423) 770385.

P S Enterprises, P.O. Box 268, Poole, Dorset BH14 8DE, telephone (0258) 840224

Panda Promotions, 24 Westgate, Honley, Huddersfield, West Yorkshire HD7 2AA, telephone (0484) 666144

The Park Lane Hotel Antiques Fair, London House, 271-273 King Street, London W6 9LZ, telephone 01-741 8011

Ralph Paulett, Peak Fairs, Hill Cross, Ashford, Bakewell, Derbyshire DE4 1QL, telephone (062981) 2449

Mrs. Caroline Penman, Penman Fairs, Cockhaise Mill, Lindfield, Haywards Heath, West Sussex (mail to P.O. Box 114, Haywards Heath, West Sussex RH16 2YU, telephone Lindfield (04447) 2514 and 4531

Philbeach Events Ltd., Exhibitions Centre, Warwick Road, London SW5, telephone 01-370 8205, fax 01-244 7617

Lindy Berkman, Pig & Whistle Promotions, 53 Muswell Ave., London N10, 2EH, telephone 01-883 7061 and 01-249 4050

Antony Porters Fleamarkets, Whitegates, Netherton, Huddersfield, Yorkshire, telephone (0484) 662429

Provincial Booksellers Fairs Association, P.O. Box 66, Cambridge CB1 3PD, telephone (0223) 240921

Mrs. Lorna Quick, Four Seasons Fairs, 6 Post Office Lane, Glemsford, Sudbury, Suffolk CD10 7RA, telephone (0787) 281855

A. Robins, Chapel Cottage, Cubert near Newquay, Cornwall, telephone (0637) 830566

Sherman & Waterman Association Ltd., 12/13 Henrietta Street, Covent Garden, London WC2 8LH, telephone 01-240 7405/6

Silhouette Fairs, 25 Donnington Square, Newbury, Berkshire, telephone (0635) 44338

P. Smith, 87 Pembroke Street, Sevon Port, Plymouth, telephone (0752) 668837

Sports Centre, Keele University, Newcastle-under- Lyme, Staffordshire, telephone (0782) 621111

Step in Exhibitions, 105 Warwick Road, London SW5, telephone 01-370 1267

Taunton Antiques Center, 27-29 Silver Street, Taunton, Somerset TA1 3DH, telephone (0823) 289327

Top Hat Exhibitions Ltd., 66 Derby Road, Nottingham, Nottinghamshire, England

Treasure House Antiques Market, Mrs. D. Henderson, 31b High Street and Crown Yard, Arundel, West Sussex BN18 9AG, telephone (0903) 883101

Unicorn Fairs, P.O. Box 30, Hereford, Hereford & Worcester HR2 8SW, telephone (061) 773 7001

Upper Gardner Street Traders' Association, 47 Hove Park Way, Hove BN3 6PW, telephone (0273) 505560

Fred Hynds, Wakefield Ceramics Fairs, 1 Fountain Road, Rochester, Kent ME2 3SJ, telephone (0634) 723461

Waverly Fairs, Boreley Cottage, Boreley, nr. Ombersley, Worcester, telephone (0205) 620697

West Country Antiques & Collectors Fairs, The Dartmoor Antiques Centre, off West Street, Ashburton, Devon TQ13 7DV, telephone (0364) 52182

Westfairs, P.O. Box 43, Weston-super-Mare, Avon BS23 2DS, telephone (0934) 33596

Geoffrey Whitaker, Antique Fairs, 25B Portland Street, P.O. Box 100, Newark, Nottinghamshire NG24 1LP, telephone (0636) 702326

Keith Atkins, General Manager, Wolverhampton Markets Department, Heantun House Salop Street, Wolverhampton WV3 0SH, (0902) 21571 and 26528

Alan Kipping, Wonder Whistle Enterprises, 1 Ritson Road, London E8, telephone 01-249 4050

Auctioneers

All of these auction houses have sales of antiques and collectables. Auction schedules and sales are usually available upon request.

Abridge Auction Rooms, Market Place, Abridge, Essex, telephone 01-849 2107

Albert Andrews Auctions, Farm Building, Maiden Lane, Crayford, Kent DA12 4LX, telephone (0322) 528868

Aldrige's, 130 Walcot Street, Bath, Avon BA1 5BS, telephone (0225) 52839

George Allen, Tudor Sale Rooms, 8 Hillcrest, Skellow, Doncaster, South Yorkshire, telephone (0302) 725029

Allen & Harris, The Planks Salesrooms, Old Town Swindon, Wiltshire SN3 1QP, telephone (0793) 615915

Allman Auctions, 10 Middle Row, Chipping Norton, Oxfordshire OX7 5NH, telephone (0608) 3087

Ambrose Auctions, 149 High Road, Loughton, Essex ILG10 4LZ, England

Anderson's Auction Rooms, 28 Linenhall Street, Belfast, County Antrim BT2 8BG, Northern Ireland, telephone (0232) 221401

The Auction Rooms & Furniture Warehouse, 101 Hoe Street, Walthamstow, London E17, telephone 01-520 3215

Edward Bailey & Son, 17 Northgate, Newark, Nottinghamshire NG24 1EX

Bainbridges Auctioneers and Valuers, St. Johns Yard, St. Johns Parade, Mattock Lane, Ealing, London W13, telephone 01- 840 7177

Ball & Boyd, 17 Madoc Street, Llandudno, Gwynedd, Wales, telephone (0492) 77239

T. Bannister & Company, Auctioneers, Market Place, Haywards Heath, West Sussex, telephone (0444) 412402

Barbers Fine Arts Auctioneers Ltd., The Mayford Centre, Smarts Heath Road, Mayford Green, Woking, Surrey GU22 0PP, telephone (04862) 28939

Bearne's Auctioneers, Rainbow, Avenue Road, Torquay, Devon TQ2 5TG, telephone (0803) 296277

Bell Court Auction Rooms, 67 High Street, Bidford-on-Avon, Warwickshire, telephone (0789) 772611

Berkeleys of Brentwood, 45 North Road, Brentwood, Essex, telephone (0277) 224599

Biddle & Webb, Ladywood, Middleway, Birmingham B16 0PP, telephone (021) 455 8042

Bigwood Auctioneers Ltd., The Old School, Tiddington, Stratford-upon-Avon Warwickshire CV37 7AW, telephone (0789) 69415, fax (0789) 292686

Black Horse Agencies—Geering & Colyer, Highgate, Hawkhurst, Cranbrook, Kent TN18 4AD, telephone (05805) 3181
Black Horse Agencies—Locke & England, 18 Guy Street, Leamington Spa, Warwickshire CV32 4RT, telephone (0926) 27988, fax (0926) 450242

Bloomsbury Book Auctions, 3/4 Hardwick Street, London EC1R 4RY, 01-833 2636 and 01-636 1945

Bonhams Knightsbridge, Montpelier Galleries, Montpelier Street, Knightsbridge, London SW7 1HH, telephone 01- 584 9161, fax 01-589 4072, telex 916477 BONHAM G

Bonhams Chelsea, 65-69 Lots Road, London SW10 0RN, telephone 01-351 7111, fax 01-351 7754, telex 916477 BONHAMS G

Boulton & Cooper Ltd., St Michaels House, Malton, North Yorkshire YO17 OLR

Michael J. Bowman, 6 Haccombs House near Netherton, Newton Abbot, Devon TQ12 4SJ, telephone (0626) 872890

Bracketts, 27-29 High Street, Tunbridge Wells, Kent, telephone (0892) 33733

Brown & Merry, 41 High Street, Tring, Hertfordshire HP23 5AB, telephone (044282) 6446, fax (044282) 7743

William H. Brown Auctions, Westgate Hall, Westgate, Grantham, Lincolnshire, telephone (0476) 68861

Andrew McCann, Burlings St. Mary's Auction Rooms, Buxton Old Road, Disley, Stockport SK12 2BB, telephone (0663) 64854

Burstow & Hewett, Abbey Auction Galleries, Lower Lake, Battle, East Sussex TN33 0A7, telephone (04246) 2374 or 2302

Butler & Hatch Waterman, The County Group, 102 High Street, Tenterden, Kent, telephone (05806) 3233

Capes Dunn & Co. Auction Galleries, 38 Charles Street, Manchester M1 7DB, telephone (061) 273 1911 and 273 6060

Cheffins, Grain & Comins, 25 Market Place, Ely, Cambridgeshire CB7 4NP, telephone (0353) 662266

Christie's & Edmiston's, 164-166 Bath Street, Glasgow G2 4TG, Scotland, telephone (041) 332 8134/7, telex 779901

Christie's, 8 King Street, St. James's, London SW1Y 6QT, telephone 01-839 9060, fax 01-839 1611, telex 916429

Christie's South Kensington, 85 Old Brompton Road, London SW7 3LD, telephone 01-581 7611, telex 922061

Clarke & Le Quesne, 3 Victoria Road, Coventry, West Midlands, telephone (0203) 23377

Cobbs Burrows & Day, 39/41 Bank Street, Ashford, Kent, telephone (0233) 24321

Cooper Hirst, Goldlay House, Parkway, Chelmsford, Essex CM2 7PR, telephone (0245) 258141

S.W. Cottee & Son, Wareham Markets Sale Rooms, East Street, Wareham, Dorset BH20 4NR, telephone (09295) 2826

Crow's Market Auction, High Street, Dorking, Surrey RH4 1AQ, telephone (0306) 740382

Dacre, Son & Hartley, Victoria Hall, Little Lane, Ilkley, West Yorkshire LS29 8EA, telephone (0943) 816363, fax (0943) 816086

Dee & Atkinson, The Exchange, Driffield, East Yorkshire YO25 7LD, telephone (0377) 43151, fax (0377) 241041

Dowell Lloyd & Co., 118 Putney Bridge Road, London SW15, telephone 01-788 7777

A. E. Dowse & Son, Scotland Street, Sheffield, South Yorkshire S3 7DE, telephone (0742) 725858

Henry Duke & Son, 40 South Street, Dorchester, Dorset, telephone (0305) 65080

Eddisons Auctions, 4/6 High Street, Huddersfield, West Yorkshire HD1 2LS, telephone (0484) 533151, telex 55169 EDDLDS G

Elliott & Green, The Auction Sale Room, Emsworth Road, Lymington, Hampshire, telephone (0590) 52310

F.H. Ellis & Sons, 44-46 High Street, Worthing, West Sussex, telephone (0903) 38999

H. Evans & Sons, 1 Parliament Street, Hull, Humberside HU1 2AR, telephone (0482) 23033

Ely Auction Market *(Please see Cheffins Grain & Comins)*

Fellows & Sons, Bedford House, 88 Hagley Road, Edgbaston, Birmingham B16

Fox & Sons, 31 Chatsworth Road, Worthing, West Sussex, telephone (0903) 205566

John Francis Antiques & Fine Arts, King Street, Carmarthen Dyffed, Wales, telephone (0267) 233456

Fraser, Glennie & Partners, Cirencester, telephone (0285) 3938

G.A. Property Sales, The Canterbury Auction Galleries, 40 Station Road West, Canterbury, Kent CT2 8AN, telephone (0227) 763337

Garth Denham & Associate, Horsham Auction Galleries, The Carfax, Horsham, West Sussex, telephone (0302) 43837

Glendining's, 7 Blenheim Street, New Bond Street, London W1Y 9LD, telephone 01-493 2445, fax 01-629 8876, telex 298855 BLEN G

Gorringe's Auction Galleries, 15 North Street, East Sussex BN7 2PD, telephone (0273) 472503 or 472382

Andrew Grant, 59/60 Foregate Street, Worcester, Hereford & Worcester, telephone (0205) 52310

Graves, Son & Pilcher Fine Arts, 71 Church Road, Hove, East Sussex BN3 2GL, telephone (0273) 735266

Grays Auction Rooms, Alfred Street, Grays, Essex, telephone (0375) 31181

Gribble, Booth & Taylor, 32 The Avenue, Minehead, Somerset TA24 5AZ, telephone (0643) 2281, fax (0643) 7523

Hamptons Fine Art, 93 High Street, Godalming, Surrey GU7 1AL, telephone (04868) 23567, fax (0483) 426392

Hamptons Pocock & Lear, 20 High Street, Marlborough, Wiltshire SN8 1AA, telephone (0672) 55181, fax (0672) 55882

Hanbury Williams Auctions, 34 Church Street, Cromer, NR27 9ES

Hatton Garden Auctions, 36 Hatton Garden, London EC1 HP, telephone 01-242 6452

Heathcote Ball & Co. Fine Art Auctioneers, Castle Auction Rooms, 78 St. Nicholas Circle, Leicester, Leicestershire LE1 5NW, telephone (0533) 526789

Heathcote Ball & Co. Fine Art Auctioneers, Albion Auction Rooms, Commercial Street, Northampton, Northamptonshire NN1 1PJ, telephone (0604) 22735

Hobbs & Chambers, "At the Sign of the Bell", Market Place, Cirencester, Gloustershire GLl7 1QQ, telephone (0285) 4736

Hobbs Parker Auctioneers, Romney House, Ashford Market, Ashford, Kent TN23 1PG, telephone (0233) 62222, fax (0233) 46642

Hogg Robinson Auctioneers, 82a Eden Street, Kingston-upon-Thames, Surrey KT1 1DY, telephone 01-541 4139, fax 01-541 1360

Holloway's, 49 Parsons Street, Banbury, Oxfordshire OX16 8PF, telephone (0295) 53197

Edgar Horn, Auctioneer, 47 Cornfield Road, Eastbourne, Kent, telephone (0323) 22801

Raymond P. Inman Auctioneer, 35 & 40 Temple Street, Brighton, East Sussex BN1 3BH, telephone (0273) 774777

James of Norwich, 33 Timberhill, Norwich NR1 3LA, telephone (0603) 24817

Jeffreys, The Auction Rooms, 5 Fore Street, Lostwitheil, Cornwall, PL22 0BP, telephone (0208) 872245

Kennedy Wolfenden, 218 Lisburn Road, Belfast, County Antrim BT9 6GD, telephone (0232) 681775

Kent Sales, "Giffords", Holmesdale Road, South Darenth, Kent DA4 AF, telephone (0322) 864919, telex 896691 KENT SALES G

King & Chasemore Auctioneers, West Street, Midhurst, West Sussex GU29 9NG, telephone (073081) 2456

Lacy Scott Fine Art Auctioneers, Risbygate Street, Bury St. Edmunds, Suffolk, England

Lawrences Fine Art Auctioneers, Norfolk House, High Street, Bletchingley, Surrey RH1 4PA, telephone (0883) 843323

Lawrence of Crewkerne, South Street, Crewkerne, Somerset TA18 8AB, telephone (0460) 73041

Lefevre & Partners, 80 Grosvenor Street, London W1X 9DE, telephone 01-408 0578

Leigh Auction Rooms, 88-90 Pall Mall, Leigh-on-Sea, Essex SS0 1RG

Lewes Auction Rooms, 56 High Street, Lewes, East Sussex, telephone (0273) 478221

Locke & England *(Please see Black Horse Agencies—Locke & England.)*

London Bridge Auctions, 6 Park Street, London SE1, telephone 01-407 9577

Lots Road Chelsea Auction Galleries, 71 Lots Road Chelsea, London SW10 0RN, telephone 01-531 7771 and 531 5784 and 531 2349

Loves of Perth (Thomas Love & Sons Ltd.), 6 South St. Johns Place, Perth, Tayside PH1 5SU, telephone (0738) 24111

Lowery's Antique Auctions, 24 Bridge Street, Northampton, Northamptonshire NN1 1NT, telephone (0604) 21561

Frank R. Marshall & Co., Church Hill, Knutsford, Cheshire, telephone (0565) 41872

Michael Matthews Auctions, Dowell Street, Honiton, Devon, telephone (0404) 41872

McKennas Auctioneers, Bank Salerooms, Harris Court, Clitheroe, Lancashire BB7 2DP, telephone (0200) 22695 and 25446

Moore's Auction Rooms, 217/219 Greenwich High Road, London SE10, telephone 01-858 7848

Morgan Evans & Co. Ltd., 28-30 Church Street, Llangefni, Gwynedd, Wales, telephone (0248) 723303

Morphets of Harrogate, 4/6 Albert Street, Harrogate, North Yorkshire HG1 1JL, telephone (0423) 502282

Neales of Nottingham Auctioneers, 190-192 Mansfield Road, Nottingham, Nottinghamshire NG1 3HX, telephone (0602) 624141, fax (0602) 607456

Neale Sons & Flecher, 26 Church Street, Woodbridge, Suffolk 1P12 1DP, telephone (03943) 2263

D. M. Nesbitt, 7 Clarendon Road, Southsea, Portsmouth PO5 2ED, telephone (0705) 864321

Newington Green Auctions, 55 Green Lanes, London N16 4TD, telephone 01-246 4222

Michael Newman Fine Art Auctioneer, Kinterbury House, St. Andrews Cross, Plymouth, Devon PL1 2DQ, telephone (0752) 669298

B. J. Norris, The Quest, West Street, Harrietsham, nr. Maidstone, Kent, telephone (0622) 859515 and (0860) 819335

Norris & Duvall, 106 Fore Street, Hertford, Hertfordshire SG14 1AH, telephone (0992) 582249

Northampton Auction Galleries, The Old Albion Brewery, Commercial Street, Northampton, telephone (0604) 37263

Nuttal Richards & Co., The Town Hall, Axbridge, Somerset, telephone (0934) 732969

Old Amersham Auctions, British Legion Hall, Whielden Street, Old Amersham, Buckinghamshire, telephone (02403) 22758

Osborne King and Megran Auctions, 17 Castle Arcade, Gilford, BT63, telephone (0232) 240332

Outhwaite & Litherland, Office 3, 43 Houghton Street, Southport, Merseyside, telephone (0704) 38489

Parkins Auctioneers & Valuers, 18 Malden Road, Cheam, Surrey SM3 8SD, telephone 01-644 6633

Pearsons Ormistons, 54 Southampton Road, Ringwood, Hampshire, telephone (04254) 3333

Phillips at Blenstock House, 7 Blenheim Street, New Bond Street, London W1Y OAS, telephone 01-629 6602, fax 01-629 8876, telex 298855 BLEN G.

Phillips (Bath), 1 Old King Street, Bath, Avon BA1 2JT, telephone (0225) 310609 and 310709, fax (0225) 446675

Phillips (Cardiff), 9-10 Westgate St., Cardiff, Wales CF1 1DA, telephone (0222) 396453

Phillips (Chester), New House, 150 Christleton Road, Chester, Cheshire CH3 5TD, telephone (0244) 313936 and 313937

Phillips (Colwyn Bay), 9 Conwy Road, Colwyn Bay, Clwyd LL29 7AF, Wales, telephone (0492) 533406

Phillips (Cornwall), Cornubia Hall, Par, Cornwall PL24 2AQ, telephone (072681) 4047, fax (072681) 7979

Phillips (Edinburgh), 65 George Street, Edinburgh EH2 2JL, Scotland, telephone (031) 225 2266

Phillips (Exeter), Alphin Brook Road, Exeter, Devon EX2 8TH, telephone (0392) 39025 and 39026, fax (0392) 410361

Phillips (Folkestone), Bayle Place, 11 Bayle Parade, Folkestone, Kent CT20 1SQ, telephone (0303) 45555

Phillips (Glasgow), 207 Bath Street, Glasgow G2 4HD, Scotland, telephone (041) 221 8377, fax (041) 226 4441

Phillips (Ipswich), Dover House, Wolsley St., Ipswich, Suffolk 1P1 1UD, telephone (0473) 55137

Phillips (Knowle) *(Please see Phillips Midlands.)*

Phillips (Leeds), 17a East Parade, Leeds, West Yorkshire LS1 2BU, telephone (0532) 448011

Phillips Marylebone, Hayes Place, Lisson Grove, London NW1 6UA, telephone 01-723 2647

Phillips (Midlands), The Old House, Station Road, Knowle, Solihull, West Midlands B93 0HT, telephone (056) 456151

Phillips (Morley), 20 Fountain St., Leeds, West Yorkshire LS27 9EN, telephone (0532) 523888

Phillips (Oxford), 39 Park End Street, Oxford, Oxfordshire OX1 1JD, telephone (0865) 723524, fax (0865) 791064

Phillips (Plymouth), Armada Street, North Hill, Plymouth, Devon PL4 8LS, telephone (0752) 673504

Phillips (Sherborne), Long Street, Sherborne, Dorset DT9 3BS, telephone (0935) 815271, fax (0935) 816416

Phillips West 2, 10 Salem Road, London W2 2BU, telephone 01-221 5303

Phillips Sanders & Stubbs, 32 The Avenue, Minehead, Somerset

Prudential Fine Art Auctioneers, Bristol Auction Rooms, Oakfield Road, Bristol, Avon BS8 2BE, telephone (0272) 734052

Prudential Fine Art Auctioneers, Baffins Hall, Baffins Lane, Chichester, West Sussex PO19 1UA, telephone (0243) 787548

Prudential Fine Art Auctioneers, Portland St., Hereford, Hereford & Worcester HR4 9JE, telephone (0432) 272413

Prudential Fine Art Auctioneers, 49 London Road, Sevenoaks, Kent TN13 1AR, telephone (0732) 740310

Prudential Fine Art Auctioneers, 114 Northenden Road, Sale, Manchester, Greater Manchester M33 3DH, telephone (061) 962 9237

Prudential Fine Art Auctions, Cinque Ports Street, Rye, Sussex, telephone (0797) 222124

Prudential Fine Art Auctioneers, Station Road, Weston-super-Mare, Avon BS23 1XU, telephone (0934) 33174

Prudential Property Services (Fine Art/Chattels Division), The Salerooms, The Market, St. Ives, Cambridgeshire PE17 4JA, England, telephone (0480) 68144

Reeds Rains, Trinity House, 114 Northenden Road, Sale, Manchester M33 3HD, telehone (061) 962 9237

Riddetts Auctions, Richmond Hill, Bournemouth, Dorset, telephone (0202) 25686

Rowse, Jeffery & Watkins, 5 Fore Street, Lostwithiel, Cornwall PL22 0BP, telephone (0208) 872245

Russell, Baldwin & Bright, 38 South Street, Leominster, Hereford, telephone (0586) 4123

Sandgate Auctions, 42 Fort St, Ayr, Ayrshire, Scotland

Simmons & Sons, 32 Bell Street, Henley-on-Thames, Oxfordshire RG9 2BH, telephone (0491) 571111, fax (0491) 579833, telex 847621

L.S. Smellie & Sons Ltd. Auctioneers, Auction Mart, Lower Auchingramont Road, Hamilton, telephone (0698) 282007

Sotheby's, 34-35 New Bond Street, London W1A 2AA, telephone 01-493 8080, fax 01-409 3100, telex 24454 SPBLON G

Sotheby's Chester, Booth Mansion, 28-30 Watergate Street, Chester, Cheshire CH1 2NA, telephone (0244) 315531, fax (0244) 46984, telex 61577 SOBART G

Southeby's Scotland, 146 West Regent Street, Glasgow G2 2RQ, telephone 041-221 4817

Sotheby's Sussex, Summers Place, Billingshurst, West Sussex RH14 9AD, telephone (040381) 3933, fax (040381) 5153, telex 87210 GAVEL

Southgate Antique Auctions, Southgate Town Hall, Green Lanes, London N13, telephone 01-886 7888

Henry Spencer & Sons, 20 The Square, Retford, Nottinghamshire DN22 6KJ, telephone (0777) 708633, fax (0777) 709299

Stanley, Alder & Price, The City Auction Rooms, 4 Prince Buildings, George Street, Bath, Avon.

Stewart, Gore Auctioneers, 102 Northdown Road, Margate, Kent, telephone (0843) 221528

J. Straker Chadwick & Sons, Market Street, Chambers, Abergavenny, Gwent NP7 55D, Wales, telephone (0873) 2624

Stride & Son, Southdown House, St. John's Street, Chichester, West Sussex PO19 1XQ, telephone (0243) 782626

Summerley Auction Rooms, Limmer Lane, Felpham, Bognor Regis, West Sussex PO22 7LF

The Sussex Auction Galleries, 53 Perrymount Road, Haywards Heath, Sussex RH16 3DS, telephone (0444) 414935, telex 87650

Taylor Lane & Creber, 38 North Hill, Plymouth, Devon, telephone (0752) 670700

Temple Auctions Limited, 133 Carryduff Road, Boardmills, Lisburn, County Down BT27 6YL, telephone (0846) 638777

Tennant's of Yorkshire, 26-27 Market Place, Leyburn, North Yorkshire

James Thompson, 64 Main Street, Kirkby Lonsdale, Lancashire LA6 2AJ, telephone (0468) 71555

Duncan Vincent, 105 London Street, Reading, Berkshire RG1 4LF, telephone (0734) 589502 and 594748

Wallington Missionary Auctions, Crusader Hall, Stanley Park Road, Wallington, Surrey SM5 4PP, telephone 01-647 8437

Wallis & Wallis, West Street Auction Galleries, Lewes, Sussex BN7 2NJ, telephone (0273) 473137, fax (0273) 476652, telex 896691 TLXIR G

Waltham Forest Auctions, 101 Hoe Street, Walthamstow, London E17, telephone 01-520 2998

Ward Price & Co., 14/15 Queen Street, Scarborough, North Yorkshire YO11 1HQ, telephone (0723) 3533581

Warren & Wignall, The Mill, Earnshaw Bridge, Leyland Lane, Leyland, Lancashire, PR5 3PH, telephone (0772) 453252 and 451430

E. Watson & Sons Auctions, Heathfield Furniture Salerooms, The Market, Heathfield, East Sussex, telephone (04352) 2132

Weller & Dufty Ltd., 141 Bromsgrove Street, Birmingham B5 6RO, telephone (021) 692 1414 and 1415, telex 338024 WELDU (answer back BIRCOM)

Wellington Salerooms, Clifton House, Mantle Street, Wellington, Somerset, telephone (082347) 4815

Noel Wheatcroft & Son, Old English Road, Matlock, Derbyshire, telephone (0629) 4591

P.F. Windibank Auctions, 18-20 Reigate Road, Dorking, Surrey RH4 1SG, telephone (0306) 884556

Woolley & Wallis Auctioneers, The Castle Auction Mart, Castle Street, Salisbury, Wiltshire, SP1 3SU, telephone (0722) 411422

Wright-Manley Auctioneers, Beeston Sale Centre, Beeston nr. Tarporley, Cheshire CW6 0DR, telephone (08293) 2151

Wright-Manley Auctioneers, Wem Market Hall, High St., Wem, Shropshire, telephone (0939) 32471

List of Maps

List of Illustrations

Index

Will You Help?

Time passes, events change. Almost as soon as this book went to the printer, things changed: some shows moved location, others were cancelled, others increased in size or scope, others gained a focus on a particular type of item. Some flea markets may move because of urban renewal or other reasons.

Won't you please let us know? If you do, we'll be able to improve the next edition of this book. Then, future readers can benefit from your findings.

Either tear out this page, or feel free to use other sheets of paper.

Sincerely,

Peter Manston

What did you find different?

What problems did you find?

Is there any way to avoid this problem?

What markets or fairs moved time or place?

What was your greatest success and most wonderful find?

Thank you very much!

Please send your comments to:

Peter Manston
c/o B.T. Batsford
4 Fitzhardinge Street
London W1H 0AH

Will You Help?

Time passes, events change. Almost as soon as this book went to the printer, things changed: some shows moved location, others were cancelled, others increased in size or scope, others gained a focus on a particular type of item. Some flea markets may move because of urban renewal or other reasons.

Won't you please let us know? If you do, we'll be able to improve the next edition of this book. Then, future readers can benefit from your findings.

Either tear out this page, or feel free to use other sheets of paper.

Sincerely,
Peter Manston

What did you find different?

What problems did you find?

Is there any way to avoid this problem?

What markets or fairs moved time or place?

What was your greatest success and most wonderful find?

Thank you very much!

Please send your comments to:

Peter Manston
c/o B.T. Batsford
4 Fitzhardinge Street
London W1H 0AH